INSIGHT
GUIDES

CReTe

Directed and Designed by Hans Höfer
Original edition by Gerhard Sasse
Translated by Marianne Rankin

APA
PUBLICATIONS

CRETE

Second Edition
© **1991 APA PUBLICATIONS (HK) LTD**
All Rights Reserved
Printed in Singapore by Höfer Press Pte. Ltd

ABOUT THIS BOOK

Crete, the cradle of European civilisation, the legendary island where Asia and Africa meet, is a place of many contrasts. After the *Insight Guides* to *Greece*, *The Greek Islands* and *Athens*, it was only a matter of time before another *Insight Guide* title joined this prize-winning series.

Crete has been the subject of many portraits and pictures, but the writers of *Insight Guide: Crete* have made every effort to capture the island's many different aspects in a new and original way, drawing on their own often-specialised knowledge of the place. But above all, their aim is to convey their own love for Crete and its people.

The Authors

The project editor of *Insight Guide: Crete* and author of most of the chapters in the book is **Gerhard Sasse**, who while travelling in Africa and North and Central America, learned about very different and exotic cultures. Fascinating though these cultures are, they are normally viewed from a distance. Crete, however, is different; one becomes involved in the classical "Minoan" civilisation as one learns about it.

Gerhard Sasse's "love affair" with Crete has endured since his first visit to the island in 1969. He knows and loves the islanders, but has no illusions about them either, and appreciates their individualism and strength of character.

Gerhard Sasse's enthusiasm for Crete is equally shared by his wife, **Nadja Sasse**. A Bulgarian born in Sofia, she has lived in the Federal Republic of Germany for more than 15 years. During that period, hardly a year has passed without a lengthy stay in Crete. The sketch pads and notebooks of this writer and artist are proof. Because she speaks Greek like a native, she is able to explore aspects of life in Crete which remain hidden from the ordinary tourist, whether it be an association of hothouse growers or a scholar out in a remote part of the island digging for remains of an ancient culture.

The author of the historical section, **Hans-Gerd Schulte**, has written essays on pre- and early history. However, he has also worked on several radio plays which focuses on contemporary history. He is a lawyer by profession. His wide range of talents was exactly what was required for probing an elusive subject such as early Cretan history. Faced with a lamentable lack of facts, the historian turns detective, searching for clues and details.

Author and sociologist, **Gerhard Wilhelm**, combines a keen interest in great explorers (Evans and Schliemann, as well as Freud and Jung) with studies of matriarchal societies. This combination of factors related to the Minoan civilisation have always fascinated him. His work on Arthur Evans on the one hand, and the social system of the Minoans on the other, enabled him to bring these threads together for *Insight Guide: Crete* in a coherent, descriptive manner.

Takis Touglitos hails from Athens and is now a Berlin-based film-maker and scriptwriter. He has some pertinent comments to

Gerhard Sasse

Nadja Sasse

Hans-Gerd Schulte

make on the subject of superstition and has in fact compiled a lucid picture of everyday life on the island. He plans to elaborate on this penchant for mysticism of the Cretans and other Greeks in a book he is currently working on.

The youngest contributor, **Stella Stephaniki**, was born on Crete. She lives on Haniá and works as a travel agent in Paleóhora. As a courier, she was able to furnish details which were extremely useful in the compilation of this *Insight Guide*. Stella Stephanaki also advised on the sections about Haniá, Réthimnon and West Crete.

The numerous maps in this book were drawn up by **Kai Berndtson** in Munich. He is responsible for many of the maps in *Insight Guides*, which make the books indispensible when travelling.

The Photographers

The popularity of *Insight Guides* with travellers is not only due to the interesting and well-researched text. A great part of the appeal of these travel guidebooks is the wonderful photography. APA Publications aim to give the photographs a role far beyond one that is merely illustrative: the pictures blend with the text, like a dialogue and are an integral part of the whole, giving the adventure-seeking reader an opportunity to think and dream of visiting faraway places.

The team working on this book was a combination of seasoned APA photographers and enthusiastic newcomers. Together they have succeeded in capturing the varied and elusive, even illusive atmosphere of the island: the true character of the island without the usual clichés.

Marcus Brooke had already shown his talent in *Insight Guide: Greek Islands*, as had **Michele Macrakis**, who comes from Athens. It is the first time, however, that the sensitive photographs taken by **Regina Hagen**, who hails from Munich, have been included in an *Insight Guide*. She also had the arduous task of compiling the photographic material for the final choice to be made by the publisher in Singapore.

The photographer and artist **Udo Gerner**, who has known Crete for many years, was able to dip into his own well-stocked archives for material. He is capable of giving well-worn scenes and themes a completely new perspective.

Nomi Baumgartl is yet another contributor who has had her photographs published regularly in leading international magazines.

Once again **Gerd Pfeiffer** proved himself a friend in need and contributed photographs in areas where certain subjects were found lacking.

Other valuable photographic contributions came from **Jens Schumann**, **Stefan Seidel** and **Hans Wiesenhofer**.

Under the patient guidance of **Dr. Dieter Vogel**, manuscripts and photographs finally found their way, often by circuitous routes, to Munich, and into this final volume. Many thanks to all, especially to those in Jahnstrasse, whose unselfish support so greatly contributed to *Insight Guide: Crete*.

– APA Publications

Gerhard Wilhelm   *Stella Stephaniki*   *Udo Gerner*

HISTORY & CULTURE

PLACES & FEATURES

TRAVEL TIPS

The shape of Crete is reminiscent of a gnarled branch, or perhaps a snail. A wise old Cretan likened the island to the crown of King Minos – tempered and battered by numerous battles and wars but, above all, ravaged by time.

With an area of about 8,350 sq. km, it is the largest of the Greek Islands and, after Sicily, Sardinia, Cyprus and Corsica, the fifth largest island in the Mediterranean Sea. From west to east, the island is over 256 km long, and between 15 and 60 km wide.

Crete lies between the 34th and 35th degrees of latitude, on a plane with Tunisia and Syria and, with more than 300 days of sunshine a year, it's the most pleasant of all the Mediterranean islands. It is, without doubt, also the most significant of the islands; for here, more than 4,000 years ago, European culture first blossomed with the "Minoan" civilisation.

There are so many different sides to Crete that there is certainly something here for everyone. The northern coast is the tourist area, with wonderful beaches, while the southern coast is still relatively deserted and undeveloped. Those looking for solitude can take refuge in the peninsulas of Gramvoússa, Rodopoú and Akrotíri, or just go up into the mountains.

There's beautiful scenery wherever you look, but it's not of the soft and gentle kind. It is quite a rugged place, in stark contrast to the friendly openness of the inhabitants.

Plant lovers can find many different species unique to the island. If you are interested in caves, there's no lack of choice: there are more than 3,000 of them, all different. Then there's the Samaria Gorge, 18 km long, which makes it the longest in Europe, and several shorter gorges, no less spectacular.

Crete is exceptionally rich in places to see. Most of these can be easily reached on the 2,000 km of asphalt road. Apart from excavation sites of the Minoan period – especially Knossós, Festós, Agía Triáda, Mália and Káto Zákros – there are many interesting Greek-Dorian and Roman sites; then a wealth of Byzantine cultural monuments – over 1,000 churches, chapels and paintings; in the towns there are old buildings from the time of the Venetian and Turkish occupations. Between Hrissoskalítissa in the far west and Toploú in the east, there are more than 30 impressive monasteries strung out across the island.

Left, the legendary bull carrying Europa.

Up until the second half of the 19th century the early history of Crete lay buried in the myths of late Greek civilisation. It lay hidden beneath the more than 4,000 years which had elapsed since the building of the first of the splendid palaces. But even the earliest legends attest to the high level of cultural development. We hear of the godlike Minoan dynasty and their great sense of justice and beauty. The Minoans loved dancing and sport and their settlements reflect their abil-

The sensational discoveries made by the archaeologist Arthur Evans after 1900, the numerous other finds and continuing excavations while not providing evidence of the godliness of the Cretan kings, certainly point to the existence of an independent culture far in advance of the later Mycenaean civilisation.

Today the evidence revealed by excavation and research completes a picture of the art, architecture, religion and everyday life

ity to combine the practical and the aesthetic. It was this social complexity which made Crete the first great historical centre in Europe, now so richly documented in Crete's museums and excavated sites.

Homer, Herodotus, Horace and Ovid all tell of Zeus, who took on the form of a bull and won the daughter of the Phoenician king. He carried her on his back over the sea to Górtin. Under the evergreen plane tree they created Minos, Sarpedon and Radamanthys. Foremost among their offspring was the mythical demigod/king, Minos, wise and just yet powerful and severe.

of Europe's first very advanced civilisation. Revelations about the Cretan-Minoan epoch have led to a revision of previous theories on early Greek history. But despite this, articles and pamphlets still abound in which the history of Europe merely has its prelude in Crete. In some, Cretan culture loses its unique attributes and is seen as merely part of a "Minoan-Mycenaean" culture.

Neolithic Period (up to 3000 BC): Up to now there has been no evidence of Palaeolithic or

Preceding pages: fresco from Knossós. Above, courageous Europa takes the bull by the horn.

Mesolithic habitation of Crete. It is assumed that in Neolithic times a hunting and gathering culture immigrated to the island, perhaps as early as the 7th millennium. At first these early islanders lived in caves, such as the Eileithya Cave near Amnissós or the Gerani Cave near Réthimnon. Later they built primitive dwellings of stones and bricks. This development took place before the "Neolithic Revolution" – the advent of cultivation of the ground.

With the introduction of agriculture, the use of fire for the production of pottery and the taming of wild animals and cattle breeding – cows, sheep and goats – a unique island civilisation developed. Through fishing and sea voyages, contact was made with the neighbouring islands of Gávdos, Día and the Cyclades. Tools such as hammers, cudgels and axes were made from stone, occasionally from bone. Pottery vessels were made without the aid of a wheel. The pots had a rustic appearance with a simple shape, and were decorated with polished patterns and slits. Some discoveries of marble and baked idols (Neolithic pieces in the Archaeological Museum in Iráklion – abbreviated as "AMI," in cabinets 1 and 2) point to the worship of the Mediterranean Goddess of Fertility, the Great Mother, Mother Earth. But there was still very little indication of the unique way in which early civilisation on Crete was to develop in the future.

Prepalatial Period (3000–2000 BC): At the beginning of the Cretan Bronze Age, in the early 3rd millennium BC there was a further wave of immigration to the island from the Aegean and Asia Minor. The newcomers were relatively more advanced. They had the potter's wheel, and also had experience in obtaining and working copper, which soon became a valued commodity for the far-reaching sea trade. Furthermore, glassy, volcanic obsidian was imported from the islands of Melos and Yiali. New trading routes and cultural links were established with Anatolia and Syria, Cyprus, the Cyclades, Libya and Egypt.

These contacts with neighbouring civilisations, some of which were indeed highly developed, combined with Cretan receptivity and inventiveness, led to the rapid development of the highly original and unique Mediterranean culture of the Minoan palatial civilisation.

It was probably during this period, referred to as Prepalatial, that Knossós and Festós got their names, both of which reflect the influence of Asia Minor. The first mansions such as Mírtos and Vassilikí were occupied, and larger buildings were erected, some with a second storey. The practice of burying the dead in beehive tombs began, as was shown by finds in Lébena and Krási and in Fourní near Arhánes. These innovations show the process of change during the early years of Minoan culture. The architectural high point of this burial culture will be seen later in Pylos and Mycenae.

The ceramics of the Prepalatial period still show signs of the New Stone Age as the wheel was seldom used in the early period and the pieces were not baked in an oven but on an open fire. The Pírgos style, which was influenced by the rich Cycladic culture (AMI, cabinet 3), shows distinct further development of late Neolithic ceramics. A vivid example of the polished lattice pattern is the often reproduced dark chalice-like cup (AMI, No. 74855).

Dating from the same period too, is an example (AMI, No. 2719) of a pyx, a shallow, round steatite box with a lid, decorated with slit patterns and with a handle in the shape of a dog lying down. Other variations in the style of creative works in clay are the Agios Onoúfrios style, with its profusion of line decorations, the early Vassilikí style characterised by uneven baking, and the Barbotine style with three-dimensional decoration (examples in AMI, Room 1, cabinets 3, 4, 6, 9, 12).

Just as remarkable as the ceramic art, was the technique of stone working which developed. The stone pitchers found on the island of Mólchos in Mirabello Bay (AMI, cabinet 7) are notable for their attractive shape and the natural texture of the material. The harmony of shape and decoration of the vessels is particularly impressive.

There were also innovations in the art of seal moulding. Small *objets d'art* used for decoration or protection were made in a variety of designs. Precious stones, rock crystal and ivory were used, and shaped into geometrical and figurative forms, pyramids or cylinders. The rich variety of ideas is astonishing. The seal makers produced graceful animal representations or even, more rarely, depictions of human figures.

In metallurgy too, there were new trends. Goldsmiths had reached a high level of skill as early as the Prepalatial era (AMI I, cabi-

building, the hilltops were first carefully flattened. Then the unique and unprecedented residences were built, with hundreds of rooms adjoining in labyrinthine form.

Later, on the same sites, new palaces were erected, making excavations under the foundations difficult. Sometimes parts of the courtyard were accessible, however, as in the old palace theatre arrangement in the West Courtyard at Festós, and at the Louloures in Knossós, where round, well-like sacrificial shafts, were built on Prepalatial foundations. In general the new palaces dif-

nets 5, 14, 16, 17, 18a). The Cyclades were still the leaders in the artistic field (cf. AMI I, cabinet 18a, found on Crete) but by the end of the Prepalatial period they had been superceded by Crete.

Early Palatial Period (2000-1700 BC): At the beginning of the 2nd millennium, there was a further successful development in Cretan life. As the population increased in the island settlements, the first palaces were built, and set in prominent positions, such as on the heights of Knossós and Festós. The palace of Mália was built on somewhat more modest lines. In order to prepare the ground for

fered little from the old, except in one major respect: the new palaces were far larger, and eventually took on the dimensions almost of small towns.

Archaeological finds lead to the assumption that there was a monarchical central power in Knossós. The growing influence of the Cretan rulers paved the way for the development of a thalassocracy, an island kingdom, giving Crete economic and political pre-eminence in the whole of the Aegean. This in turn led to the "Pax Minoica," an extended period of peace, during which extensive fortifications were unnecessary and all the arts reflected the people's peaceful way of life.

Due to its favourable situation at the intersection of east Mediterranean trade, Crete's fleet was able to make wide-ranging contacts. Cretan ships sailed as far as Italy and Ugarit, Troy, Melos and to Lerna in Argolis.

At these Mediterranean trading posts, many Kamáres style pots have been found. The name was derived from the original site of origin on Crete, a grotto in the Ida Mountains, below the snow-capped peak of Psíloritis where the infant Zeus is said to

of pilgrims. People laid down offerings to placate the goddesses of fertility and maturity, and those of birth and death. Finds from this period also reveal the way the pilgrims were dressed. The women had wide skirts and elaborately coiled hair. The men wore loin cloths and carried daggers in their belts. Some offerings – depictions of sick parts of the body, hands or chest – indicate the extent of the power ascribed to the goddess of nature.(This tradition of votive offerings to the deity has continued on Crete, unbroken, since Minoan times.)

have grown up. In ceramic terms, the Kamáres style denotes the Late Palatial period. But decorative elements from an earlier period are still in evidence. The main features of the Kamáres style are its great variety, wide range of colours and, above all, the beauty of the pieces.

Grottos such as the Kamáres Cave and other mountain shrines were the destinations

Left, partridge fresco from a caravanserai; the colourful "eggs" are symbols of fertility. **Above**, griffin fresco from the small throne room in Knossós.

The palaces were not merely the dwelling places of the rulers, but were also centres of production and administration. It has been discovered that even at the beginning of the Early Palatial period, a script composed of hieroglyphics was in use, but this was only preserved on a few objects and tablets (AMI II, cabinet 25). All documents in ink have been lost. This still undeciphered first European picture writing possibly had its origins in Egyptian hieroglyphics. In this script each word had a sign, whereas in the Linear-A script which developed from it, from about 1700 BC onwards, each syllable had a sign.

Despite many years of study, this script has still not been deciphered either. It most probably corresponded with the far reaching bureaucratic necessities of the palatial trade organisation. It is assumed that the few clay tablets which have been preserved contain references to stocks and trade. However, it is the invaluable and singular Festós Disc which documents the transition to the Late Palatial Minoan period. This is a clay disc, embossed on both sides with hieroglyphics, the text of which, reading from the outside to the centre in spirals, would perhaps give

more cultural information. The text is composed from 45 syllables but, unfortunately, it has never been deciphered. It has been dated at about 1600 BC.

The end of the early palaces came suddenly. In about 1700 BC they were all destroyed almost simultaneously. Their destruction is generally attributed to a massive earthquake, although it has been put forward that a warring invasion from North Africa could have been responsible. But the rapid rebuilding of the palaces and the continued development of Minoan civilisation contradict that theory.

Late Palatial Period (1700–1400 BC): The extensive sea trade which provided the basis for the flowering of Minoan culture, also served to supply the island with any materials it lacked. Lead, silver, copper, steatite, jasper, rock crystal, manganese and ochre, all essential for the paintings, were extracted from the island itself. There was local timber too; cypress trees abounded. But copper was imported from Cyprus, gold from Nubia, ivory from Syria, obsidian from the island of Melos and from Egypt papyrus. Tin was of great importance as it was increasingly used in bronze alloys, and it was imported from Asia Minor.

In fact the whole development of Minoan civilisation can only be understood against the background of this economic exchange. In the civilised lands of the Near East, particularly in Egypt, Cretan products were greatly sought after. Not only was wine in high demand, but also olive oil, timber, ceramic pots, bronze weapons and many other products. Foreign trade from Crete was extensive, reaching as far as Ugarit and Phoenicia, and is attested to by finds of Cretan wares in Syria and Yugoslavia as well as in inscriptions found in Egypt.

After the destruction of the old palaces, new ones were built, including Knossós, Festós and Mália – which have for years been the destination of numerous visitors. In 1900 the English archaeologist Arthur Evans and his team, led to the site by Greeks, caused a sensation by unearthing the palace of Knossós. At almost the same time, Federico Halbherr and Luigi Pernier were at work in Festós. Those excavations were continued after 1950 by Doro Levi.

Mália was revealed by the Cretan archaeologist Joseph Hatzidákis from 1915 until 1920, when French teams took over. A fourth palace was not discovered until 1960–61 although its existence had been suspected for some time. It is in Zákros in eastern Crete, and since 1962 has been systematically researched by Nikolas Pláton. These excavations are of particular interest as large parts of the palace, some preserved beneath the sea, have been found untouched.

One can safely assume that Crete will come up with further archaeological finds in the future. The number of excavation sites is considerable and in some recently revealed building complexes, researchers believe they have found more Minoan palaces: Tourkoginotia/Arhánes, Prophítis Iliás, Monastiráki and Hamálevri and Haniá.

The four palaces already excavated are similar in some respects, but they are not imitations of the residences of Mari or Ugarit nor are they comparable to the palaces of Anatolia, Egypt or Mesopotamia. Most notable are the north/northeast facing quadrangles and the asymmetrical layout of the buildings and the irregular shape of the outer walls. There are no facades to provide outside shelter while extending the living space. This gives a clear indication of how the Minoans lived.

Other unique features are the palace halls, open at the sides, and the enormous staircases, the "bathrooms" too, lying lower than the adjoining rooms, the light shafts and outside, gardens in terrace form with porticos. The upper rooms were used for offices, sanctuaries and staterooms.

The whole ensemble is quite spectacular. The labyrinth-like arrangement of the building is evident from the ground-plan. Huge *pithoi* fill the storerooms, there are cult rooms, workshops of various kinds within the palace complex, administrative offices and, finally, the royal staterooms. The whole ensemble gives a unique indication of a palace life, which endured for more than half a millennium.

Outside the palace building, both at Festós and Knossós, there were theatre-like courtyards and stairways, with "processional paths" leading at an angle (Festós) or at right angles (Knossós) linking the steps to the "small" palace, which at Knossós was at a distance from the main building.

Around the palaces, but also in other parts of the island, townships grew up with several

thousand inhabitants, which became regional centres and marketplaces. The freedom loving nature of the Cretans was reflected in the towns. Of course, the architecture of a town was greatly influenced by its location; for example whether it was built on a slope (Festós, Psíra, Arkolohorí) or on a level plain (Mália).The geographical position of Zákros, Gourniá and Palékastro called for narrow streets, while at Mália and Knossós there were blocks of houses divided by courtyards and gardens.

In this completely original and varied style

of building even the mostly flat roofed stone town houses showed a highly developed sense of creativity. Excavations have revealed more details, as in the simple two-storey brick house in Gourniá with a storeroom on the ground floor, and living rooms above. Its counterpart is House E at Mália. This "villa" has about 50 rooms on the ground floor, with bathrooms and a room decorated with murals. It is respectfully, if inaccurately, called the "Small Palace."

The variety of housing at Knossós can be seen from about 50 faience plaques, part of a complete picture, giving an indication of the

Left, a nice find from Soúnia – an octopus decorates the drinking vessel. **Right**, richly ornamental cup in Kamáres style.

facades of the houses at the beginning of the Late Palatial period (AMI II, cabinet 25). The two and three storey houses are of varied design; the ochre-coloured windows indicate that there was a covering of transparent material. A clay model of a typical, fairly large house complete with light shaft and balcony was found in 1970 at Arhánes. Even more attractive are the houses of Akrotíri on the island of Santorini (Théra), which were preserved in the volcanic matter, and which reflect the building designs on Crete (Late Palatial period, phase II, late Minoan Oia).

between rich and poor. Houses from the area between Kouse and Siva were poor, without kitchen, lavatory or even a stable. Then there was the typical country house in Achládia, with servants' rooms and a reception room next to the entrance, and then at the top of the spectrum, the splendid and plush Minoan villas. Each of the "manor houses" of Tílissos comprised many apartments with a two-roomed porter's lodge (Villa B); they also had running water. It was also noticeable, however, that country life gradually became more refined and civilisation developed, as a

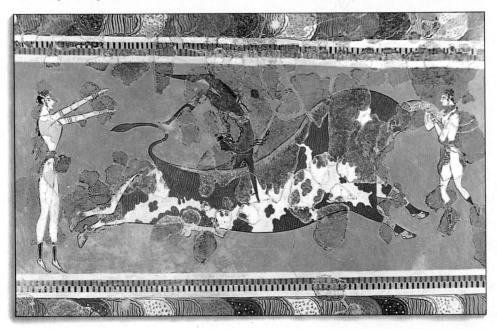

In the countryside, life was less varied and free. Although on the length and breadth of the island there was no one olive tree exactly like another, the eternally repeating demands of the viticulture and olive harvest, and the uniformity of agriculture and cattle raising left little scope for the development of the individual. Various forms of collective ownership, as well as clan associations had been a feature of Cretan life for centuries. But now clear social divisions became evident and the old order was broken up. This is shown in various excavated country houses, which clearly reflect the difference

consequence of the cultivation of nature.

Life in the new Palatial society unfolded in many directions. There were bull fights and processions, dances and plays, which can clearly be seen as early forms of the different categories of sport, religion and theatre. Religious life was primarily influenced by the cycles of nature, and the seasons of the year which determined growth. Despite the fact that Crete was an important trading and sea power, for the people the fundamental growth of plants and ripening of crops was still a mystery. The autumnal withering and dying was observed with awe, and hope was always renewed with the advent of rebirth in spring. The wonder at nature's regeneration had early found expression in the concept of a great Mother Nature. She was the mother, and also the wife of the younger, lesser god who died each year, yet always came back to life. As Diktynna, Briómartis or Eileithyía, with regional variations, this goddess was also recognised in neighbouring regions and she appeared impressed on seals and golden rings, which are among some of the most valuable finds of the Late Palatial period.

Some of the scenes captured on such rings

Arhánes, AMI VI, cabinet 88, No. 989). There is still much to learn about the origins and early history of European theatre.

Ceremonies and processions also featured in the religious sphere. With the development and transformation of new Palatial customs, the significance of the holy caves, the importance of which dated back hundreds of years, began to diminish. Some were still revered, but new centres of worship had sprung up as well. In the caves, the power of the great goddess was manifest. In the Grotto of Eileithyía the goddess of

– and again the difference between country and Palatial life is evident – indicate that many events took place out of doors, as shown on the golden ring of Isópata (AMI VI, cabinet 87, No. 424). Other cult events, however, are depicted as taking place in stone areas (golden ring from Mycenae, National Museum Athens No. 3179), or staircases, which lead one to visualise a theatre-like central courtyard (ring from

Famous exhibits from the Museum of Iráklion: left, the bull fight fresco of Knossós; above, the Festós Disc.

women in labour, the birth helper, was sought. Even the poem Homer told recounted this. The Cave of Psichró was thought to have been the birth place of the young god who later became known to the Greeks as Zeus. Numerous votive objects, sacrifice tables, small statues, tools and double axes give an insight into this religion of nature, which endured for a considerable period of time.

The bull games, where the worldly and religious ceremonials were inextricably bound, were held in the theatre area. The bull was worshipped in Eastern cultures as a god-

33

like creature. In Catal Hüyük in South Anatolia, stylised bull horns were found, dating from the 6th millennium BC. On Crete the bull was probably the embodiment of virility. The god of heaven in Mesopotamia was a bull. The myth of the union of the beautiful bull and Pasiphae, the wife of Minos, may have its origin, in a Minoan belief in the holy marriage between the god of heaven and the Great Mother which resulted in the fertility of the earth and its flowers, plants and trees. The ubiquity of bull worship is indicated by sculptures and horns and their proximity to

the double axes. This cult aspect must not be overlooked when one admires the agile athletes and incredible acrobats.

The bull games certainly caused the deaths of athletes from time to time. Occasionally there may have been a sacrificial offering of one of the bulls, but on the whole the games were nowhere near as gory as present day bull fights. The venue for these tests of courage seems to have been the so-called "royal road," a narrow street leading to the wider theatre area, which was itself probably less suitable. The finding of a long stone foundation along the street, which could

well have offered seating for spectators, would seem to indicate this arrangement. Details of the games are shown in various representations: one of Crete's most beautiful murals has the games as its subject (AMI XIV). The unique representation of movement, one of the most important characteristics of Minoan art, is nowhere more evident than in the ivory sculpture of the suspended somersaulting bull leaper (AMI IV, cabinet 56) which is prized as one of the first examples of such movement in art. The cult container from the small palace in Knossós, the stone bull's head with lifelike rock crystal eyes, the golden horns and the wonderful slit and relief decoration of the head, show the special place held by this revered animal (AMI IV, cabinet 51, No. 1368).

A totally different aspect of Minoan art is seen in a ceramic model, dating from a somewhat later period, from Palékastro (AMI X, cabinet 132, No. 3903). Three women are dancing a round, with a lyre player in the centre. They are holding hands, and make a circle around the musician. Their long, bell-like robes accentuate their light swaying movements, described by Homer with the words: "...circling round, just like the rounded wheel the seated potter wields..."

In the ancient world, Crete was the cradle of dance, and several signet rings show ecstatic dancers. Some dances have even been handed down to the present day. Scenes of dancing are documented in the miniature frescoes at Knossós. Almost a thousand years later, the Greek poetess Sappho wrote in verse:

The Greek women,
Harmony in their light feet,
Danced around the altar of Eros,
Stepping on softly swelling flowers.

The dance for the protection of the newborn offspring of Zeus has its origin on the island of Crete. So too the choral songs in praise of Dionysos, from which Attic drama was to develop.

Special mention must be made of some

treasures of the purely Minoan Late Palatial works of art. In ceramics, where the forms become more slender, two new styles emerged with the building of new palaces. The flora style came a little earlier, with its dark colours on a light background. Very naturalistic, particularly in the depiction of grasses (AMI IV, VIII), it was used to portray the world of plants. The marine style eloquently expressed the other side of island life: octopuses, corals, shells and starfish. Here, particular attention should be paid to the works from East Crete (AMI IX, cabinets 120, 125; AM Agios Nikólaos, room 3).

However, some of the most remarkable pieces of art in the world must be the famous snake goddesses from the central sanctuary of Knossós (AMI IV, cabinet 50) whose interpretation as depicting mother and daughter is still controversial. Even though the third figure, like some of the others, is not complete, the clothing of these sacred figures clearly indicate the various fashions of the Late Palatial era. The arms and upper parts of the older goddess are covered with snakes, cult-like attributes of the female godheads. They may be seen as chthonian animal companions of the Earth Goddess, although in Minoan times they were looked upon as protective house demons.

Some of the most glorious work of Minoan art is seen in the unique murals. It is here, above all, that the whole depth of the love of life and the glorious creativity of Cretan artists is expressed. Here the combination of the grace and originality in the depiction of the themes and the rich colour composition are shown at their height. Alfresco, but also applied dry, the paintings adorned the walls and filled the surfaces of the rooms. Simple but durable mineral and metallic oxide colours glowed red, blue and green. They conjured up ornamental spirals and lines, painted over stucco relief work with bull scenes and pictures of cult festivals in the miniature frescos. Here and in the

Left, large portrait of a beauty of Knossós in blue. **Above**, Earth Mother with snakes from the Palace of Knossós.

Mycenaean versions as well, above all in the Minoan paintings which were uncovered on Santorini, the attractive youthfulness of this art has been well preserved and can still be appreciated today.

Even Níkos Kazantzákis was spellbound by the murals: "large almond shaped eyes, black swaying braids, noble, dignified women with bare breasts, with lush, sensual lips, and birds, pheasants, partridges, blue apes, kings' sons with peacock feathers on their heads, wild holy bulls, maiden-like priestesses with snakes winding around their

arms, blue boys in wonderful gardens: joy, strength, wealth, a secret world, Atlantis arisen from the depths of Cretan soil looked at us with huge black eyes, but with sealed lips. What world is this, I wondered, when will she open her mouth and speak? What great deeds had been performed by these ancestors from the soil of Crete upon which we stand?"

In about 1450 BC, this colourful splendour came to a sudden end. The cities and palaces of the Minoan civilisation collapsed in ruins. What actually happened? Was it the eruption of the volcano of Santorini, which was more devastating than the eruption of Krakatoa in 1883 (which left 36,000 dead), and the ensuing earthquake and tidal wave which caused the destruction of Minoan culture? Today, the catastrophe of Santorini is dated at about 1500 BC, 30 or 50 years before the destruction on Crete. It is, however, still possible that there were indirect repercussions, as the Cretan trading fleet must have suffered great losses. But the complete destruction of all the palaces – apart from Knossós – and the cities? The theory of an islandwide fire following the eruption of the volcano can no

social inequality may have led to disputes bordering on civil war, but there is no evidence to suggest an islandwide destructive battle. So it is possible that Crete came under Mycenaean influence in two stages.

First – we assume – Knossós and other places were conquered, much of them destroyed or possession taken of them. The influence of the political seizure of power on the culture, its tolerance of, and simultaneous adaptation to particular ideas and interests may have taken place as described centuries later by Horace, referring to the re-

longer be upheld today. The facts do not support any other thesis, so one is left with hypothesis. What is certain is that after this set-back, but perhaps even much earlier, Mycenaean regents ruled in the palace of Knossós which they altered and they themselves developed in quite a different way.

At Haniá too, the Linear-B clay tablets were found (up to then only secured in Knossós). The discoveries in Tourkogitonía/ Arhánes and Agiá Triáda from this period (1600–1450 BC) point to a Mycenaean presence in numerous other places in Crete – perhaps even earlier, as is now argued. Great

placement of Greek predominance by the Romans: "The Greek land was conquered, elevating the rough possessor."

It is at Knossós above all, that the slow process of change can be seen. The previously unknown and all-conquering Mycenaean war chariot is in use – although the Cretans used it mainly for outings. The throne room in the palace of Knossós was erected in this period. The royal grave of Isópata, to the north of Knossós, is definitely Mycenaean, as can be seen from its unfamiliar construction and arrangement of rooms. The war-like, masculine character of the new rulers is also evident in the knights' graves near Festós, which contained swords, daggers and spears – unusual grave furnishings on peaceful Crete. Also attributable to this warring spirit are the mercenary figures in the fresco scene "Leader of the Blackamoors" from Knossós (AMI XIV, No. 3); and in general the subjects of the murals became harsher (for example the Procession Fresco, AMI XIV, No. 21).

Even in Egypt, which continued to be a trading partner of the island, the change in Cretan clothing to a loin cloth, tapered at the

These valuable script documents were mainly the book keeping lists, although mention was made of some of the Greek gods. On the Knossós tablet V-52, four godheads are referred to, among whom was almost certainly the goddess Athena. There is dispute over the exact dating of the Knossós tablets, and over the date of the change from Linear-A to Linear-B, as well as over the deciphering itself.

In the field of ceramics, too, in the centres of foreign domination, a new style evolved: the so-called Palace Style. Although the

front, was observed. The script used for the palace book-keeping, Linear-A, was replaced by the more fitting Linear-B. This script, preserved on baked clay tablets, records an early form of the Greek language.

This was discovered, in a sensational effort of deciphering, by Michael Ventris in 1952. In Pylos in the Peloponnese, where similar tablets were found, the same language, Mycenaean Greek, was spoken.

Left, a sarcophagus found in the Palace of Agía Triáda. Above, a golden ring from a chamber tomb in Mycenae.

Minoan creative skill is still in evidence, in the art of stone working for example, there are, unfortunately, signs of decay. Now, instead of the octopus motif, reflecting the graceful Minoan style of movement, on a palace style amphora we see a swarm of battle helmets.

Around the year 1375 BC, the Palace of Knossós was destroyed – this time completely – and with it disappeared several other Minoan settlements and Mycenaean centres on the island, all of which served as invaluable testimony to the first great European civilisation.

Post Palatial Period (1375–1000 BC): Here again, the cause of the destruction is obscure. It is possible that there was an ultimately unsuccessful uprising on the island, against the foreign overlords. Perhaps the governor was evicted by Mycenaean mainland forces. The Mycenaeans now held parts of central Crete and were extending their influence.

Other Greek tribes forced their way onto the island, and Crete's influence abroad

were used and further developed in the new centres of power. Cretan artists who had emigrated contributed to this development. Thus the dramatic depiction of the conquest of a walled city on a silver rhyton from Mycenae (National Museum of Athens, Mycenaean Room, cabinet 27, No. 481), is probably an example of Cretan metal-working. This is in fact the oldest example of historical representation in the Occident.

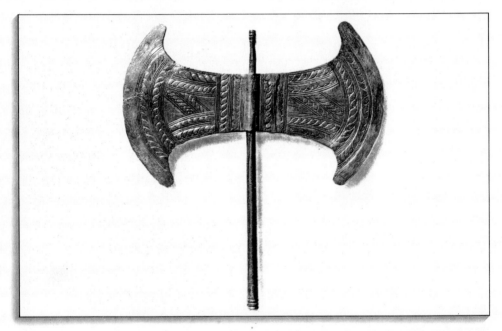

began to decline. The significance of what was now essentially a Mycenaean province of the Greek "community" (Koine), which included other islands such as Samos, Rhodes and Chios as well as parts of Thessaly and Asia Minor (e.g. Milet), was no longer what it had been. Mycenae and Tyrins, Thebes and Pylos, Sparta and Athens were now far more important as fortified centres of Mediterranean power, the internal disputes of which are recorded in the *Flight of the Atreids*.

While Crete was in decline, politically, culturally and artistically, Cretan artefacts

The lesser importance of Crete does not exclude the presence of a Mycenaean king on the island. Cretan participation in the Trojan War, considered more likely since grave findings in Besik Bay near Troy, with a fleet only slightly smaller than that of Agamemnon, would indicate this to have been probable. Homer relates, in the second book of the *Iliad*:

*But the renowned spear thrower Idome-
meus led the Cretans,
Who came from Knossós and the fortress
of Gortyn,*

Lyktos, Milet and Lycastos on chalk shim-
mering cliffs,
Phaestos, Rhytion too, those populous
towns
Others too, from Crete of a hundred cities,
These Idomeneus led, he of the skill with
the lance,
And Meriones, like the murderous Ares,
They were followed by a squadron of
eighty dark ships.

This time of decline, which may be referred to as the "Cretan-Mycenaean Civilisation", is also known as the time of "Reoccupation", when the palaces and buildings which had been destroyed were resettled. Unfortunately there is very little documentation of this period. The erection of a new palace cannot be proved, although it is assumed, but the small shrine of the double axes does date from this time. Life went on as usual in the cities of Festós, Knossós, Górtis and Agía Triáda and life began in a new way in what were, according to tradition, cities founded by the new rulers, such as Tegea, Pergamos and Lappa.

The sudden turning point is nowhere more clearly evident than in the far-reaching changes in artistic expression. The typical Mycenaean stylisation in ceramic decoration and the degeneration in thematic representation is clear evidence of artistic decline, particularly in stone work. A typical example of Mycenaean art is the "Goddess with uplifted hands."

The decline of Minoan culture, which had so long stimulated and enriched the Mycenaean, caused a cultural paralysis in Mycenaean artistic development, which was evident further afield than Crete. Art cannot be taken captive; culture cannot be conquered. The destruction of the artistic prerequisites led to the destruction of the culture itself. Crete shared with other places the history of Mycenae, which was not to last much longer.

Left, this golden double axe was found in the cave of Arkalochri. **Right,** the poppy goddess from Sazi is believed to be the goddess of fertility and healing.

In room X of the Archaeological Museum in Iráklion, the works of art and craft dating from this period are on view, and their uniformity is evident, despite slight traces of Minoan influence.

The greater political picture is known in general: the deadly feuds between Greek tribes may have led to the brutalisation and weakening of the Minoan kingdom. The vagabonds, sea robbers and plunderers to whom the destruction of the cities and palaces of Hattuscha and Ugarit, Mycenae and Tyrins, Pylos and Thebes is attributed, may

have included Cretan and Mycenaean adventurers in their number (Achaeans, Pelasgers) as indicated in Egyptian inscriptions from the time of Ramses III (1196–1166 BC). But the Trojan War is dated at this period of Mycenaean decline too. The legends of the journeys of the Argonauts and the return of the Heraclidae indicate momentous mass movements of peoples. Thucydides writes: "After this war (against Troy) the Hellenes moved and went to live elsewhere, and so there was no peace in the land and no power was gained. The late return of the warriors from Troy brought

39

much strife. The conquered felt the need to leave and to found new cities."

At this time members of another Greek tribe, the Dorians from the north, migrated to Crete. Eteorcretans (the "real" Cretans), Pelasgers, Kydonians (West Cretans) and Dorians made up a multilingual mix of peoples, amongst whom in the ensuing centuries, the Dorians were dominant.

The original inhabitants fled to remote and inaccessible parts of the island, there to guard their own cultural identity. They preserved ancient customs and forms of expression which were their own, although showing Mycenaean influence (AMI XI, cabinets 148, 154). Above all they kept their own original language.

sub-Minoan times (1100–1000 BC) and in the Protogeometric period, the beginnings of which lie before the turn of the millennium, cultural schisms are evident with traces of Minoan customs in the regional development of the new Dorian "three-class system" (see Homer, *Odyssey*, XIX, 171). The successful newcomers and their warriors became the new ruling class; the burghers were guaranteed specific rights by a binding legislation. Then there was a third group of non-Dorians which seems to have constituted an oppressed servants' class.

By the end of this Post Palatial period, the Minoan dream of peaceful coexistence in a flourishing culture was lost. But the efforts of archaeologists, who have painstakingly unearthed traces of this civilisation, have revealed that Minoan culture did in fact remain unconquered and that, above all, its influence on the historical consciousness in the present century can easily be traced.

Geometric Period (1000–700 BC): Even in

Slowly a political system of "Spartan" strength was formed on Crete. The towns were heavily fortified and youths eligible for military service were trained. Tougher and more reliable weapons were produced with the use of iron, which now superseded bronze. Burial of the dead was replaced by urn cremation. The somewhat clumsy Protogeometric ceramic works are displayed in the Archaeological Museum in Iráklion, Room XI. With the development of the early geometric style which followed, starkly stylized figures, which differed from those of the mainland, were created (AMI, cabinets 146,

155). In the later, mature geometric phase there was a reawakening of original creativity, although the works cannot compare with the Attic amphoras or the Olympic bronze sculptures of the same period. The impression of a provincial, reactionary place, poor in ideas slowly receded, and a period of isolation drew to a close for Crete. As a Dorian port of transshipment and centre of maritime trade, it did not find itself completely cut off from the neighbouring Mediterranean cultures.

Archaic Epoch (700–550 BC): In the following Homeric and post-Homeric century and a half, Crete, as part of the Greek world, was drawn into the upheaval and radical change which characterised this period of strife, poverty and over-population. A colonisation movement led to the formation of almost 1,500 city states, some of which were tiny. This movement of peoples stimulated the region, both politically and economically. The high turnover of goods through the new trading centres of Ionian Asia Minor, and throughout the Levant, brought about an economic upsurge.

In the realm of art, it can be seen that the years of relative isolation were over, and that the stereotyped repetition of circular and rectangular ornamentation and uniform geometric figures was at an end. In the visual arts, Homeric myths were presented and in a more varied and livelier way, which freed them from the constraints of the ornamental and decorative style, and breathed new life into long-buried creative ability.

Left, the little horses of the pyxis are from the geometric epoch. **Above**, graphic imitation of Mycenaean armour.

Perhaps Crete had already been stimulated artistically by the completely different cultures of Syria or Assyria, for there was much trade between those countries, or perhaps its location had attracted foreign artists to settle, enriching the artistic creativity on the island. Whatever the reason, for the last time in its long history, Crete developed its own form of artistic expression: the Daedalic Style. Among the numerous workshops on the islands in the Aegean and on the mainland, the school of Daedalus and his pupils was considered of decisive importance in the renewal of Greek sculpture. And the name lives on, giving lasting renown to the style and to that legendary time.

In the grotto long associated with the birth of Zeus, unique bronze shields and tympana (sound cymbals) were discovered, first by Cretan shepherds and later as a result of systematic excavation, by Fabricius, Halbherr and Aerakis in 1885. Because of their oriental relief work, they were ascribed functions in the cult of Zeus: legend has it that a warlike noise was made while dancing to drown the cries of the infant Zeus, hidden in the grotto, in order to save him from being

(AMI XVII, cabinet 193) which was found at Górtis in a holy place on the Acropolis, is generally taken to represent the goddess Athena. Notable too, are the Sphyrelata from Dréros near Neápolis, three cult figures which depict Apollo, Leto and Artemis. Hammered bronze once covered their wooden cores like a skin. The cores have long since rotted away. Although damaged, the 80 cm high central figure is impressive, with her oriental cap, as are the goddesses who are adorned with early Daedalic hair ornaments (AMI XIX, 210).

swallowed by his father Kronos.

The bronze work shows a transformation of oriental form and content. From the oriental hero Gilgamesh, the hand of either a Cretan or an immigrant North Syrian master has fashioned a wonderful drawing of the Cretan Zeus (AMI XIX, cabinet 209).

The importance of early Cretan sculpture is evidenced by the stone sculptures of the goddesses of Górtis, a town in the region of Festós, which was growing ever more powerful (AMI XIX). This may be a representation of Artemis and Leto, in Minoan-Dorian oriental style; the statuette with a helmet

The oldest of the temples built in the archaic period with Minoan architectural elements have been excavated near Priniás on the eastern foothills of the Ida Mountains. The unique late Daedalic portal sculptures of two goddesses seated opposite one another clearly reflect traces of Egyptian and Syrian/Phoenician iconography.

The picture of the archaic epoch may be completed by a visit to the Dorian city of Lató in the district of Mirabéllo, which was founded at this time. With its streets lined with houses and its ground plans of the stores, above all the Agora and the show staircase area, it gives a significant insight into the early history of Greek city life and theatre. If one looks at the old steps, which are reminiscent of the arenas of Festós, Gourniá or Agía Triáda, one seems to feel, across the dark ages, something of the *joie de vivre* of the Minoans which Homer so vividly describes:

> *Glowing youths there and much acclaimed young women danced around, hand in hand.*
> *Soft clothes covered the youths, light as oil's soft glow, and the maidens were veiled in linen.*
> *Every dancing girl was adorned with a lovely garland, and the youths had golden daggers at their sides in silver belts...*
> *Many were those crowded around the lovely dancers, rejoicing with all their hearts...*

–Homer, *Iliad*, XVIII, 5593/604

As the archaic epoch drew to a close, Crete sank back into the obscurity of an island province.

Classical Hellenistic Period (550–67 BC): In the following period, the political and cultural focus was finally established on the mainland. Attica became the new centre of Greece. Athens, which rivalled Sparta, had for centuries waged war, not only against the threatening enemy of Persia. With the birth of Greece from the Aegean (Gaitanides), Crete was relegated to the cultural and political sidelines. Although tradition and poetry enabled the island to maintain its high reputation, there was no new outstanding creativity in the field of art.

There is, however, one extraordinary document which must be mentioned: a stone inscription which affords the visitor a glimpse into the ancient Cretan legal system. "King Minos" was renowned for his wisdom, although he was also known as a stern law maker and judge. It is said that the legendary Spartan law maker Lykurg studied on Crete. Even Solon enriched early

Greek legislation from Cretan law. So, for the ancients, Crete was also an island with a high reputation in the field of law.

In 1884, Federico Halbherr – soon to be assisted by Ernst Fabricius – found the great inscription of Górtis. Standing in the mill canal of Déka, they deciphered a total of 17,000 signs carved in broadstone which was the legal script of the rising Cretan town of Górtis.

This settlement on the Messará plain had long lain in the shadow of the older royal residence of Festós, but now the city was on

its way to becoming the centre of this fertile region. With its two trading ports of Mátala and Levín in the south, it was able to outstrip Festós, and possibly the other cities of the island too. There are 12 columns, each with 52 lines, expertly carved in the stone, in a special "printed carving", in the language of an old Dorian dialect. The lines follow a so-called "ox turn", that is, the lines turn like the ox when ploughing (Bustrophedon). They do not simply follow each other but alternate and reverse, with the letters set in the mirror image. In the early Greek alphabet, the letters Phi, Chi, Psi, Zeta, Eta and Omega are

Left, remains of the once lively stage in Agía Triáda. **Right**, the caves of Mátala, so often inhabited in times of need.

43

missing. The 20 tablets of law, each about 70 cm wide and about 170 cm high, make up the longest Greek inscription ever found, and reflect a hitherto unknown and very ancient set of laws. The inscription is generally dated at about the first half of the 5th century.

There is no clear separation of the different branches of the law. The work deals with civil and criminal law, substantive and procedural law, and deals with the punishment for adultery and claims following a death. Different sanctions were imposed for (free and unfree) burghers (by the latter one assumes the descendants of the old suppressed Minoan peoples are meant). Here is an example: "Whoever assaults a free male or female, must pay one hundred strate... If a slave assaults a free male or female, he must pay double... Whoever assaults his own slave, must pay two strate..."

Even the rights of possession of the children of slaves had been dealt with. They were as follows: the child of an unmarried slave woman was allocated to her father's master; the child of a married slave woman, to her husband's master.

It was correctly assumed that this body of laws was of more than regional importance. The reference to the old laws showed interesting developments in the new laws. In this period, influenced by the Dorians, there are no longer any indications of a matriarchal society, and the rights of women are hardly better than those of slaves.

Interesting information is also provided on the methods of giving evidence: "If the case concerns a slave (or any other possession) and each party maintains that he is the owner then, if a witness testifies, the judge will rule in accordance with that evidence;

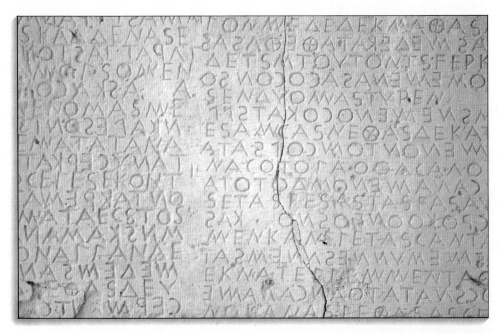

but if witnesses support the claims of both parties, or of neither, then the judge must rule in accordance with his conscience under oath." (I, 16–24).

Not much took place on or around Crete at this time. Górtis had almost attained its goal of becoming the main city, and in the changeable Cretan city state history there were many often short-lived agreements and contracts. Sometimes they backed the wrong horse, as in the support for the Persian fleet in the sea battle against Alexander the Great in Issos (333 BC). He remained unvanquished. The Hellenic events which influenced world history, from the death of Alexander the Great (323) to the death of Caesar, were only followed from a distance on the island of Crete.

Roman Occupation (67 BC–AD 337): The following almost 2,000 years were determined by foreign occupation and by rulers who saw Crete as a bread-basket or as an important strategic naval base. The years were of course marked by the resistance of the Cretans to these unbidden intruders and their hostile armies.

For about 400 years the new Mediterranean power (and later world power) of Rome

Roman province (Crete-Cyrere) with Górtis as its capital. Górtis had been friendly to the Romans, aiding them in their occupation, and was thus rewarded.

Ruins and archaeological finds give evidence of a Roman way of life, but also reflect the restraints imposed on the foreign rulers by the people, and the compromises they were obliged to make after many years of suppression and rebellion. That the island experienced a modest flowering is indicated by the theatres and temples, villas and water systems, especially in Górtis and the new

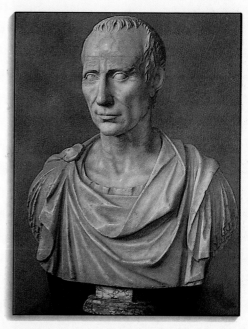

nean power (and later world power) of Rome was the determining factor in Cretan life. One of the first measures taken was against the hordes of pirates whose bases were on Crete and in Cilicia and who were in part supported in their efforts by the islanders. In the year 67 BC the Praetor Quintus Caecilius Metellus and his troops landed near Haniá and after several years of resistance, conquered the island which then became another

Left, the law carved in stone at Górtis. **Above**, Gaius Julius Caesar, 100–44 BC (right) raised eyebrows when his face was put on a coin (left).

garrison city of Knossós. Crete also played a part in the early history of Christianity: Paul, whose companion Titus became the first bishop of Crete, on his way into captivity in Rome in the year AD 59 stopped at Kalí Liménes. The conversion of the island to Christianity had its martyrs, such as the "Holy Ten" (Agii Déka), beheaded in AD 250 for refusing to worship the Roman gods. With the decline of Roman imperial power, Pax Romana and the temporary suppression of piracy came to an end. As early as the year 67, Pompeius had prepared for a decisive blow, with 500 ships and 120,000 soldiers.

Byzantines (AD 337–826): Crete maintained its non-central role during the rule of the Byzantines, who became responsible for this Mediterranean region from AD 337 onwards, before the Roman Empire was divided into West and East Rome (AD 395). The day of 11 May 330 saw the inauguration of the old city of Byzantium as Constantinople, the Christian capital of a state system which was to last for a thousand years. Crete was administered from there, and was left to its shadowy existence. Christianity was allowed to flourish on the island.

Many churches were built, of which the most important architecturally and from the point of view of ecclesiastical history, is perhaps the domed basilica of Holy Titus in Górtis. This dates from the 6th century, and was probably erected on the site of a more ancient building near the Roman odeon and theatre. In general it can be assumed that the political situation was stable.

Crete, and the rest of the Aegean, remained unaffected by the first convulsions which shook the East Roman Empire, the assaults by Germanic tribes between the 4th and 6th centuries. But in AD 623 the island was shaken by the Slav migrations. From the mid 7th century, Crete was the scene of Arab attempts to move northwards to conquer Constantinople, which was the cultural and political centre of the world at that time. After decades of fighting for supremacy, East Rome lost Sicily and Crete in 827. Both islands were ceded to the Arabs.

Arabs (AD 826–961): The ports of Crete soon became used by the Saracen pirates, who made life dangerous throughout the whole Aegean, up to the Dardanelles. This became a permanent feature of life under the Arab occupation. More oppressive, however, was the complete destruction of all Christian monuments, and the grim pursuit and persecution of Cretan Christians and the rigid exercise of Arab power for more than a century. Once again many islanders retreated to hide-outs in the mountains.

In AD 828 the Arabs set up their headquarters near the present-day city of Iráklion, the fortress el-Khandek. The old city of Górtis was irrevocably destroyed. It was not until 961, after several attempts which came to nothing, that the East Roman army, led by Nikefóros Fókas, was finally able to retake Crete. As East Rome began to display its power, Crete was again ruled from Constantinople.

Return of the Byzantines (AD 961–1204): The retaking of the island was extremely bloody, even by the standards of those days, and Saracen heads were used as catapult ammunition against the fortresses of Rab-el Khandek. According to the chronicles there were more than 200,000 dead, and as many captives after a siege which lasted for months, resulting in a great famine which was followed by the eventual storming of the city. It was thanks to the retaking of Crete and of Aleppo (926) that Fokás was made emperor two years later.

By then Crete was a relatively independent military and administrative region. Its location led to a certain isolation and agriculture soon became refeudalised. Merchants from the capital city, and from allied neighbouring lands came to Crete, and reinvigorated the sea trade, which was mainly controlled by Genoese families. As life became more stable on Crete, both politically and culturally – architecture and fresco painting experienced a revival – so the power of Constantinople declined. This was illustrated in the complete tax exemption of the big landowners and the emergence of a bureaucracy. According to tradition, an attempt to gain autonomy took place at the time of the Byzantine defensive action against the Seldschuks (1090–92). But it ended with the arrival of the imperial sailing fleet, commanded by Johannes Dukas.

century) or in Kritsá (Panagía-i-Kerá, 13th–14th centuries).

Venetian Rule (1204–1669): The historical background of the change of ruler which heralded the decline of the Byzantine Empire was the occupation of Constantinople during the Fourth Crusade. Venice now acquired the island, by a contract of purchase from the Genoese owners (a gift of the last Byzantine Emperor Alexios III Angelos). The Venetians were able to make good use of the island in their maritime expansion. By means of only a few representatives sta-

Byzantine art was dated from the dominant period of Constantinople (up to 1202–04). The Byzantine church buildings of Miriokéfala (Panagía Church, 11th–12th century) with its many frescoes, was built during the period of the reconquest of Crete. Byzantine art treasures from the following Venetian epoch are more numerous, and equally admirable, in Assómatos (Arhánes, Church of the Archangel Michael, 14th

Left, view of the excavation site of Górtis. **Above**, stone-cold structure: monument to Byzantine rule at Moni Arkádi.

tioned on Crete, these new strong and dictatorial rulers managed to put down 14 major uprisings and a rebellion during the next four and a half centuries, and at the same time expand the economy. The island of Crete was completely transformed and brought in line with Venetian ideas. Place names were changed – Crete took the name of Candia, as did the old capital (Chandax). Building began, in order to change the face of the island – not entirely to its detriment, it must be admitted. Politically, the Cretans were able to escape Venetian influence, at least in some parts of the island. In other parts, the

47

islanders rose up against the nobles of the ruling class and proclaimed a "Republic of St Titus." A concession for religious tolerance of the Eastern Christians ensured the solidarity of the people, but the gruesome end of the uprising in 1363–64 was inevitable.

Only after the final fall of Constantinople (1453) did Byzantine artists and learned men come to Crete. They were to enrich this Greek and East Roman influenced island considerably. Some ships and volunteers had, in fact, taken part in the defence of Constantinople against the Turks. Now this

tured capital (1326), to the most important power in the Eastern Mediterranean, with Constantinople (1453) as their last capital city. As they pushed westwards, the Ottomans encountered fierce resistance (Battle for Vienna 1683). Their conquest of the island was brutal, and succeeded despite the resistance led by Francesco Morosini. There were persistent attempts by the islanders to break free.

For the Turks, the island was a source of tax revenue but, more crucially, a base of great military importance, so that even when

meeting of the Latin early Renaissance spirit and the Greek Orthodox antique heritage was to bring forth its own results. This was most clearly evidenced in the new capital where features still visible today, such as the Morosini Fountain, the Loggia and the Agios Markos Church, reflect this new culture. The Turks took the island in 1669, after three harsh years of siege at Candia. Afterwards, about 150,000 dead were counted.

Turkish Occupation (1669–1898): By the time Crete was conquered, the Ottoman Empire had grown from a band of Turkish clans with Bursa/Brussa as their first cap-

the islanders refused their economic cooperation and the towns grew desolate, the retention of this island, so dearly paid for, always seemed justified.

In Cretan lore the famous attempted uprising of 1770 has never been forgotten. Before the Cretan Dhaskalojánnis could make use of a coalition with the enemy of the Turks, Russia, during the Russo-Turkish War (1768–74), he was tricked by the Sultan, who, announcing himself ready to negotiate, took him prisoner and tortured him to death.

But Crete remained an inspiration to revolt for the other islands of the Aegean, and the numerous battles necessary to safeguard conquered territory slowly wore down the Ottoman Empire. Gradually a Greek national consciousness was born. In 1821 the Greek mainland and some of the islands rebelled. The Peloponnese was free.

In the winter of 1824–25, Mohammed Ali, viceroy of Egypt and the new commander in chief of the occupational fleet landed on Crete, which had been given him by the Turks as a reward for his punitive expedition against the Greeks. Once again the island was conquered. Meanwhile, other great

chafing under the rule of a Bavarian king's son (Prince Otto). But there was no peace on Crete, which the British had taken from Egypt and returned to Turkey in 1841. In 1869 the Paris Conference extended Cretan autonomy. However, three years earlier, on 8 November 1866, in the monastery of Arkádi, hundreds of Cretans had blown themselves to bits by exploding a cache of arms rather than be captured.

To this day, Crete celebrates its own National Day on 8 November. Freedom or death – for decades this was the only honour-

powers of Europe had decided to attempt to deal with this centre of conflict. On 6 July 1827, an armistice was arranged between Russia, Great Britain and France, and Greece (without Crete) was guaranteed autonomy, albeit under Turkish sovereignty.

It was not until 1830, after continued acts of war, that a peace settlement came into force. In 1832 Greece was a kingdom, now

able maxim for survival through times of rebellion and heroism when retaliation was part of everyday life.

In 1897 an attempt by the mainland to win back the island failed. Then in the following year Crete acquired "autonomous status" under Ottoman supremacy, with the full support of the great powers. The high commission of Prince George became the party responsible for the administration of the island. An almost incidental event, when some British soldiers were killed, finally led to the end of the Turkish presence on the island in November 1898.

Far left, icon of Mary, the Holy Mother of Jesus. **Left**, Turkish Cretans. **Above**, an old Cretan tells the story of the Turkish occupation of Crete with a couple of visual aids.

49

Life on Crete during this century has essentially been influenced by three main political events. First, union with the mainland of Greece (*Enosis*) aroused passions, and no foreign interference was wanted. In World War II the people were suppressed by German troops of occupation; finally there was the terror perpetrated during the years 1967–74 by the colonels who had siezed power in Athens.

At the beginning of the century Crete was

still under international protection. True autonomy and the *Enosis* which everyone awaited for so long still had to be fought for. The struggle for independence was led by the Cretan Elefthérios Venizélos. He was head of the liberal party and later minister of justice and foreign affairs in the relatively powerless Cretan national government of Prince George. His goal was finally achieved on 30 May 1913, after the abdication of Prince George (1906), the dissolution of the high commission (1908) and, finally, the withdrawal of international forces from the island (1909). Venizélos' attempt to occupy

the Turkish capital and to found a new Byzantium ended miserably in bloody failure. Crete was obliged to take 13,000 Greeks from Asia Minor in exchange for 11,000 Cretan Turks (the more than 1.55 million Greeks who had lived in Turkey had to leave the country).

More drastic for the islanders was the occupation during World War II by German troops. On 20 May 1941, German parachutists and mountain infantrymen landed near Haniá, where they attempted to provide security for further airborne contingents. This risky operation resulted in far more casualties than expected, because the British, who were defending the island, had been well prepared for the invasion. On 2 November 1944, the occupying troops left the island, although the last units did not leave West Crete until after the war. During the occupation, the island had been ravaged, and hundreds of men and women fell victim to the Nazis.

When the Cretan resistance fighters initiated guerrilla actions against the German occupational forces, the latter retaliated by destroying whole villages and arbitrarily shooting Cretan civilians. German orders were "10 Cretans for every German shot." In some mountain villages the male population was wiped out. Today, young Germans who know the history of the island can only marvel at the great hospitality which is shown them nowadays by the Greeks.

The long occupation and terror did not succeed in breaking the resistance of the Cretans. On the contrary, the island became the very centre of Greek resistance. Many of the actions taken by the Cretan people were courageous ones. They paid for them in blood during the rigourous punishments inflicted by German occupying forces. The older people still remember these incidents vividly, particularly the surprise action by partisans which caused the capitulation of the German headquarters in October 1944. But even this led to a terrible revenge, and the mountain village of Anógia was completely destroyed. The effects of such persistent resistance, bringing much grief and sorrow, were felt long after the war. The late official recognition of this was of widespread importance.

It was not until 1945 that the last troops departed from Crete, leaving burnt villages, bombed out cities and destroyed roads. The island was in economic ruins.

The last important chapter of the struggle for freedom lies in the recent past, and some visitors can still clearly remember it. Greece has now become a republic with parliamen-

On 21 April 1967, a group of right wing colonels staged a *coup d'état* against the elected government, and destroyed the liberal politics of the centrist coalition under George Papandreou, establishing a military dictatorship. Any opposition was rigourously suppressed, detention camps were set up, and the regime supported the foreign policy of the American protecting power.

Following student unrest (1973) and the Cyprus adventure (1974), the dictatorship was overthrown. In 1981 a cabinet determined by PASOK was voted in in an attempt to

tary democracy, with Crete as one of its ten administrative provinces. At first the bloody civil war had led to an unstable quasi protectorate status.

In 1974, the United States of America replaced Great Britain as "protecting power". A controversial alteration of electoral law, effected by the Americans in 1952, afforded stable conservative majorities in the Greek parliament until 1963.

Left and **above**, monuments to the freedom fight of the Cretans. Venizélos was in the forefront during the fight for independence.

break free of American influence. The internal politics of the new government of Andreas Papandreou mirrored the age old Greek longing for freedom and social justice. But this aim was not realised in actuality. In June 1989 PASOK, which had been shaken by corruption, scandals and private upheavals, lost its majority. An interim coalition of conservatives and communists took over. The US military bases on the island (Timbaka in the Messará plain and Goúves near Iráklion) still present a political problem for Crete which is bound to come to a head in the next few years.

Crete, an island of sunshine equidistant from Asia, Africa and Europe, has become a major tourist attraction. What's more, its popularity continues to increase, a trend not likely to change for some years yet.

The many battles fought over Crete serve to reinforce the historical importance of this central point of the Mediterranean. It is still a very important place today. In the old days, it was a necessary base from which the safety of trading routes could be ensured, whereas nowadays it is the strategic military importance which takes precedence. With its air force and rocket bases and the fleet in Soúda Bay, it is now one of the most vital NATO bases in Europe.

Here on the island of Crete, about 4,000 years ago, the first great European civilisation developed. It was named the Minoan civilisation, after the mythical king Minos, son of Zeus and Europa. Numerous excavations have yielded a great deal of information about this period, but much of the life of the Minoans still remains obscure. What is certain is that the Minoan palaces and places of worship constitute some of the main attractions of the island. Even Homer was full of admiration:

Crete is a land set in the dark billowing seas,
Fertile and charming and surrounded by water. There live
Numerous people, and their cities are ninety,
People of many races and many languages! There live
Achais, Kydones and native Cretans,
Dorians of three different groups, and noble Pelasgers,
Their royal city is Knossós, where Minos ruled,
Who spoke nine years long with Zeus, the great god.

Thus the description in the *Odyssey*. But even for Homer (8th century BC) the Minoan epoch was ancient history and shrouded in that same mystery which captures and fascinates visitors to Knossós to this day.

Explorers assume that the 90 cities referred to had about 1.2 million inhabitants. Today there are only about half a million people who live on the island, but the mixture is still as colourful. The appearance of Crete has, however, changed dramatically. Ancient authors tell of huge cypress and pine forests, but centuries of plunder have denuded the island, leaving bare limestone scenery. Only further inland, mainly in the west, are there any wooded areas.

Geography and Economy: There are four high mountain ranges which form the character of the island: the Lefká Ori in the west (Pánhes 2,452 metres); the central Ida or Psilorítis Mountains (Tímos Stavrós 2,456 metres); the Díkti Mountains (Díkti 2,148 metres) in the central west and further west, the Sitía Mountains (Aféndis Stavoménos 1,476 metres). Then there are the lower ranges such as the Asteroússia Mountains in the south, so that, in all, 51 percent of Crete is mountainous and another 26 percent hilly.

The remaining 23 percent of flat land is devoted to agriculture, which next to tourism is the main industry on the island. Vegetables, olives, vineyards and citrus fruit are cultivated. On the Messará Plain, with its vast expanse of about 140 sq. metres, and in other smaller flat areas, production has been increased by the introduction of greenhouses which enable the farmers to reap more than one harvest per year.

The fertile high plains of Lassíthi, Omalós, Nída and Askífou provide not only a sharp contrast to the karstic mountains, but offer the only ground where potatoes and cereals can be grown, although the bulk of these still has to be imported.

Organisation and Population: Crete is divided into four administrative districts. The four capital cities of these districts lie on the north coast of the island. It is quite impossible to say which is the most typical city, as was Knossós or Kydonia in ancient times, for the four are as different from one another as are the four humours. Iráklion with its oriental colour and confusion epitomises the choleric, effervescent temperament; Haniá by contrast is sanguine. Réthimnon has a melancholy aspect, while Agios Nikólaos is phlegmatic and opulent.

As the best beaches are on the northern coast, it is here that the tourists congregate. Almost 50 percent of all holiday makers are to be found on the 70-km stretch between Iráklion and Agios Nikólaos. The current

126,000 inhabitants is full of contrast; Lassíthi with 70,000 people in a large area, is the least densely populated, and Réthimnon with 62,000 people, is the smallest and most mountainous district.

Climate and Weather: Blue skies and a glorious view over fields, mountains and sea: most brochures picture Crete as having only eternal summer weather. In fact there are three climatic zones on the island. The north has a typical Mediterranean climate, the interior has mountain weather and the south is subtropical, with desert climate at times.

Crete and Southern Greece

tourist capital is the town of Agios Nikólaos.

Iráklion, with its capital city of the same name, is the colossus of the districts. About 244,000 people live here, almost half the total population of the island. Here too more ancient sites are found than on the rest of the island districts put together, which indicates that even in the early days this was the most populous region. Of course other districts have their own attractions: Haniá with its

Preceding pages: view of the Lassíthi Plateau; sheep and snow on Psilorítis; the Cretan carries out his day's work in the café.

There are only two seasons, the dry season from May to October with July and August as the hottest months, and the rainy season from November to April, with constant rain and storms in November and December. While there is no real autumn, spring arrives briskly in March/April. However, the spring is very short, and there is no period of gradual growth as in northern climes.

These climatic changes do, of course have an effect on the choice of holiday period. The summer months are the best for beach holidays, as the sometimes almost unbearable heat precludes walking and sightseeing. In

April there is a lot of rain, and bathing is cool – perhaps a good time to try the south coast. But the glorious flowers which bloom in profusion are a wonderful compensation. The sea is warm right up till October, but by autumn the colours have faded and the fields after the harvest are empty and brown.

Then there are the unpredictable winds, which can change suddenly. The hot, dry south winds which often carry sand from the Sahara can be felt even in the north. The north winds, however, bring a welcome breath of cool air in the baking summer heat.

knows to whom the island belongs, least of all the Cretans, who in the past, and in recent times have shed so much blood trying to free themselves from the yoke of Islam, but in vain. The valiant sons of this classic isle fight this national battle bravely, and at the head of the warriors, as in Ireland, Poland and Tirol and elsewhere in similar struggles, are enthusiastic priests for whom the fight for freedom of the land is consecrated to God. The capital city, Candia and the important port of Canea have little attraction for us today as things stand, we'll leave them be-

If you go out boating, you really do need to pay special attention to the extremely changeable nature of the winds in the waters around the island.

Tourism: About 100 years ago, according to the *Illustrated Manual of Geography and Ethnology*, this was the sight which greeted the traveller arriving by sea: "In the distance the jagged mountains of the isle of Crete appeared, with the highest peak the Ida, where Cretan Zeus was born. From these people, the Cretan Dorians, Lykurg took his strict laws for the Spartans, and today the island is a sad reflection of unlawfulness. No one

hind, and sail to the island of Milo, where there is peace."

This impression seems to have lasted for a long time. Up until the 1950s, travellers would pass Crete by. In 1953, for example, only 450 visitors were counted. Since then the numbers have steadily increased and in 1983-84 they passed the million mark: 1988 saw between 1.3 and 1.5 million tourists on Crete and the numbers are still growing.

In accordance with Arthur Koestler's remark that "tourists are more easily milked than cows" (here it's sheep and goats, of course) the revenue from tourism has almost equalled that of agriculture, traditionally the most important branch of the economy. This change has brought with it a range of problems, some direct, others less so. It's quicker to earn money as a waiter than as a farmer, so many young people are leaving the villages, which then suffer a rise in the ratio of old people. In the long run this could bring about the decline of the rural economy. There has definitely been a decline in local traditions, most notably from the tourists' point of view, with regard to hospitality. In fact the legendary Cretan hospitality in olden days

Prosperity alone has altered things too. But it also has to be admitted that the same people who bring prosperity also alter things, and bring new ideas like naked bathing and sexual freedom. Moreover, the difference in the standard of living between those people directly involved in the tourist trade, and those who are not, may lead to wider social divisiveness. This is happening today, not just in the coastal areas, but also within the villages and towns and even in quite isolated mountain settlements.

was only offered to certain foreigners, who in those days were to a certain extent "the minority passing through." Nowadays, if one arrives alone, particularly in the interior, or visits older folks, everything is still as it used to be. However, certain things, particularly in the gastronomic field, have changed. It can happen that one is given an orange upon arrival, only to discover the "gift" has

Left, pupils from the Music School of Réthimnon acquainting themselves with Cretan folk music. **Above**, viticulture is one of the most important sources of income.

There are also other quite unexpected difficulties. As most tourists don't just come for the Minoans or the climate, but want to experience something of the "real" Crete, they are irritated that their money has had the effect of changing the country in a way which is actually not in their interest at all. Motorways, of great benefit to everyone, are seldom criticised, but when whole village communities tear down their old houses, which were uninhabitable by our standards, and rebuild themselves villages in the finest concrete, then one can understand the irritation of the public, for surely we want everything to stay nice and picturesque. At least on holiday, one wants to enjoy unspoiled beauty. Many places are financially far better off than before, but this new competitive thinking often leads to quarrels. In Paleóhora, which has for years been prone to such bickering, a rather bitter joke used to go around – that the Cretans were going to leave their little town to the tourists and retreat into the mountains.

Despite what one sees in Hersónissos or Mália, Crete is in no real danger of being spoiled. Regular visitors can see immense

iter, or foreign workers. No, all in all, one has to admit that tourism is as much a blessing to the island, as the island, with its Mediterranean climate and natural beauty, is a boon to the tourists. One just has to try to ensure that the development is kept within limits, so that it can all remain a blessing, and the intrinsic charm and loveliness of the island survive well preserved.

The Church: Almost all Cretans are adherents of the Greek-Orthodox Church, which has always played a special role on the island. During the long periods of foreign

changes: some remote village which has been established suddenly, or another daring dream of the Cretan planners come true. This trend of thought led Ierápetra, perhaps with an envious look at the sophistication of the Riviera, to build a promenade of overly grand proportions. But it would be a mistake to see only the negative side of tourism on Crete. There are no natural resources on the island and, apart from a few food and textile factories, no industry either. Thus jobs are extremely scarce here. It is noticeable just how many Cretans speak German – as a result of working in Germany as *Gastarbe-*

domination, the Church was much more than merely a community of believers. It became a social institution, running schools and hospitals; above all it was the focus of unity and resistance to oppression.

In a novel by P. Prevelákis, the following dialogue takes place between a worker and a monk. The two are locked in an argument with each other:

Worker: "And to think I took you for a holy man."

Monk: "Here one is a man first, and only then holy."

This original and somewhat profane interpretation of Christian teaching (think of "turning the other cheek") is typically Cretan. The struggle of the people against the various foreign rulers over the centuries has always been closely bound up with the Church. The many attacks on the island's 34 monasteries are a clear indication of just where the enemy suspected the centres of resistance to be.

Just how seriously the Cretans took their maxim "freedom or death" was never more clearly demonstrated than at the monastery of Arkádi. Although there have been similar

waning. The younger generation is not prepared to grant the Church its traditional influence. Church greed is criticised. There has also been criticism of the attitude of the Church during the Turkish occupation, including charges of co-operation.

Civil marriage was introduced in 1983, and many of the younger Cretans now prefer this alternative. But among the older folk, and particularly in more remote areas, the influence and standing of the Church are as great as ever. None of this is of course a uniquely Cretan phenomenon.

struggles and battle cries elsewhere (in Germany, for example, in the ballad of *Pidder Ling* by Detlev v. Liliencron, 1883, the cry was "rather dead than slave"), nowhere has the duration of suppression equalled that which has taken place on Crete over the centuries. Thus the bonds between Church and people became particularly strong.

But nowadays the influence of religion is

Left, the Lassíthi Plateau is the centre of agriculture. **Above**, tourism makes money ever important both as a means of payment and as a status symbol on Crete.

Politics: It could be said, as an analogy to what the monk said, that "here one is first a Cretan, and only then a Greek." It is true that the Cretans have always worked towards *enosis*, union with Greece, but for reasons of security, not because of any deep feeling of solidarity. There's a saying, "The English are megalomaniacs: they think they are the best in the world. The Irish are more modest – they merely feel themselves superior to the English."

Those sentiments so neatly expressed, could apply equally well to the relationship between the Cretans and the Greeks, who are of course not megalomaniac. As they lack their own skilled football teams, the Cretans, despite their feelings of superiority, will on occasion cheer teams from Athens or Thessaloniki, particularly if they are beating 11 players from another European country.

Fundamental to this feeling of superiority is the longing for freedom. Anything which appears to a Cretan as a curtailment of liberty is rejected. The course of their history has forced the people to become experts at discerning enemy intentions. It's no wonder that at Greek election time, the results from

The Cretan Character: There's an interesting theory that, in time, human nature takes on the characteristics of the weather. When one hears that Cretans are brave, proud, passionate, self-sacrificing and hospitable, then one can see the resemblance of these traits to the climate. But of course, there's another side to the coin.

When studying the Cretan character, one could be forgiven for thinking that the words "Cretan" and "critical" were related, or even had exactly the same meaning. (Etymologically however, there is no connection: criti-

the administrative district of Crete are always markedly different from those returned by the rest of the country.

When a referendum on the abolition of the monarchy was held in 1974, 69 percent of the Greeks voted for abolition, but 91 percent of the Cretan population returned a vote against the monarchy. And where else would ordinary people go into the streets armed, to protest against the removal of art treasures from their museums? That's what happened in 1979 in Iráklion when then Prime Minister Karamanlís wanted to loan part of the Minoan collection abroad.

cal comes from the verb *krínein*, to separate). Cretans are definitely highly critical. As they are interested in any kind of politics, the main target of their criticism is clear. But not far behind is their propensity for criticising each other. Cretans are proud to be Cretans, and this is evident in their criticism of other groups and nationalities. But internally, this critical attitude leads to a kind of hierarchy of superiority. The educated feel superior to the uneducated, the city dwellers to the farmers, those who live in the mountains to the fishermen, the rich to the poor, which again makes Crete rather like the rest of the world.

Over 2,000 years ago, Epimenides remarked that "all Cretans are liars, lazy-bones and bad hats." As Epimenides himself was a Cretan, the saying takes on another dimension. What might just have been an objective truth becomes something more. The philosopher would not have made such a remark casually. At the time, Crete was ruled by the Dorians, and one can imagine that his remark was meant to sow the seeds of doubt in the minds of the rulers, making them feel that there was nothing that in either character or action of the Cretans which they could take at face value.

It was only after St Paul had quoted this phrase of Epimenides, (Epistle of Paul to Titus, 1:12) adding "This witness is true," that the remark took on the gravity of a judgement. How do the Cretans stand these days, as regards their attitude to the truth? Well, all things considered, the following picture emerges: Cretans are given to showing off and making up stories. They talk a lot, promise a lot, and the next day they've forgotten it all, or it doesn't matter any more. And whether from necessity or for fun, they do tell lies. Reliability is just not their strong point. They are undisciplined and seldom finish what they start. If you arrange something with a Cretan, you can be pretty sure it won't come off. The result of this unreliability is an atmosphere of instability and nervousness, because no one knows whether he can rely on anyone else. "He who doesn't cheat stays poor." That's an old saying on the island. The author D. McNeil Doren, who lived on Crete for a long time, wrote of a Cretan girlfriend who completely changed character when he entered her shop to buy something. Having just helped him as a friend, she immediately tried to diddle him as a customer. This strange phenomenon is apparently quite common, as Cretans try to find out in their own way just how clever someone is.

So, feeling disillusioned, you go to the

Left, in Iráklion Cretans and non-Cretans alike spend hours in the cafés. **Right**, iced coffee is refreshing on hot days.

beach and cast your longing eyes at a succulent grape, and the next minute, it is yours. Or, in the evening, you ask the waiter at a café or bar of the hotel the name of a particular song that is being sung on television and the next morning there's the cassette at Reception, as a gift for you.

Generosity and indifference, spontaneity and calculation. How can these attributes be so intertwined? It's probably best simply to accept the Cretans, rather than to try to understand them. Perhaps they really are like the weather – where out of a clear blue sky,

a sudden squall can blow up, or without warning, the temperature change – and who can honestly say that they have ever understood the weather?

Once Again – The Minoans: The singularity of Crete was accurately summed up by Henry Miller when he wrote in 1940: "Greece is that which everyone knows, even if they have never been there... Crete is something else. Crete is a cradle, an instrument, a test tube in which a volcanic experiment is taking place." One could add the paradox, Crete is that which no one knows, however many times he has been there.

While in Greece architecture, politics, philosophy and religion all have clear-cut contours, on Crete so much is still lost in the mists of time. If you are looking for well preserved monuments like the Parthenon temples, you will probably be disappointed. For on Crete there are only fragments, but these set no limits on the imagination.

Despite the successful excavations, there is still so much which is unknown about the Minoan civilisation, and so much which may never be known. Was there in fact a monarchical system? If so, then what kind of monarchy was it that literally dared to place itself in the midst of the people, as is so clearly evident in Káto Zákros? What was the function of the buildings we refer to as palaces, and what was their relation to each other? If one assumes a matriarchy, then were the supposed kings actually priests, and the priestesses perhaps in fact queens? So many questions still remain unanswered.

This mystery, together with the lack of clear-cut facts, is in itself an attraction. It's not that everyone can exactly make up their own picture of the Minoans, but the relative lack of hard facts gives an unusual leeway for personal theories.

The Cretan authority J. Gaitanides went one step further when he asserted that Crete was a continent. Those few square miles – a continent? Such excess must surely have been influenced by the Cretan love of exaggeration. But what else can one call the sites of the Minoan culture, rising like huge monoliths out of the surrounding wilderness? Even later periods of foreign rule concentrate such a fill of historical events on the island as are in fact normally only found on whole continents. Last but not least, a world of consummate independence has been created by the fiercely individualistic Cretan people. In a word: the man is right! And you cannot really get to know a continent in one brief visit.

A Practical Start: It's best to be mobile on the island of Crete. The public bus service is good, and one can reach quite remote places on buses, but they are rather slow. So it is much better to hire a car, although more expensive. As one can move freely in a car, one tends, particularly in mountain areas to underestimate the distances. Only the New Road between Haniá and Agios Nikólaos is worthy of the name of motorway. On other well built stretches of road, from Iráklion in the Agía Varvára direction, for example, one can make quick progress.

But perhaps when you are exploring the island you should allow enough time for time itself to become unimportant – and simply enjoy the holiday. Or how about riding on a motorbike or moped? It will carry you – perhaps not quite as safely – to your destination, with the refreshing Cretan wind blowing in your face.

There are bicycles too for hire in certain places. If you want to enjoy the scenery more intensely, then try shank's pony. It pays to plan your days. If you have only a little time, but want to see a lot, there's a danger of missing the essential nature of the island, while ruining your holiday. The maxim of "better to enjoy the beach than traipse around the monuments in boredom" has turned many a Crete visitor into a Crete lover. Antique monuments have the enormous advantage that they won't walk away. If you visit them, don't cram too many facts and figures. Just remember that under the bright Cretan sun, everything changes. It's best to travel light – that goes for your mind as well as for your luggage!

Festivals: The Minoans enjoyed celebrations, if H.G. Wunderlich is to be believed. He was inspired by a mural to describe a harvest festival. As he saw it, the people had gathered in the palace courtyard, the women dressed in their best and their dark hair elaborately styled. The sign for the beginning of the tournament was about to be given by the priestess with the holy snakes held high in her hands. Seven young men and women were to perform a breakneck leap over the bull. Then the people would go outside until the evening, when they would all reassemble in the theatre to watch the dances of the girls.

Cretans today like nothing more than a celebration. Any excuse will do. Most festi-

vals are in honour of the saints, and on their name days, a service is held in the church dedicated to the saint, which is followed by a public festival.

The most important festival of all is a wedding. Before the roads were properly built, wedding celebrations often lasted a week. As travel was difficult, people would take the opportunity of a wedding to enjoy each other's company for a while. At the beginning of the century, a wedding would be conducted as follows. An "inviter" chosen by the relatives of the bride and bridegroom, would go to the villages where the couple came from, to announce the good news, and to invite the guests.

kaniskiá, which mainly consisted of meat, cheese, oil and wine. Poorer people often brought bread, potatoes and onions.

On Sunday morning the bride, in all her finery, would receive the guests. Many tears were shed, as the wedding also meant that the bride would leave her parents' home forever. Then the *pastiká*, *mantinádes* especially composed for the occasion, and all about the bride, would be sung. The bridegroom was not allowed to hear these songs, and they had to be finished by the time he and his relatives and friends arrived to fetch the

groom, would go to the villages where the couple came from, to announce the good news, and to invite the guests.

The wedding itself would always be held on a Sunday. On the Saturday afternoon, some of the guests would carry the trousseau, which had been on view for a few days, from the bride's house to that of the groom. *Balotés* were sung, often the impromptu *mantinádes* (two or four line strophic songs with a chorus).

On Saturday evening, the villagers from the place where the couple were to make their home would bring symbolic gifts, the

bride and her party to the church.

After the wedding service, the dance for the bridal veil was usually held immediately outside the church. All the male relatives of the couple would dance with the bride. The last to dance would receive the veil, which meant that he too would soon be married. Then the procession, led by a lyre player, would go to the groom's house, and again *pastiká* would be sung, and this time the subject was wider, with a lot of good wishes and practical advice for the couple.

In the groom's house, the bride's mother-in-law would give the bride honey and nuts, *melokário*, as a welcoming gift. Before the bride crossed the threshold, she would dip her finger into the honey, and make a cross on the door. This ritual was performed to bring good luck to the household.

Before the guests sat down at the tables laden with good things, everyone sang a prayer like song in which the mothers-in-law were wished strength to accept their new son and daughter-in-law. Then to the sound of gunshots, the festivities would begin, and the celebrations would continue for three or four days. A great deal of crockery was broken

of the child is toasted with wine and *rakí*.

Of the church festivals, Easter is the most important. Following the winter carnival season, Lent is a sombre time of fasting and church-going; all Greeks take it seriously. Orthodox households adhere to strict dietary rules which become more and more rigorous as Easter approaches. During Holy Week, meat and eggs are forbidden; even oil is disallowed. Only on Wednesday may one use oil for cooking. After midnight mass on Easter Day, there is a traditional procession. This is the climax of the Greek religious

during the proceedings. This old fashioned kind of wedding is now only celebrated in the more isolated villages.

A christening is another important occasion for a feast, although this event is less lavish than a wedding. The celebrations always take place at night, and often everything is over just after midnight. Here too, special songs have to be sung, and the health

year. Churches are packed to bursting with the faithful, all of whom have brought along candles with which to "carry home the light" of the Resurrection. In the churchyard a funeral pyre is erected, and an enormous effigy of Judas Iscariot is burnt. Then the faithful make up for their recent deprivations, and family meals turn into festivals of music, song and dance, with traditional Easter roast lamb, tripe soup and red eggs.

Harvest festivals, too, such as the "Orange Festival" in Skinés, the "Wine Festival" in Réthimnon or the "Sultana Festival" in Sitía are relaxed and happy occasions.

Left, a group of orthodox Greeks present bread as an offering to St George. **Above**, even in this modern day and age, traditional weddings do take place.

In the beginning is chaos. From chaos, Gaea arises, bringing heaven (Uranos), the sea (Pontos) and the mountains (Ourea) to the world. For lack of any other male, Gaea weds her son Uranus, and with him begets the Titans. Soon Uranus has set himself up as ruler of the world. But he fears that his children might challenge his power, and so forbids Gaea to have any more children. But Gaea joins forces with her youngest son, Cronus, who without hesitation castrates Uranus and takes his place. Then Cronus marries his sister Rhea, and begets many children by her.

But now the same fear assails Cronus as once plagued his father: he fears for his power. As he does not want to forgo the pleasures of procreation, he decides to swallow the newborn infants. This fate befalls Hestia, Demeter, Hera, Hades and Poseidon. Rhea goes to the more experienced Gaea for advice. When another child is born, Rhea wraps a stone up in swaddling clothes, and gives it to Cronus to eat. While Cronus is lulled into a false sense of security, Rhea gives birth to a son Zeus, in the Díkti Cave. He is fed by the three nymphs Amaltheia, Adrasteie and Io, and later moves to the Ida Cave, where he spends his youth.

When Zeus finds out that some of his siblings are in Cronus' stomach, he becomes cup-bearer to his father, and slips the old god an emetic. Soon afterwards his brothers and sisters are born for the second time. They acknowledge Zeus as their leader and overthrow and ban Cronus. Once Zeus becomes the most powerful among the gods, he decides on Olympus as their home, and establishes a state and territories. This arrangement has the advantage of leaving Zeus free to pursue his main pleasure in life: love. Being a god, he can take on any form he chooses. One day he falls in love with Europa, the beautiful Phoenician princess.

The Sun God in zodiac circle and the Earth Mother with her children, the Four Seasons (Roman floor mosaic from Sassoferrato).

Disguised as a bull, he approaches the Phoenician coast. Europa leaps onto his back. He immediately jumps into the sea and swims to Crete, going ashore in the Bay of Mátala. Then, under the evergreen plane tree, he either reveals himself to Europa as a god and seduces the flattered princess, or turns himself into an eagle and rapes her. Three sons are born of this union, Minos, Rhadamanthys and Sarpedon. Soon Zeus finds other amorous pursuits. Europa marries the Cretan king Astarios who adopts her three sons.

Minos is the only son who keeps up his

Wishing to discourage other aspirants to the Cretan throne by a show of power, Minos asks Poseidon for a miracle: a white bull is to emerge from the waves. Poseidon grants him his wish but the bull is so beautiful that Minos cannot bring himself to kill it, and offers a different one to Poseidon. However, Poseidon is not deceived and punishes him by making Pasiphae, Minos' wife, fall in love with the bull. In her anguish, Pasiphae confides in the court engineer Daedalus. He ingeniously constructs a model of a cow. Pasiphae then hides herself inside the model,

relationship with his father. He spends nine years in the Díkti Cave, learning the art of leadership from Zeus. Armed with tablets of law, Minos returns to humankind, banishes his brothers, and becomes the sole ruler of Crete. Even the critical historian Thucydides was impressed by the unanimity of opinion handed down by tradition, which portrays Minos as a wise man. It was not until later that contradictions appeared and he was seen as a power hungry tyrant, a shameless wooer of women: Briómartis threw herself into the sea to escape him, and was saved by the fishermen's nets.

which is immediately mounted by the bull. The Minotaur is born of this union, half man half beast. Minos is beside himself with fury, and wants to kill the monster instantly. But Ariadne, his daughter, begs for mercy for her half brother.

The white bull, saved from sacrificial offering, gains fame as an exceptionally strong and dangerous Cretan bull.

Later, Heracles, who in a fit of mental disturbance killed his children, is ordered by the Delphic Oracle to perform 10 heroic deeds, one of which is to capture the Cretan bull. Heracles succeeds, and takes the bull to the Peloponnese, where it does much damage. At this time, Androgeus, the son of King Minos, has just won the pentathlon in the Panathenian Games. While out hunting the bull, Androgeus is ambushed and murdered by a jealous rival. As soon as he hears of this wicked deed, Minos sends his fleet against Athens. After a long struggle, the Athenians surrender. As recompense for his son's murder, Minos demands the sacrifice of six youths and six maidens each year. Under the Palace of Knossós, Minos has ordered Daedalus to construct a labyrinth, where the

On Crete, Theseus falls in love with Ariadne. She reciprocates his feelings, and promises to help him. Once the deed is done, they will marry and flee to Athens. Actually Dionysos has a claim to Ariadne, and she herself has no idea just how she can help Theseus. She turns to Daedalus for advice, and he suggests that she should give Theseus a ball of thread. Theseus fastens the thread at the beginning of the labyrinth, feels his way to the end, kills the Minotaur and, with the aid of the thread, returns to daylight.

Then Theseus and Ariadne flee. While

Minotaur lives. Whoever enters is faced with two adversaries: the confusing labyrinth and the monster itself.

One day Theseus, the son of the King of Athens, is chosen as a sacrifice. It is more likely, however, that Theseus took it upon himself to go to Crete to fight the Minotaur. As he leaves he hoists a black flag on his ship. If his mission is successful, Theseus is to hoist a white flag on his return.

Left, figurines of the mythological bull. Above, a modern representation of the figure of the Earth Mother.

they are resting on Naxos, Dionysos appears, demanding his rights. He abducts Ariadne to Lemnos, where she later bears him four sons. Theseus is in such despair at the loss of his love, that he forgets the agreed-upon sign on his journey homeward. When Aegeus sees the ship returning with a black flag aloft, he assumes that Theseus has been killed by the Minotaur. Despondent, he throws himself into the sea, which has since that time been called the Aegean.

Later, Minos discovers that it was Daedalus who helped Ariadne and Theseus to flee. As punishment he locks Daedalus and his son Icarus in the labyrinth. But Daedalus easily finds his way out. His only problem is how to escape from the island. He makes wings for himself and Icarus. Daedalus warns his son not to fly too high, for the sun will melt his wings, nor too low for the damp sea air will make the feathers too heavy. Icarus ignores the warning and flies higher and higher. The wax melts and Icarus falls into the sea. That is why that part of the Mediterranean is called the Icarian Sea.

Daedalus is a different kind of father from Aegeus. He does not commit suicide from grief, but flies as planned to Sicily. There he goes to the court of King Kokalos and, as a man of ideas, is received with open arms.

Minos has in no way forgotten the shameful deception. Eager for vengeance, he sets out to search for Daedalus. To find him, Minos thinks up a trick: he takes a spiral formed shell and offers a big reward to anyone who can pull a thread through the shell. During his travels, Minos comes to Sicily. One day he comes to the court of King Kokalos and sets his task. Kokalos takes the shell and says he can pull the thread through. Kokalos goes to Daedalus. Now it is clear Minos has the measure of his erstwhile court engineer. In his vanity Daedalus is of course determined to solve the problem. He ties the thread to an ant, bores a hole in the shell, and lets the ant creep through the shell attracted by a trail of honey.

When Kokalos shows him the shell, with the thread pulled through, Minos knows he has reached his goal, and demands the surrender of Daedalus. Kokalos agrees, but before carrying out his promise, he offers to hold a feast in honour of his illustrious guest. Now Minos' end is drawing near. While taking his bath to prepare for the grand feast, he is murdered by the daughters of King Kokalos, who pour boiling water over him. Thus, Minos, the son of Zeus, meets his end in a Sicilian bath. He disappears from the scene as suddenly as the civilisation which bore his name.

Inner picture in an Attic clay bowl from Duris (about 470 BC), Athena and Heracles.

SUPERSTITION

The atomic physicist Niels Bohr was just putting a horseshoe up in his house when a friend arrived. "What are you doing that for?" asked his friend, amazed. "Surely you're not superstitious?" "Of course I'm not," answered Bohr, "but I've heard it works all the same."

It is generally thought that superstition is a relic of the distant past, of pre-Christian times, when each natural phenomenon had its own god or "prime mover". But just as Christmas was "created" in 336 by the Church to counterbalance the winter solstice, so probably the early, disparate gods have been united in our one almighty God. When, from time to time, one of these emerges from obscurity, and throws into relief the underlying disunity of the Christian faith, we call it superstition.

Apart from the summer solstice, other heathen customs have been so completely integrated into orthodox belief and practice, that people are in fact quite unaware of their origin. The plea for deliverance from suffering and infirmity must be one of the most ancient expressions of religion. It was for this purpose that several thousand years ago, different parts of the body were fashioned in clay and set up in the holy places. Votive offerings were linked to this, as the gods did nothing for nothing. The process has hardly changed, except that nowadays the sacrificial offering is money, and light metal plaques are used instead of clay. In Hrissoskalítissa there are many such votive offerings.

A popular dictionary defines superstition as "belief in unnatural processes, as opposed to valid religious and scientific concepts." Just think about a "miracle" in this context. There belief and superstition are inextricably linked; in

A grotesque tree root, believed to work miracles and protect the inhabitants of the shore of Préveli.

fact the one defines the other. For a miracle is by definition that which is not explicable in terms of "valid religious and scientific concepts" or, in other words, concepts which have arisen from experience of life and an interpretation of the laws of nature. Belief and superstition are in fact very closely linked, but not always quite as closely as on Crete. But people here don't think they are superstitious at all – despite "clear indications to the contrary."

For the peasant woman for example, who manages to calm a screaming child in a few seconds, without any kind of hypnosis, but simply using a belt and some kind of secret ritual, this is nothing less than a God given gift. Whether the "girdle of the mother goddess" had anything to do with it, she wouldn't say.

Here are more examples of what would elsewhere be called superstition:

1. On the first day of the quarter and, in some areas, also on the first day of the month, it is most important to note who first crosses your path. If the first person is bad, that will bring bad luck. So on those days, a family member who is, of course, a good person, is sent out onto the road, to test the ground. Without this precaution, no superstitious person would set foot outside the door.

2. If an unexpected guest arrives, someone creeps outside the door and spills salt on the ground. This is supposed to ensure the speedy departure of the guest.

3. At Epiphany, after mass, believers take home candles lit from the holy flame, and replace the cross burnt on the door lintel. This protects the house from bad luck and evil spirits the whole year.

4. Kazantzákis in *Zorba the Greek* refers to a "Mara" who is supposed to be the spirit of evil, and a cunning pimp.

5. Black cats and broken mirrors have no meaning on Crete, but it is considered lucky to own a black hen.

Votive offerings: representations of afflictions cured as a result of prayer.

LITERATURE

Modern Cretan literature is stamped by the influence of the writers Níkos Kazantzákis and Pantelís Prevelákis. Kazantzákis was born on 18 February 1883 in Varvári. The first play written by this qualified lawyer was performed in Athens in 1906. He spent the next few years in Paris studying political science and philosophy (under Henri Bergson). In 1915 he was a volunteer in the Balkan War. In 1919 Venizélos appointed him Minister of Welfare.

On leaving politics, Kazantzákis travelled to England, Spain, Russia, Japan and China. These journeys inspired him to write a series of critical travel books. In addition he wrote lyrics, stories, novels and tragic plays with predominantly historical or religious themes as well as philosophical essays and epic poems such as the *Odyssey*, which appeared in 1938. In 1945 he returned to politics and took a ministerial position in Soufoulis' cabinet, but soon resigned because of inter-party quarrels.

International fame came to Kazantzákis with his later works, above all through his novel *Zorba the Greek*. There are, however, several misunderstandings regarding his work. It is often maintained that the character of Zorba was heavily influenced by Nietzsche and is a superhuman creation, as well as to some degree a second side of Kazantzákis' character, much embellished and with delusions of grandeur. In fact, although the novel cannot be regarded as a factual account, Zorba is at least in part the portrait of a man with whom Kazantzákis lived and worked on a Cretan beach for six months in 1917.

A further misunderstanding arises from the fact that Alexis Zorba is more widely known through the somewhat shallow film of the book than through the original. He is often thought to be the archetypal noble Cretan. But Zorba is, in fact, not a Cretan at

Preceding pages: upholding tradition. Left, Anthony Quinn and Alan Bates in the Michael Cacoyannis film Zorba the Greek.

all, but a Macedonian. Zorba, a Greek from the mainland, brings a breath of freedom to the Cretans, caught up in their ghostly traditions. Even on Crete, Zorba only became known through the making of the film, and it is said that those who saw the film were shocked at the representation of earlier conditions on the island.

In the novel, the man of action, Zorba, comes face to face with the intellectual ditherer, Kazantzákis. Zorba stands at the centre of life, and just takes things as they are. He has no inclination to improve the world.

into practice. He fails to "come alive".

Here we come to a further misunderstanding: the book is no mere adventure story, but a philosophical novel dealing with existential questions, questions of life and death. As in all Kazantzákis' works, the central theme is that of the relationship of man with God.

There's no doubt, however, that in his indisputable love for his homeland, Níkos Kazantzákis himself is the archetypal Cretan. He is always aware of the special nature of the island, and of its past. "Being a Cretan is a duty," he says. This conduct, almost that

Taken in isolation, this is a conservative standpoint, which could well arouse criticism. But, on the other hand, Zorba does in fact alter the world around him – even if unintentionally. He is a kind of "mystical realist", who views things in daily life always as new and wonderful. He does not separate this sense of wonder – as would a believer or an intellectual – from reality; for him it is the substance of reality itself. This infatuation is infectious. In contrast there is the "boss." He is full of questions, doubts and problems. He makes grandiose plans, none of which ever come near to being put

of a representative, is strongly reminiscent of Thomas Mann, a similarity which extends beyond their wide education and range of interests to certain physiognomic similarities. It is certainly in no small measure due to this whole-hearted patriotism that Kazantzákis (despite the criticism) embodied in his works that he became and has remained so popular on Crete.

However, in the depiction of his contemporaries, particularly of former friends, Kazantzákis is sometimes very severe. If someone has surrendered to fate, become complacent and stopped fighting, Kazantzákis' contempt and despair is plain. In his autobiography, *Report to El Greco*, he describes a small rural scene: a bluebird has just flown past and Kazantzákis wishes to know what kind of bird it was. The peasant he asks replies, "Why do you want to know? You can't eat it." To mollify the reader, Kazantzákis adds, "I was no misanthrope; I always loved people, but from a distance…"

Almost as well-known as *Zorba the Greek* is *Freedom or Death* (1953), an exceedingly pessimistic depiction of the uprising of 1889 against the Turks. Here a different charac-

literary world, that it was decided simply to put both works on the Index.

What is amazing is not so much the fact of the church's initiative, but the timing. As early as 1928, in his book *Askitikí*, Kazantzákis had expressed what he saw as insurmountable contradictions in the so-called message of salvation: it is not God who saves man, but man who must save God. In his novel of 1948, *Christ Recrucified,* Kazantzákis takes up Dostoyevsky's dark vision according to which it is the Church above all which is in need of the crucifixion of Christ,

terisation of God is given: "If you are a wolf, eat; if you are a lamb, let yourself be eaten! And who is God? He is the Great Wolf – who eats both lambs and wolves and all their bones!" Certain passages in this book and many parts of the later novel, *The Last Temptation of Christ*, have offended the Church. However when the Vatican announced that it intended to excommunicate Kazantzákis, there was such an uproar in the

Far left, Giorgis Zorba, model for the novel. Left, Dimitsana with Prevelákis. Above, hundreds paid their last respects to Kazantzákis.

which may need to be repeated throughout all eternity.

After the filming of the novel *The Last Temptation of Christ* by Martin Scorsese, more than 30 years after it had been put on the Index, the inability of the church to come to terms with Kazantzákis is remarkable. The objections raised today sound like a parody of the earlier criticism. Kazantzákis brought out the human side of this exceptional being, Jesus Christ, and portrayed him as "the animal that questions," a man who thinks but who also has natural desires. For anyone partially free of prejudice, it is clear

83

that neither in the novel nor in the film, is Jesus disparaged. Scorcese has interpreted the novel entirely as the author intended.

The opinion that the mystery of the Passion is lessened by this interpretation echoes the same false argument as those who maintain that modern scientists have eliminated the wonder from religion. They ignore the fact that the more the scientists discover about nature, the more wonderful it becomes. Great thinkers, notably Einstein and Heisenberg, have made penetrating comments on this subject.

In 1955 Kazantzákis was nominated for the Nobel prize, by Albert Schweitzer among other eminent persons. The Church managed to prevent this honour being bestowed upon him. From 1950 onwards, Kazantzákis and his wife lived in Antibes on the Mediterranean coast. On 26 October 1957 Kazantzákis died in Freiburg in Breisgau. The coffin was received by enormous crowds in Iráklion a few days later.

The grave of Níkos Kazantzákis lies in southern Iráklion in the Martinengo Bastion of the old city wall. In the background is the striking profile of the Joúchtas. On the tomb-stone are the words of Kazantzákis: "I hope for nothing. I fear nothing. I am free."

It is often maintained that Kazantzákis was posthumously "banned" to the Martinengo Bastion and that he was denied burial in consecrated ground. None of this is true. In 1957 a proper funeral service was held. In 1977 a memorial mass was celebrated, and it is a custom on Crete to allocate special burial places to prominent citizens.

Pantelís Prevelákis: It was surely an omen – he was born 26 years to the day after Níkos Kazantzákis, on 18 February 1909. Prevelákis studied philology in Paris and Thessaloníki and from 1939 to 1975 was professor of Art History at the Academy of Arts in Athens. All his life he remained in close contact with his birthplace of Réthimnon. This fascination can still be understood today, for in no other Cretan city is the "geological layering" of time so clearly in evidence as here.

So perhaps it is no wonder that Prevelákis became known as an author of "historical dimensions". For the interpretation of the changes wrought by time, he invented a new category, that of "Mythistory", a mixture of historical interpretation and subjective mythological impressions.

In 1938 his first effort in this direction, *Chronicle of a City,* appeared to great acclaim. Later novels received a varied reception by critics and readers. There was, however, widespread agreement that the historical and the subjective mythical did not complement one another and in the end should be treated as separate entities.

While Kazantzákis' international fame lives on, Prevelákis was soon eclipsed after his death in March 1986. Bookshops and librarians no longer remember his name. But while not enjoying the same level of recognition, Prevelákis is nevertheless an interesting and gripping writer.

Reading works by these two native sons is indispensable if you want to gain an understanding of Crete before your visit.

Left, Kazantzákis – still revered in Crete. Right, taking after the legendary Alexis Zorba.

It is not even 100 years since adventurers and archaeologists first set out to discover the secrets of Crete, the birthplace of European civilisation. For thousands of years this sunny island, the fifth largest in the Mediterranean, just 320 km from the shore of Africa, has cast its spell over foreign invaders.

In recent times there has been a different kind of invasion of Crete. Searching for the origins of our culture and also for a kind of lost paradise, visitors of different kinds have attempted to take possession of the island. This time things are different. The intention of the new "invaders" is peaceful, and their aim is to benefit mankind by safeguarding the birthplace of European civilisation.

What began as a matter of scientific interest revealed a glorious culture which shattered the historical notions held until that time about the development of the Occident. The joy of life and the love of peace evident in the Minoan epoch as well as the superior place of women at that time were extraordinary revelations to the world.

But it was during the 1960s that the youth of the industrialised nations, tired of a materialistic, Americanised lifestyle, made their way to a life of natural purity. Attracted by the world of Zorba, they saw Crete as a place where dreams came true. There, they arrived and enjoyed a casual, happy lifestyle in idyllic surroundings.

The invaders of today usually land in Iráklion, disembarking from countless ferries and charter flights. Modern tourism has left its mark on Crete in many ways. There are now six flights a day from Athens to Iráklion, four from Athens to Haniá and thousands arrive each year on ferries from Piraeus.

Preceding pages: calmness of the sea revealed through a hotel window; white and blue, the Greek national colours; storm over Iráklion.

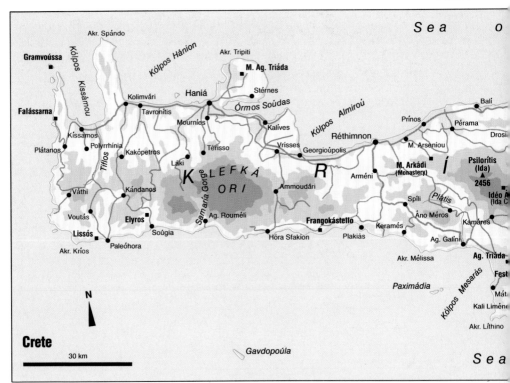

Concrete and asphalt have altered what not so long ago was the unspoilt charm of the island. But if you take the time and make the effort, the world of the Minoans and of Zorba is still there, far from the madding crowd. Off the beaten track a fascinating and unique island is waiting to be discovered.

To aid you in this discovery, the following chapters have been compiled, offering inspiration as well as practical advice. The starting point is Iráklion, where almost all visits to the island begin. If you wish to avoid the heat, dust and tourist rabble, then you should attempt a cool, quiet visit to the two excellent museums of archaeology and history in Iráklion, where you will gain insight into the turbulent history of Crete's largest city.

From Iráklion, you can go on to Knossós, the most important excavation site on Crete. More Minoan palaces can be found in Arhánes, Mália, Agii Déka and Festós, as you leave the environs of Iráklion and follow the road south towards the Libyan Sea.

From Réthimnon you can follow a trail of discovery which leads to numerous old Cretan monasteries before the route carries on westwards to the city of Haniá. The highlight of the journey through this part of the island is a visit to the spectacular Samaria Gorge.

Then it's back eastwards, to the tourist centres, the bustle and the liveliness of the beach resort of Agios Nikólaos, and on to southern, coastal Ierápetra and Sitía. For those interested in art, there is another fascinating Minoan palace located in Káto Zákros.

Last, a visit to the Lassíthi Plateau, the centre of Cretan agriculture and the Díkti Cave, the birthplace of Zeus, and the tour comes to an end.

Detailed information on travel, accomodation and dining can be found in the Travel Tips section.

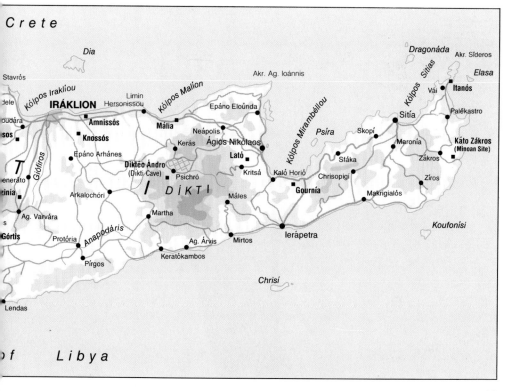

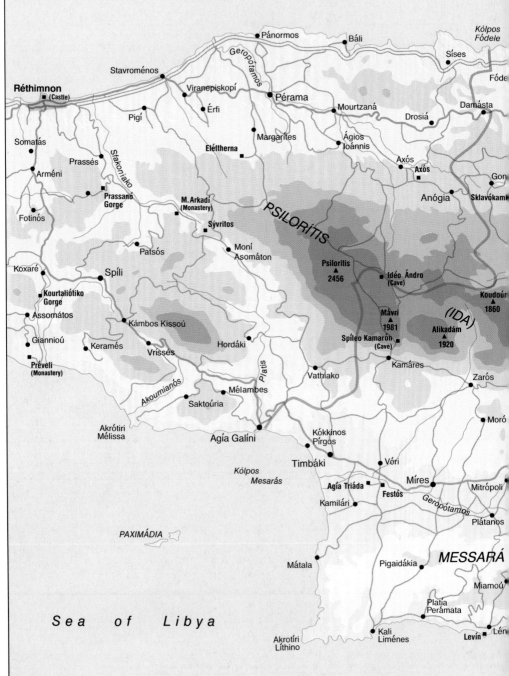

Kritikó   Pélagos

S e a   o f   C r e t e

Kólpos
Fódele

Pánormos   Báli

Síses

Geropótamos

Stavroménos   Fóde

Réthimnon   Viranepiskopí
■ (Castle)   Damásta

Pérama

Érfi   Mourtzaná

Pigí   Drosiá

Margarítes   Ágios
Ioánnis

Somatás

Eléttherna   Axós

Prassés   Axós

Arméni   Gon

M. Arkadí   Anógia   Sklavókam
Prassanó   (Monastery)
Gorge

Fotinós   Sývritos

Patsós   Moní
Asomáton

Koxaré   **PSILORÍTIS**

Spíli   Psiloritis   Idéo Ándro
▲ 2456   ■ (Cave)

Kourtaliótiko
Gorge   Koudoúr
▲ 1860

Assomátos   Kámbos Kissoú   Mávri
▲ 1981   (IDA)

Gianniou   Keramés   Hordáki   Spíleo Kamarón   Alikadám
Vrissés   (Cave)   ▲ 1920

Préveli
(Monastery)   Kamáres

Platis   Vathlako   Zarós

Akoumianós   Mélambes

Saktoúria   Moró

Akrótiri   Kókkinos
Mélissa   Agía Galíni   Pírgos

Timbáki   Vóri

Kólpos   Míres
Mesarás   Agía Triáda ■   Mitrópoli
Festós
Kamilári   Geropótamos
Plátanos

PAXIMÁDIA   **MESSARÁ**

Mátala   Pigaidákia

Miamoú

Platía
Perámata

S e a   o f   L i b y a   Kali
Akrótiri   Liménes   Levín   Lén
Líthino

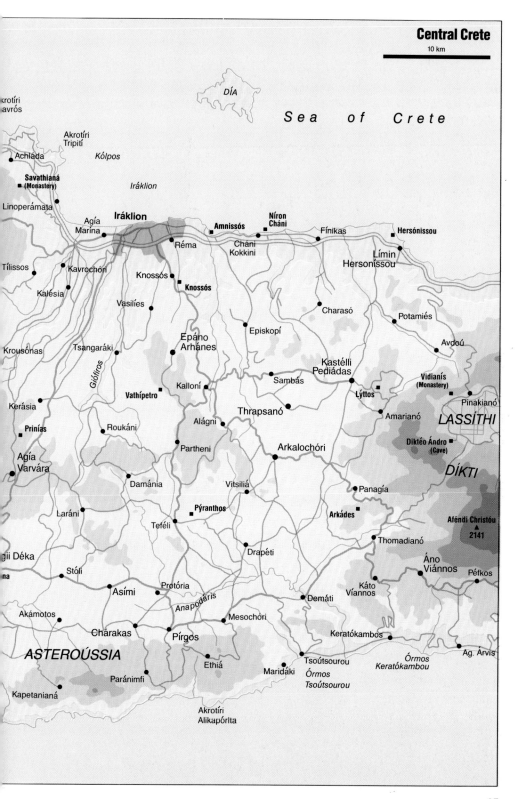

DÍA

S e a   o f   C r e t e

krotíri
avrós

Akrotíri
Tripití

Achláda

Kólpos

Savathianá
(Monastery)

Iráklion

Linoperámata

Agía
Marína

Iráklion

Amnissós

Níron
Cháni

Fínikas

Hersónissou

Réma

Cháni
Kokkini

Límin
Hersoníssou

Tílissos

Kavrochóri

Knossós

Knossós

Charasó

Potamiés

Kalésia

Vasilíes

Episkopí

Avdoú

Krousónas

Tsangaráki

Epáno
Arhánes

Kastélli
Pediádas

Vidianís
(Monastery)

Kerásia

Giófiros

Kallóni

Sambás

Lýttos

Pinakianó

LASSÍTHI

Prinías

Vathípetro

Thrapsanó

Amarianó

Agía
Varvára

Roukáni

Alágni

Arkalochóri

Diktéo Ándro
(Cave)

DÍKTI

Partheni

Damánia

Vitsiliá

Panagía

Laráni

Pýranthos

Arkádes

Aféndi Christóu
▲
2141

gii Déka
na

Stóli

Teféli

Drapéti

Thomadianó

Áno
Viánnos

Péfkos

Asími

Protória

Káto
Víannos

Demáti

Akámotos

Anapodáris

Mesochóri

Keratókambos

Chárakas

Pírgos

Ag. Árvis

ASTEROÚSSIA

Ethiá

Maridáki

Órmos
Tsoútsourou

Tsoútsourou

Órmos
Keratókambou

Paránimfi

Kapetanianá

Akrotíri
Alikapórlta

97

IRÁKLION

There was a city named Iráklion on Crete as early as in the Minoan epoch. Greek mythology tells that it was here that Heracles performed the seventh of his 12 deeds: the slaying of the fire-breathing Cretan bull. The Greeks probably named the city Herakleion or Herakleia, in honour of their hero. In the following period, under the Romans and Byzantines, this region was only sparsely populated. It was not until after the conquest of Crete by the Saracens that Iráklion once again gained importance. It was expanded and fortified. The new name Rabd-el-Khandek, which meant castle with moat, was descriptive of the architectural alterations of the city.

In 961 Nikefóros Fokás reconquered Crete for the Byzantine Empire. By doing so, he completely destroyed Rabd-el-Khandek, which was later rebuilt and named Chandax.

The Venetians took Crete without bloodshed in 1204. They bought the island, but it took them until 1210 to supplant the Genoese. Chandax became Candia, and not long afterwards the whole island was given that name. In the four centuries of Venetian rule, Candia became a centre of culture. In practice this meant that the new rulers lived in the main city, in wealth and plenty, while the native Greek inhabitants were stripped of their land and possessions and reduced to slavery.

After 1536 the Veronese fortifications engineer Michele Sanmicheli built a great fortress around the city, which withstood the attacks of the Turks for 21 years. But eventually the Venetians could hold out no longer, and in 1669 the Turks took Crete. Once again the city of Candia changed its name. It was then called Megálo Kástro, meaning great fort, but again its influ-

ence waned. The Turks selected Haniá as their centre of activity, and in 1850 its status was elevated to that of the new island capital. Even today, Haniá retains its Turkish character.

When the Turks had to leave Crete in 1898, Megálo Kástro once again became Herakleion, in Modern Greek, Iráklion. After the annexation to Greece, Iráklion took on the aspect of a metropolis. In World War II the city suffered heavy bombing by the Germans and British. It was not until 1972 that Iráklion once again became the capital city of Crete.

Many travellers have the same problem with the city of Iráklion as they do with Greek cuisine. They are disappointed before ever really having got to know it. However, there's no denying that Iráklion is difficult to fall in love with at first sight. Particularly in the city centre, it seems to be exactly what the tourist is trying to escape – filth, noise-

Preceding pages: the fortress of Iráklion stretches along the shore. Left, storm clouds loom over the fortress. Right, the Venetian lion in the castle.

and nothing but traffic and ugliness. But if you look behind the scenes, you'll discover the true nature of the city. It has, in fact much that is pleasant to offer; not least its people, who manage to combine metropolitan open mindedness with unspoilt warmth.

A city tour could begin at the **Market Place**, where the unusual oriental atmosphere makes a visit an interesting experience. It is located on 1866 Street, to the south of **Nikefóros Fokás Square** and is quite small. It is usually incredibly crowded, as locals as well as tourists come to do their shopping here. Although the prices are not the lowest, the quality is high. You can buy fruit, sweets, bread, fish and drinks as well as clothes, and reproductions of antique works of art and souvenirs.

Halfway down the market street, **Fotioú Street** leads off to the left. This used to be the place to enjoy the relaxed atmosphere of little *tavérnes*, but nowadays everything is cool and profit orientated. The food is still not bad, but far too expensive. The market street leads to **Kornáros Square** with its lovely Turkish well house and the **Bembo Fountain**. The headless statue from Roman times was brought from Ierápetra by Z. Bembo.

If you turn to the right just before the end of the market street, you will find yourself at the handicraft centre of the city. Here the quaint shops are huddled together as they were 100 years ago in the times of the guilds.

There's plenty of life in **Eleftherías Square** and plenty of traffic too. This semicircular area to the south of Fokás Square is lined with cafés and restaurants where culture enthusiasts can relax and enjoy a drink after visiting the Archaeological Museum.

On **Dedálou Street**, one of the few pedestrian precincts in the city, there are shops to suit every taste. This street

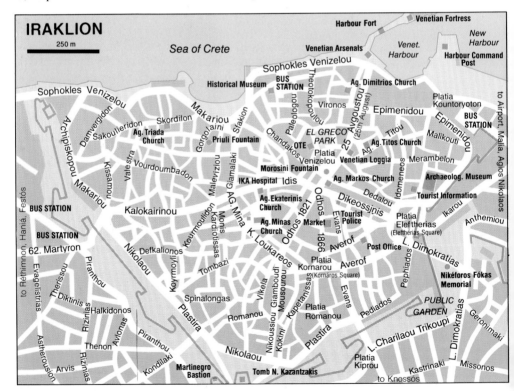

100

leads to **Venizélos Square** which, with its huge traffic junction, is clearly the centre of **Iráklion**. Here in the evenings, the youth of the city gather, and as most of the stores stay open for business until nine in the evening, there are always crowds of shoppers, not only during the high season.

The **Morosini Fountain** was built by the Venetian governor Francesco Morosini in 1628, at the end of a 15-km-long water pipe. This aqueduct (parts of which can be seen behind Knossós above the motorway) brought water to the city from Mount Joúchtas. The four water-spouting lions' heads are the emblem of the city, but few notice that the fountain is decorated as well, with scenes from ancient mythology.

Hándakos Street leads due north from the fountain. The first part of the street is also a pedestrian precinct. Here cafés and restaurants stretch for about 50 metres.

On the eastern side of Venizélos Square is **Agios Markos Church**. This basilica with three aisles is the oldest Venetian church on Crete and impressively illustrates the eventful history of the island. It was built in 1239 in honour of the patron saint of Venice and restored several times after earthquakes in 1303 and 1508. From 1669 to 1915, it served as a mosque. Later it was used as a warehouse, then as the branch of a bank and finally as a cinema. After renovation to its original Venetian style in 1961, it is now an exhibition centre for icons and copies of frescoes from Byzantine churches on Crete.

If you keep right after Agios Markos Church, you reach the Venetian **Loggia**. This two-storey building was also built by Francesco Morosini, in 1626–28, and was a club (*loge*) for the Venetian aristocracy. In World War II the Loggia was so badly damaged that the authorities decided to pull it down

Mystical atmosphere in the square of the three churches; St Mínas Church in the background.

101

and rebuild it in the original style. Behind, the former **Armeria**, the Venetian armory, is the Town Hall.

Agios Títos Church, dedicated to Titus, the patron saint of Crete and its first bishop, was for many years the seat of the Archbishop of Crete. It was after the expulsion of the Saracens that the bishopric was moved from distant Górtis to Chandax (Iráklion) and this basilica was built. As the metropolitan church, it was for a long time spared by the Turks, but eventually was turned into a mosque.

The earthquake of 1856 so damaged the church that the renovation project of 1972 almost turned into one of rebuilding. During these changes elements of Ottoman style were incorporated. In many ways Agios Títos is an unusual church. Among its treasures, the iconostasis and the skull of St Titus in a golden vessel are of particular note.

After crossing **25th August Street**,

you can go down to the Venetian Port, where nowadays there are not many fishing boats but plenty of private luxury yachts. On the right are the enormous cylindrical vaults of the socalled **Arsenal**, which are now mainly used as shipyards and docks. A breakwater leads to the impressive harbour fort of **Koules**.

If you turn southwest from the Morosini Fountain, that's away from the harbour, and keep going straight on, passing through 1821 Street, you reach a square with three churches. The largest of these is **Agios Mínas Cathedral** (1862–95). Apart from its huge dimensions and the fact that it is the metropolitan seat, it has nothing special to offer. Nearby is the little **Agios Mínas Church**. Inside is the remarkable iconostasis, which is not always on show, as the church is usually locked. In the northeast corner of the square is **Agía Ekateríni Church**, which was built in

Harbour skyline.

the year 1555 as part of the "Convent School of Mount Sinai." This unusual school produced among others the writers V. Kornáros and G. Hortátzis and the painter El Greco. During Turkish rule this church too was turned into a mosque. Today Agía Ekateríni is used as an exhibition hall for Christian art. The greatest treasures are the six icons of Michail Damaskinós, painted in 1580 for the Vrondissi Monastery.

From here you can cross Markopoúlou Street and carry on in a southerly direction to see the grave of Níkos Kazantzákis in the **Martinengo Bastion**. It is not easy to find, and the way there leads through fascinating little lanes and alleyways; just ask for directions now and then.

The **Archaeological Museum** of Iráklion is as controversial as the "restored" site of Knossos. Some say it is the most beautiful museum in the world; others maintain that it is quite the

opposite. Here in one single museum is the ultimate documentation of the Minoan civilisation. The presentation of the exhibits does, however, definitely leave much to be desired.

A major design fault of the museum is the poor ventilation in the building, and visitors sink down on benches outside completely exhausted after their visit. Although going round the museum can be as strenuous as a 5-km jog, it is still a must for the tourist.

Here one can see traces of a culture which substantially contributed to Crete's being labelled the "Cradle of European civilisation." If one studies the Minoan culture closely, one can conclude that this civilisation marked a high point of achievement from which there seems to have been a continual decline right into modern times.

The **Historical Museum**, which chronicles the Post Minoan epoch up to the present day, is also worth a visit.

Harbour activity.

KNOSSÓS

Five km south of Iráklion lies the **Palace of Knossós**. The best way to get there is by turning into Demokratías Street from the south side of Eleftherías Square, and then driving straight on.

The site of the palace must have been popular even in Neolithic times, as the layer of rubble beneath the palace, lying almost 6.5 metres deep, indicates dense and continued settlement. Where the west wing stands today was the location of an older palace, built like the early palaces of Festós and Mália in about 200 BC. This was probably destroyed by the earthquake of 170 BC. In around 1600 BC, the later palaces were built, and they were larger and more beautiful than the earlier ones.

In the Palace of Knossós the architectural apogee of the "Golden Age" of Minoan culture is on view. The site of the palace extends over 20,000 sq. metres. There were apparently 1,300 rooms, arranged in four storeys. It is thought that about 80,000 people once lived here. In around 1450 BC all the palaces were destroyed by another natural catastrophe, caused by the eruption of the volcano of Santorini. Only the Palace of Knossós was rebuilt, possibly by Mycenaean invaders. But in 1400 it too disappeared, and with it the whole Minoan civilisation. Whether this was the result of another earthquake or of battle is still unclear.

The Greek designation of part of the palace, if not the whole of it, as the Labyrinth, could also mean "House of the Double Axe", if the derivation of the word labyrinth from the Anatolian word *Labrys* (double axe) is accepted.

At Knossós several of these artefacts were found, in the so-called "Shrine of the Double Axe," and the holy sign of the double axe was scored into pillars and on votive objects – as at other Cretan palaces. Of the 90 towns mentioned in Homer's *Odyssey*, Knossós is named "the Great", in the sense of "the most famous". That Knossós was great in size as well was established in Roman times by the geographer Strabo. The 30 stages, by means of which he calculated the diameter of the city, indicate a distance of almost 6 km.

In all the credit and controversy surrounding the archaeologist Arthur Evans, the actual discoverer of Knossós, Minos Kalokerinós, is usually forgotten. This merchant from Iráklion, whose hobby was archaeology, completed a total of 12 excavations, which revealed large parts of the west wing and six storehouses. Then his activities were halted by the Turkish governor, who forbade further digging. Kalokerinós had been inspired to undertake his excavations by Schliemann's success. It was Schliemann who came to Crete and tried to buy the site. The Turkish owner, however, declined the offer,

Preceding pages: part of the grandeur that once was – the interior of the Palace of Knossós. Left, fresco of the Prince of Knossós. Right, Minoan stairway at Knossós.

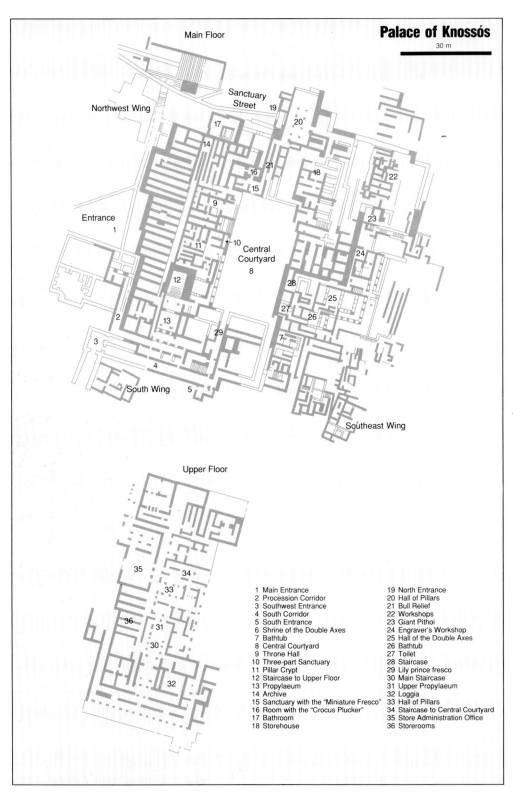

Palace of Knossós

30 m

Main Floor

Sanctuary Street

Northwest Wing

Entrance

Central Courtyard

South Wing

Southeast Wing

Upper Floor

1 Main Entrance
2 Procession Corridor
3 Southwest Entrance
4 South Corridor
5 South Entrance
6 Shrine of the Double Axes
7 Bathtub
8 Central Courtyard
9 Throne Hall
10 Three-part Sanctuary
11 Pillar Crypt
12 Staircase to Upper Floor
13 Propylaeum
14 Archive
15 Sanctuary with the "Miniature Fresco"
16 Room with the "Crocus Plucker"
17 Bathroom
18 Storehouse

19 North Entrance
20 Hall of Pillars
21 Bull Relief
22 Workshops
23 Giant Pithoi
24 Engraver's Workshop
25 Hall of the Double Axes
26 Bathtub
27 Toilet
28 Staircase
29 Lily prince fresco
30 Main Staircase
31 Upper Propylaeum
32 Loggia
33 Hall of Pillars
34 Staircase to Central Courtyard
35 Store Administration Office
36 Storerooms

108

luckily, for what would have become of Knossós had Schliemann put his plan into action? He wanted to excavate the Palace of Knossós "…in a week, using a hundred workers."

So it was extremely fortunate that the purchase of Knossós was first made by Arthur Evans. He was highly ambitious, and had plenty of time to devote to his project. Of the 90 years of his life, 35 were spent in Knossós, and several more were devoted to the study of Minoan civilisation. In considering the wonders he worked at Knossós, it is often forgotten that he never did achieve his actual aim, which was to decipher the ancient Cretan script. Linear-B was not deciphered until six years after his death, and disagreement about it persists to this day. Despite some wilful and misguided interpretations (for example "Megaron of the Queen," "Prince with the Feather Crown" etc.) and falsifications (the "Bath of the Queen" – a vessel without a drainage hole, found far from the bathroom), the value of Arthur Evans' achievements is indisputable.

The main objections voiced against his work are always in regard to his use of colour and concrete. Evans used colour to mark the reconstructed areas, and he only used concrete after much reflection, and after trying out all the other materials available. The objection is even raised that Evans used concrete although he knew that it too would not last forever. Indeed, parts of the concrete have weathered badly. Perhaps the next criticism will be that he should have used weatherproof plastic!

Whatever else may be said, had Evans not used concrete, the Palace of Knossós would have been destroyed in the earthquake of 1926. And apart from that it would be much the poorer visually, something not to be forgotten in all the controversy.

Digging up the past at Arhánes.

ARTHUR EVANS: AN ENGLISH GENTLEMAN

When the eight-year old Arthur, playing in the garden, buried a broken doll, complete with clothes, as a burial offering, and then inscribed all the objects immured on the tombstone, his father, John Evans, tried hard to make sense of his son's strange behaviour. But the fact is, he had only to look at himself to see that it was simply a case of like father like son.

John Evans was a papermaker, a successful businessman who was to leave his son a fortune. But he was also an explorer, who at his own expense undertook excavations in France, attempting to trace the origins of man. John Evans wrote trailblazing works on geology and anthropology which made him one of the most well-known research scientists of his day.

The son took after his father, and was short-sighted and physically unimpressive at 1.57 metres. But "Little Evans", as he became known, exhibited the same vitality and stamina as his father, as well as his love of adventure and wide-ranging interests. Of course it never crossed anyone's mind that the fame of the son would soon eclipse that of the parent, nor that Arthur Evans was destined to become one of the most important archaeological explorers of all time.

By the time Arthur left school, his father was the owner of several paper factories. It was assumed that Arthur would succeed his father and become a businessman too. But Arthur declined, preferring to study history. He was just 20 years old when the world's press heralded Heinrich Schliemann's discovery of what was alleged to be ancient Troy. The young student was fascinated. Frustrated with the narrow scope of the academic syllabus, he had already begun his own research and soon published an essay on numismatics. He interrupted his studies to make frequent trips to the Balkans and, at 25 years of age, his first book was published: *On Foot through Bosnia and Herzegovina*, a politically engaged and critical account of his journey. Arthur Evans supported the Panslav freedom movement, and helped in an organisation for refugees. As special correspondent for the *Manchester Guardian*, he reported from the areas of crisis on the opposition to Turkish tyranny.

All his life, Evans was moved by the needs of others. However, he was extremely reserved in his relationships with those close to him, even his own relatives. He was 26 when he met Margaret Freeman, the daughter of an English historian. As secretary to her father, she had amassed an immense amount of knowledge and was a proficient linguist. Arthur was impressed with the calm and composure of this young woman, and Margaret liked the energetic, humorous young man three years her junior. The wedding took place in the autumn of 1878.

A short while later, Arthur Evans was imprisoned in Ragusa, present-day Dubrovnik, for his political activities. Margaret and his family stood by him and managed to secure his release after a few weeks. He returned to England and, with the publication of a second book on the Balkans, was regarded as an authority on the history and contemporary situation of that region. He wrote for specialised magazines, worked on a book on the city of Ragusa and became an expert on the subject of Greek and Roman coins.

A journey to Greece with his wife brought him into contact with the 61-year-old Heinrich Schliemann. The young couple listened in fascination to Schliemann's tales, and visited the excavation sites at Mycenae, Orchomenos and Tiryns. From that time on, Arthur Evans turned his attention to the Minoan civilisation.

In Oxford, Evans was offered the post of curator of the Ashmolean Museum. He was only 33, and was extremely happy to accept the position. In his introductory talk as the new director, he declared that ethnology and archaeology had "to a large extent, the same goal: that of throwing light upon the laws of

Right, memorial to Arthur Evans.

evolution which underlie the forms of human art." The museum, in Evans' estimation, should not be a "curiosity shop" but rather a centre of archaeological research. In a short time he doubled the number of exhibits and ordered a new heating system to ensure the best possible conditions for their preservation. The new curator, however, was often absent, away on travels pursuing his own interests.

In Greece he scrutinised Schliemann's finds of gold. There were diadems, signet rings and goblets decorated with motifs quite

offered his services in aiding a people in need. It is thanks to his social and political engagements on their behalf that the Cretans granted him permission to dig at Knossós.

In 1900 Evans began his excavations on Crete. On the second day he found some fresco fragments. Exactly a week later, the first sensational discovery was made. Clay bars covered in signs revealed the existence of a prehistoric script. In just a few days, more than 100 such script tablets had been uncovered, the oldest ever indications of a European civilisation.

different from those of classical Greece. The many octopus drawings, for example, led him to believe there was a pre-Grecian, Mycenaean culture, the origins of which were not to be found on the Greek mainland.

Four years before turning the first sod at Knossós prior to his world shattering discovery, Evans announced that "the golden age of Crete [lay] far beyond the limits of this historical period." By which period he meant the time of the Greeks, beginning with the "Olympiad chronology".

The Cretans were attempting to free themselves from Turkish rule. Once again Evans

At the beginning of April there was another amazing discovery: on the floor of one of the halls, the fragment of a fresco of a life-sized figure was revealed, which was, according to Evans, the "most notable figure of the Mycenaean period". The archaeologist telegraphed his father, and John Evans was able to share in his son's triumph.

At first, Evans did not use the concept "Minoan". But a few days later, a throne was found, made of delicately veined gypsum, alabaster. He announced his findings in an article in *The Times* and it was then that he made the connection between Knossós and the legendary King Minos. In August of the same year, the highpoint of the excavations was attained with the discovery of a coloured stucco relief: this was a glorious representation of a bull.

The discoverer's theory became a certainty. Out of the obscure past, a unique culture, the oldest European civilisation, had appeared. Evans called it the Minoan civilisation, with Minos as its ruler, like a Pharaoh, "…or whichever historical personage is the origin of the name." He was thus well aware of the dubiousness of the nomencla-

great god." Elsewhere, in the *Iliad*, Minos is referred to as the "Protector of Crete". Evans cited this, as well as the legend of the Minotaur, for bulls' horns indicated the places of worship in the palace.

A mural, which has since become very well known, was a particular mystery to Evans. He called it the "Bull Fighter Fresco", as two women and a man appeared to be executing daring acrobatics on the bull's back. Evans travelled to Spain and talked to bullfighters in order to find out if such feats were possible. The experts said no. It would

ture. He knew that mythological events and figures could not be translated, easily, into history, even if Schliemann had been remarkably successful in his findings based on the poems of Homer. However, when other written evidence is lacking, then archaeology has to fall back on mythology. In the 19th book of the *Odyssey*, Homer put these words into the mouth of his hero: "Their kingly city is Knossós, where Minos ruled, who nine years long spoke with Zeus, the

Left and above, photos from Evans' extensive archives.

be impossible to hang onto the horns and vault up and over a galloping bull. But Evans was unconvinced, and held to his belief that the mural depicted an actual event, not merely a myth. He concluded that the myth of the Minotaur, to whom young Athenians were sacrificed, might refer to gruesome spectacles which had in fact taken place at Minoan Knossós.

The excavations were in their third year. After heavy rainfall, parts of a royal villa were revealed outside the palace boundaries. But inside the palace too, there were more sensational discoveries. Evans came upon a treasure chamber, in which there were petals of gold foil, glass beads, goblets, vases and ivory carvings as well as a glazed figure of a snake goddess. In ancient times the snake was a symbol of rebirth and immortality, and of the reincarnation of dead ancestors. The snake goddess therefore emphasised the prominent position held by women in Minoan civilisation.

The same interpretation applies to a temple fresco depicting a crowd of some 500 people. The front seats are occupied by ladies in elegant clothes, apparently spectators

people. The doctors he consulted reassured him to the contrary.

In the living area of the palace, Evans discovered rooms which, because of the "feminine charm" of the murals and their luxurious appointments and comfort, he identified as "megarons of the Queen." The megaron is the main room of a house.

Special significance was accorded the symbol which appeared even more often than the bull on the palace walls, and surpassed all other symbols in its frequent depiction in relief work: the Cretan double axe.

waiting for a special display or ceremony, perhaps even "bull vaulters"?

Then the spade revealed part of a wall decoration, which when put together and completed showed an elegant young man with a kind of crown on his head. Evans didn't hesitate to interpret this as the figure of a priest-king. He was sure that after finding Europe's oldest throne, he had now discovered Europe's oldest crown.

The tight belt at the waist became the hottess European fashion for both men and women. Evans wondered if this strait-lacing might have had an effect on the health of the

According to feminist theory, it is evidence of a gynaecocratic epoch in human history, a sign of matriarchal rule.

Everywhere the sign of the double axe was found, on walls of caves or temples, whether scratched on or drawn, other discoveries seemed to reveal further goddesses and evidence of the elevated position of women. This was not a phenomenon unique to Minoan civilisation, for similar conditions were evident in paleolithic Europe and in the Neolithic period in Anatolia and Umbria. The Egyptian matriarchal succession to the throne was another indication of a gynaecocratic epoch that extended throughout the whole of the ancient world.

However, traditional archaeology has been extremely hesitant about accepting these findings. It has not denied the extraordinary peacefulness, the dominance of "feminine taste", in Minoan culture, nor has it overlooked the favoured role played by women in public, as well as in the religious hierarchy, with the "great goddess of the earth" at the head. But the scholars have stressed that a matriarchal principle in religion and society does not necessarily imply

which Arthur Evans identified on the head of the "youth" not evidence against this? In fact, the headdress is no longer thought to be a crown, so that the "prince with a crown of feathers" is not taken as an indication that there were male rulers in Minoan times.

It would be presumptuous to maintain that this question has been settled once and for all, but archaeological circumstantial evidence does seem to tip the scales in favour of there having been priestess-queens.

Arthur Evans' male contemporaries, however, were aghast at the prospect of having to

the existence of female rulers and queens.

There is a difference of opinion here, and agreement cannot be reached by imagining an equal pair regency on Minoan Crete, for in the throne room of Knossós there is clearly only room for one elevated personage.

That this person could in fact have been a priestess is a theory taken extremely seriously nowadays by scholars and is being carefully researched. But is the "crown"

Left and above, parts of the interior decoration of the Minoans in the Palace of Knossós: frescoes of fabulous animals, and pillared arcade.

share history with women. The idea was greeted with amazement, and even with condescending smiles. Here, for example, is the opinion of Sir Galahad, writing in the 1930s about the frescoes of Knossós: "Women, women, nothing but women, just like on the Riviera, overdressed, permed, in high heels, a naked young man or two around... no sign of any venerable old men. There's no place for them in a female realm... men are in subordinate positions, pages, cup-bearers, flautists, field workers or sailors... not one king, priest or hero. What was at first automatically taken to be a male ruler, on a half flaked fresco, turned out to be a woman too. Women are queens, priestesses, goddesses, rulers – never serving girls."

Arthur Evans was one of the first archaeologists to call upon building experts to help him in his work. With the aid of Theodor Fyfe, excavation and reconstruction went hand in hand. Evans spared neither cost nor effort in rebuilding the old walls. His aim was to "conserve something of the inner life of the ancient palace holy place."

The Swiss painter Emile Gilliéron was commissioned to restore the frescoes. Some

The results of this work were impressive. Most visitors feel that the Palace of Knossós gives them an insight into history which no other excavation site can equal. Denigrators, on the other hand, speak of the "film set of Knossós" and criticise Evans for his over-enthusiastic restoration and improvement of his discovery. But the majority of scholars are in agreement with Evans that reconstruction was necessary at the Palace of Knossós lest it become merely a heap of rubble.

Níkos Kazantzákis described the vivid impression made on the visitor: "The palace,

consisted of no more than a few fragments, and were in need of considerable restoration. But Evans was constantly seeking reference points and analogies. He hit on a plan of producing replicas which resembled the originals as closely as possible to decorate the palace walls just as they would have done in Minoan times.

All work was undertaken in accordance with the principle that the new additions should be clearly differentiated from the old. The supporting bars, copies of pillars and the concrete were purposefully made completely different in colour from the old walls.

half decayed, half rebuilt, was still radiant after all those thousands of years and once again delighted in the sunshine of Crete. This palace does not offer the symmetry and geometrical architecture of Greece, here fantasy reigns, and the free expression of man's creativity. This palace grew like a living organism, like a tree…"

At an archaeological congress in Athens in 1905, Evans presented the chronology of the Minoan period. This was based on the stratigraphic method, layer digging. There were in those days no laboratory tests to determine dates precisely, such as the analysis of trace elements in vessel clay with the aid of neutron activation. Evans had to rely on his geological experience and on favourable circumstances. Fortunately, the layers of earth had remained almost undisturbed over the centuries and, at important spots, archaeological finds which came to light could be accurately dated.

In one fell swoop numerous historical works on Ancient Greece became obsolete, as the dating structure submitted by Evans altered everything. Modern research techniques have since confirmed the accuracy of

left his son enabled Arthur to finance and complete his grandiose plans himself. The way in which he brought the buried past back to its former glory would today be an almost impossible achievement.

Modern archaeology is changing from a science based primarily on evidence gleaned from field research to one based on laboratory examination. The methods are ever more exacting and expensive. Growing demands are confronted with shrinking means. The urbanisation process destroys sites, and archaeologists often cannot under-

Evans' chronology. His sensational findings drew numerous archaeologists to Crete. The results of their efforts are still visible today in the many excavation sites, such as those at Festós, Mália and Káto Zákros. In all it took six years before the Palace of Knossós area was revealed. At times as many as 100 people were at work on the site.

In 1908 Evans' father died. The fortune he

Left, excavation site at Arhánes. Above, Sandy Mcgillwin, Director of the British School in Knossós, studies the drawings of important burial finds.

take thorough excavation projects.

In 1911 Evans was knighted. Sir Arthur Evans became president of the Greek Society and was elected honorary professor of archaeology at Oxford University. Another 20 years of sporadic excavation and research followed until the work at Knossós was finally deemed complete. In the meantime he drew up what was probably the best account of an archaeological discovery ever written. By the time of his death at the age of 90, he had crowned his life's monumental achievements with four volumes and an index on *The Palace of Minos*.

Around Iráklion

Arhánes: From Iráklion, there is a 14- km road which passes through Knossós. After 10 km, the road branches off, and here one must keep right. The last part of your journey takes you through a lush vine growing area. **Arhánes**, a small town of about 3,500 inhabitants, is the centre of Cretan wine production. The 1,200 or so vintners have united in a co-operative, and dessert grapes, *Rosáki,* are grown here too.

Like almost any region where wine is produced, Arhánes has a friendly and inviting atmosphere. Whether or not you are interested in the Minoans, it is pleasant to spend a few days here. In the late afternoon, life begins in the cafés and *tavérnes* around the main square of the town. The men meet over the popular Tavli (Greek backgammon, played to slightly different rules) or card games. One can just mingle with the locals, and get to know something of what Crete is really all about.

In and around Arhánes there are various excavation sites. The first is to be found in the town itself and is not difficult to find. Just after entering the town, you will see a secondary school on the right: you can't miss it. Then you go on down the main street for about 200 metres until you come to a sign "To the Palace". Here you drive about 100 metres uphill to the left, then turn right and you will soon arrive at the the site. The signpost is now revealed as a gross exaggeration. It may well have led to the expectation of a Knossós-like construction. But there's nothing like it here.

The building, which dates from about 1500 BC and has only been partially excavated, is not very impressive. There is nothing very remarkable to see here in the dozen or so rooms, apart from the bases of two pillars. Experts are divided as to whether this is in fact a palace or merely a mansion. There seems to be no chance of finding out either, as excavations have been stopped out of consideration for residents of the surrounding area.

The second site, the **Necropolis** of Fourni, is reached by a small road which branches off just by the secondary school. As the road is only suitable for cars for a short distance, it is advisable to leave your car in the town. After a climb of about 15 to 20 minutes up the slopes of the **Fourni** hills, you will find yourself in front of the gate of the excavation site, which is usually locked. It is therefore essential to obtain the key from one of the cafés in the main square before attempting to visit the site. Actually the site is supposed to be open on Mondays, Fridays and Saturdays, from 9 a.m. until the evening. Anyone asking for the key should, in point of fact, then be accompanied to the site by a guide. These guides are supposed to sit in the cafés waiting to show interested per-

Preceding pages: one of Crete's national highways. Below, vintner in the castles of Arhánes.

sons around; they are paid by the state, although they have no objection to the odd tip. (All this equally applies to the mansion site of Vathípetro.)

The Necropolis of Fourni, which was in use from the early Minoan to Mycenaean times, and thus for more than 1,000 years, is held by the experts to be the most important of such sites on Crete, if not in the entire Aegean.

Instead of a map: The entrance is on the eastern side. The slope on the left faces south; Tholos A is on the right, and so faces north.

Of the more than 20 round graves, some are particularly interesting: Tholos D (a little to the left towards the edge, a woman's grave with jewellery burial offerings, Mycenaean); Tholos E (a little higher up, a communal grave from the Prepalatial era, 31 sarcophagi, 2 *pithoi*); Tholos C (a terrace higher, a communal grave of a Cycladic group, idols and amulets of obsidian); Tholos

B (formerly two-storey layout of the Prepalatial period, a communal grave, fresco decoration); Tholos A (about 45 metres to the north, a woman's grave – perhaps that of a queen or priestess-queen – with many jewellery burial offerings, vessels, bull and horse skulls, late Minoan-Mycenaean). The finds are displayed in the Museum of Iráklion (I and VI).

The third excavation site is that of a temple on the hill of **Anemóspilia**, a rarity of the first order among the many interesting finds on Crete. The well preserved temple dates from the time of the old palaces. It is to be found on the north slope of Mount Joúchtas, southwest of Arhánes. This was a most important find, as until this site was discovered, it had only been a matter of conjecture that temples had existed at all in Minoan times. Then there was an astonishing discovery: it appeared that a human sacrifice was just about to be

Ephor Iannis Sakelarakis at the site he explored, Arhánes.

made when a huge earthquake (around 1700 BC) interrupted the procedure.

The temple consisted of an anteroom and three long main rooms of equal size. In the middle of the main rooms stood a wooden image of a deity, with clay feet, which were, ironically, the only part to have been preserved complete. In the anteroom there were 150 vessels, of which some were inscribed with script (Linear-A). In many of the pots, it was possible to detect traces of the contents: fruit, cereals, honey and wine.

Similarly, in the anteroom, skeletal remains of a human were found, and two further skeletons in another of the main rooms. They were later identified as a man and a woman. The man was adorned in such a way as to indicate the possibility that he could have played the main part in some event, perhaps as a sacrificial priest. On the stone altar, the remains of another person were found. He was lying on his right side, the lower legs bent at an acute angle – presumably tied at the upper thighs. Next to his chest lay a 40-cm-long sword or knife, with which he had probably just been killed.

Forensic medical examinations have revealed further astonishing details. The woman was 28 years old, the adorned man 30, and the sacrificial victim, 18 years of age. Although the woman was suffering from a disease of the blood, the difference in colour between the upper and lower sides of the skeleton indicated that the victim had bled to death during a blazing fire. It is possible that the following may have taken place: the ceremony was almost over when the earthquake began or intensified. A helper, who was just about to carry a vessel containing the blood of the sacrifice from the side room into the main room where the image of the deity stood, was killed by falling masonry. The priest and the woman were killed instantly by the quake right next to the sacrificial victim. The flames of the torches of the temple eventually set the place on fire. The fire made it possible to establish that the young man was not killed by falling debris, but died from loss of blood, and thus was considered to have been a human sacrifice.

This find and the results of the examinations are worthy of note, but it is still surprising when reference is made to a "sensational human sacrifice" even though such occurrences were not rare in the religions and myths of the Mediterranean area. There were the famous sacrifices which involved Abraham, Agamemnon and Idomeneus. Some of the conclusions drawn from this episode are odd, however.

It is generally supposed that the Minoans, possibly having had some indication of the imminent earthquake, resorted to the gruesome means of a human sacrifice in order to attempt to avert the catastrophe at the last minute. At the same time, research asserts that this was the first and only human sacri-

Hospitable Cretan from a small village in the Ida Mountains.

fice undertaken by the Minoans. The accuracy of this assumption is, however, questionable. If the Minoans wanted to prevent the catastrophe with a human sacrifice, surely it would be natural to assume that they did this each time there were indications of a strong earthquake. This would make it unlikely that this was an isolated incident. Archaeologist Iannis Sakelarakis, the Ephor in charge of Arhanes, made himself unpopular in the Greek archaeological world for reporting his findings, and the "evidence" is still hotly debated.

There is so much which is still unexplained. It is possible, for example, that the building was not in fact a temple, but a store for the hilltop sanctuary on Mount Joúchtas. Some experts think that the sacrificial sword or knife was actually the tip of a spear. It is also not certain that a priest was present. However, on the sarcophagus of Agía Triáda a priestess is illustrated in connection with the sacrifice of an animal.

Mount Joúchtas, 811 metres high, lies to the west of Arhánes. It can easily be reached by car. The fourth excavation site, a Minoan hilltop sanctuary, is up on the northern summit, along with a radio and weather station. Unfortunately the site is not on view to the public, but that is unimportant. The main attraction here is the glorious view of Iráklion right to the sea. This is, incidentally, the mountain you see before you from Knossós as you look south, so even for the Minoans this was no ordinary place.

The significance of this mountain is heightened when one realises that it is in one of these caves that Zeus is believed to have been buried. The mountain is thought to reflect this fact in that, whether observed from the west or east, it resembles the profile of a reclining head. Popular belief has it that it is the

The path to the Ida Cave, sheltered from the sun by clouds.

face of the sleeping or dead Zeus. On the southern summit, which is reached via a gravel path along the saddle, is the **Aféndi Church** which is a combination of four different chapels. On 6 August the Transfiguration of Christ is celebrated up here. In cloudy, windy weather this place has an aura of fascination and mystery.

Three km to the south of Arhánes is the Minoan mansion of **Vathípetro**. The way to this fifth important excavation site is well marked. The mansion was built around 1580 BC and only inhabited for about 30 years. It is assumed that a larger palace-like structure was to have been built here, and that an earthquake put paid to the plan. In one of the secluded houses, there are many large storage vessels (*pithoi*) and a wine press. One can assume, therefore, that the vineyards of this area have a very long history.

Tílissos: If you take the fast road for this short stretch westwards, you make your journey unnecessarily complicated, for at the other end there are numerous little crossroads without any signposts. It is much easier to take the old road from Iráklion towards Réthimnon. Ignore the turning to Rogdiá, and 4 km further on, take the turning to Anógia. After 3 km, you arrive at **Tílissos**. On this stretch you pass a somewhat dilapidated but impressive building with three cupolas, in which there is a workshop today. Here in earlier times travellers would spend the night if they did not manage to enter Megálo Kástro (Iráklion) before the gates were closed.

Tílissos is a small town on the eastern flanks of the Ida Mountains. The north wind blows through its lovely gardens. Here it is not fruit and flowers which are grown, but olives and vineyards which provide a living for the people of Tílissos. Despite the presence of the Minoan mansions which have been discovered

Excavated mansions in Tílissos.

here, the place is still unspoiled and is not part of the tourist route. This is probably because the town is not far from Iráklion, and visitors tend to return to their hotels there and in the surrounding area after visiting the site. Apart from the excavation site, there really is nothing else here, but an evening among the friendly people of Tílissos gives you the chance to experience a side of Crete no longer found in the tourist centres. Here, you have the chance to enjoy the pleasures of the island and the hospitality of the islanders.

To reach the site, just follow the signs. (Oh, if only Zeus had willed that every site in Crete were so well signed.) The mansions erected on the foundations of older buildings were inhabited between 1600 and 1450 BC. These, like the great palaces, seem to have been destroyed by the catastrophe of 1450 BC. It is particularly interesting to note that these detached houses, of two or possibly more storeys, were built earthquake proof. A water supply system is clearly recognisable too.

Of the many finds, three enormous bronze kettles are the most remarkable. They stood in one of the three store rooms of House C, and are quite out of proportion for this dwelling place, unless the houses were much taller, and had far more rooms than has been postulated. It is, however, quite certain that these kettles were not simply used for family cooking. The largest has a diameter of almost one and a half metres, and weighs over 50 kilos. Most probably they were used for soldiers, perhaps to prepare food for the guards of the mountain pass. The kettles and other finds, amphorae, *pithoi*, vases, double axes and the bronze statue of a praying figure are exhibited in the Archaeological Museum of Iráklion, Room VII (standing alone and in cabinet 89).

If you make your way to the neigh-

Colourful creations up for sale.

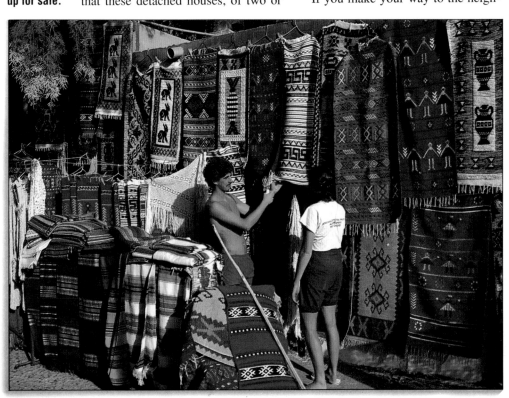

bouring *tavérna,* and are interested in unusual knitwear, you might like to take a beautiful jumper home as a souvenir. The 90-year-old head of the clan who runs the family business is a gifted knitter. Although much of the work is geared to the tourists' taste nowadays, every now and then she lets her imagination run wild and produces something truly original. Prices vary according to your bargaining skills.

Rogdiá: There are a number of wonderful trips from Iráklion into the surrounding area to the northwest, such as to the mountain village of **Rogdiá**, 16 km away. The best approach is to take the old road, and turn off after 7 km at the signpost for Rogdiá. This stretch goes past one of the few industrial areas of Crete which seems particularly hideous, lying as it does in such a wide expanse of unspoiled countryside. Some say it is a cement works, but the inhabitants of Rogdiá refer to it as a refinery. After a short breezy drive along a coastal road, with a wonderful view out over the sea, you reach Rogdiá, which lies approximately 300 metres above sea level.

It is a village which, apart from the ruins of a Venetian palace and a church, is well worth visiting for its own sake. The owner of the café opposite the palace, who was born in 1920 and is a keen reader of Kazantzákis, will happily regale the visitor with stories about the troubles at the beginning of the century and the German occupation, and he will air his opinion on the entente of nations. He has clear views on this matter, as some erstwhile members of the occupational forces are now friends of his. It is very pleasant to spend a few hours here just listening and learning.

Below the village one can see the remains of a Venetian fortress built in 1206, the **Paleókastro**. In this castle, the conditions for handing Crete over to the Turks were negotiated.

Rogdiá is a wonderful starting point for walks into the surrounding countryside. There are few people here in the vineyards, and very often there is a gentle breeze blowing. But it is better to take a car if you wish to visit the monastery of Savathianá, especially in the summer months, even if you have heard that it is only a quarter of an hour away. The truth is that the 5-km stretch involves a climb of 120 metres, and is in fact surprisingly exhausting. Many an unwary tourist has regretted taking that Cretan quarter of an hour at face value.

Although it does not lie in a bare landscape, the convent of **Savathianá** has the appearance of an oasis in the desert. It was built in a watery gully and the well tended vegetation flourishes so the white buildings are almost hidden by lush growth. You walk past glorious flower beds to the church of Agios Sávas, a building which is actually incorporated into the mountainside. There is a remarkable collection of

El Greco in Fódele, fondly remembered.

126

icons, as well as other treasures displayed near the entrance of the church. After a visit inside, you will be invited into a cosy room for coffee, quince jam and *tsikoudiá*. It is most pleasant to chat with the nuns, who sell woven cloth, embroidery, post cards and reproductions of icons. And what about that excellent Schnapps? The little nun looks quite put out – that's not for sale.

Fódele: From Rogdiá it is about 12 km to **Fódele** either straight up north on small roads, or back towards Réthimnon and on via the motorway. The village lies among orange groves, and proudly announces itself as the birthplace of the painter Doménikos Theotokópoulos (1541–1614), better known as El Greco, who later lived in Toledo in Spain. As El Greco never clearly stated in which Cretan village he was born, there was much dispute among villages as to where, precisely, he came from. Fódele presented the most credible documentation and, in 1934, it finally emerged as the victor in the dispute over this native son.

Fódele is a secretive place. As you enter the village, you have the impression that the whole place is asleep, but you soon realise that there are hundreds of people already there. They are eating and drinking in a *tavérna,* which is, of course, named El Greco's. Yes, it was definitely worth the fight. Without its famous son, the village would certainly not be on the map. The birthplace of the painter has been completely renovated, and is to be found to the north of Fódele in the isolated village of Lumbiniés, where the little 13th-century Panagia Church with its well preserved frescoes is worth a visit too. Sadly there are no original El Grecos on Crete (there is one on Syros), and the visitor has to make do with the photographs and copies in the church at Fódele.

On the return journey to Iráklion, it is

The Kazantzákis Museum is in Mirtiá.

worth making a detour to the Bay of **Agía Pelagía** where the bathing facilities are good, and the *tavérna* offers a warm welcome.

The Kazantzákis Museum: Mirtiá is reached via Knossós, and then past the restaurant at Spiliá. About 1.5 km after that, take a left turn through the vine-growing valley of Arhánes. The wine-producing village of Mirtiá gives an impression of flourishing prosperity, as one would expect from a place with such a product as its mainstay.

The museum is in the centre of the village. Looking at the pictures of its inauguration, one can only marvel at the international "community" of the writer Níkos Kazantzákis (see chapter on *Literature*, page 81).

In the museum there are many of the writer's personal possessions as well as expositions on him and his work. Of course *Zorba the Greek* is prominently featured in the exhibition and has pride

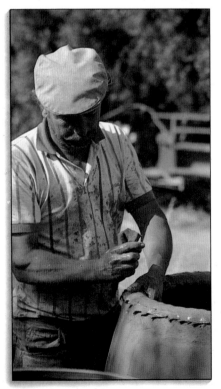

of place among the various theatre productions. There are busts, oil paintings and sketches, among them some horrendous attempts to portray the "heroic thinker" Kazantzákis as well as all sorts of meaningless trifles, which would be totally insignificant if they belonged to anyone else. There is even a tin of sweets, with bits of cinnamon sticks and a mint inside. When there is no film or television crew at work there, the museum is quite quiet. For Kazantzákis fans a visit signifies respect for the author. The rather high cost of entrance, and of a brochure, are understandable if one realises that the museum is completely self-financing; there are no subsidies at all.

Thrapsanó: On a map the way from Mirtiá to **Thrapsanó** seems quite straightforward. If only it were! A detailed description of directions would be just as confusing as the journey itself. So it is best to ask directions along the way. Everyone is aware of the problem and they all know exactly what you want when you ask for Trápsano instead of Thrapsanó. The trick is to believe people when they seem to be directing you the wrong way. They really do know the area better than you do. The roads are not in fact that complicated; they are simply wrongly drawn on the map. If you manage to find Thrapsanó from Mirtiá at the first attempt, you really have achieved the impossible.

The best pottery of Thrapsanó is to be found just before you reach the village as you come from Mirtiá. Large pots are made here. If you want to get to know the village, leave your car outside the place, for it has hardly changed over the centuries, and its cobbled streets were not designed for today's vehicles. Around the centre, which lies in a slightly elevated position, are many interesting potteries, where you can buy all kinds of arts and crafts, with tasteful work as usual displayed right next to the most awful kitsch.

Pottery today...

You really should visit the pottery at the edge of the village. Here Ioánnis Moutzákis and his wife and son work with a few helpers. There are 15 potter's wheels for large pots (*pithoi*). The clay from the surrounding area is sieved again and again to obtain as high a standard of purity as possible. After the first watering and kneading, the clay is kept under cloths until used. The axles of the wheels are set in the ground, and the wheels themselves are just above the ground. A boy down in a ditch turns the wheel while the master forms the pot on the wheel above. It really is worth a trip to Crete just to see this process. When the pot is of the right height, it is left to rest for a while, so that there is no overweight at the collar. Now the pots must regularly have water poured over them so that there are no cracks. When the pots are well dried the master goes from wheel to wheel, and from the clay strip which the perspiring boy has kneaded, and then handed to him, he expertly forms the last part of the pot, the rolled rim.

Meanwhile the fire for smaller objects has been prepared. A huge heap of sawdust is lying in front of the oven mouth. The fire is lit and one of the helpers throws one handful of sawdust after another through the stoke hole. This simple process gives an almost constant oven temperature, which ensures the quality of the pottery. It gets extremely warm just watching, even five metres away from the oven. The sawdust thrower is almost roasted, and there is a change of shift every 20 minutes. In summer, when the temperature is in the 30s anyway, the quantity of drinks consumed by the helpers is immeasurable. Even if you show no inclination to buy anything, you will be served coffee and *raki*, and the master will give you his card. He speaks in the regional dialect so that *raki* is

...and yesterday.

pronounced *ratschi*, and his name becomes Ioánnis Moutzátasch. He loves his work so much that he never takes a holiday. What, not even on Sunday, on *Kiriaki*? Well, no, he does take "Tschiriatschi" off. His speech is so infectious that one is tempted to recount a visit to the Kazantzátsch Museum, which is always a good subject of conversation, simply to get him to talk.

Amnissós: The Bay of Karterós lies 7 km to the east and offers the best bathing in the Iráklion area. The beach is divided into four parts, and only the first two can really be recommended. These are "Florida Beach" and "EOT Beach" (an admission fee is payable). The place then gets more run down further on. The noise of aeroplanes taking off and landing is ubiquitous, however.

Behind "Amnissós Beach", which is the third part, lie the ruins of the famous old city of **Amnissós** which was once the port for Knossós, and also played a prominent part in ancient mythology. It was here that Idomeneus and his soldiers left the island with a fleet of 80 ships to sail for Troy. Here, Theseus landed with the young Athenians who were to be sacrificed to the Minotaur. Homer mentions Amnissós in the 19th Book of the *Odyssey*.

As Amnissós lies in an unfavourable position buffeted by the north wind, one assumes that the place was chosen for its proximity to the Eileithyía Cave, and not for its pleasant location. Excavations on the hill of Amnissós by S. Marinatos, have revealed interesting details. Apart from the harbour and houses, a large well was discovered. On the north side, a house appeared from beneath a layer of pumice stone, the so-called "House of the Harbour Master," and because of this discovery, the "volcano catastrophe theory" was reinforced. It had been assumed that lava and ash had covered Crete, but in the

The excavated Palace of Mália.

meantime that has been refuted. On the eastern side, the "Villa of the Lilies" was discovered, named after the lilies on a fresco which are now exhibited in the Museum of Iráklion, Room XIV. The function and arrangement of the house are still unclear. The open side of the courtyard faces the sea, and small storerooms were found. The clearly more recent buildings on the hill top date from a Venetian fort, which was destroyed by the Turks.

The **Eileithyía Cave** is reached along the old road past the turning for Episkopi. After almost a kilometre, the cave entrance can be seen on the left, below the road.

Eileithyía was the Cretan goddess of fertility and birth, daughter of Zeus and Hera, sometimes equated with Hera or Artemis. The special significance of the cave is that it was a place of worship for a period of over 3,500 years.

The cave, which is 63 metres long,

and at the back almost 12 metres wide, contains stalactites (among them a stalagmite in the shape of a phallus) which are a clear indication that cult rites were practised here (AMI, I, 1). Unfortunately, the cave has been locked for some time now, and can only be visited with permission from the museum administration in Iráklion.

On the old road, further to the east, at km 14, lies the village of **Kókkini Háni**. Here in 1912, Arthur Evans and M. Xanthoudidis excavated the Minoan mansion of **Nirou Háni**, in which enormous bronze double axes were discovered (AMI, VII, standing alone) as well as many vessels, altars and lamps (AMI, VII, 89). It is supposed that these objects were intended for export, to be shipped not from Amnissós but from here. Remains of the harbour can be made out near the Knossós Beach Hotel.

Three km further along the road, there

An old section of Mália does its part for tourism.

is a turning to **Goúves** which you can take to **Skotinó**, 5 km further on. Then it is a further 1.5 km to the **Cave of Skotinó**. The speleologist Paul Faure worked here for a long time. The cave is appreciably bigger than the Eileithyía Cave (126 metres long, greatest height 47 metres, greatest width 36 metres) and it is no less important. Ceramic finds from the Minoan era right up to Roman times indicate a long, unbroken period of utilisation as a place of worship. Briómartis, the Cretan Artemis, was worshipped here.

The old road continues to **Limin Hersonissou** (km 26), which used to be a little coastal village but which is now completely swamped by tourists and new hotels. There is now nothing to differentiate it from other beach resorts in the world. The inhabitants, however, are pleased with the development and the holiday-makers, most of them on package tours, seem quite content, so

one shouldn't really complain. In the evenings, the road along the beach is full of life. Bathing along the coast here is excellent but the beach is over-crowded in high season.

At km 30 is the resort of **Stális** and at km 34, **Mália**. Mália has for some time now been divided into two parts: on the right is the old part of the town, relatively untouched, and on the left, to-wards the sea, an amusement street, presumably modelled on the Italian pattern, where there is one *tavérna*, café, bar and disco next to another, each trying to drown out its neighbour. For those looking for a nerve-shattering experience, this is the place to visit.

For those in search of peace and re-laxation, it is definitely to be avoided. The division of the town makes it rather interesting; all the visitor needs to do is just cross the road and he or she is in a different century. Attempts are being made to rectify this. Although the place

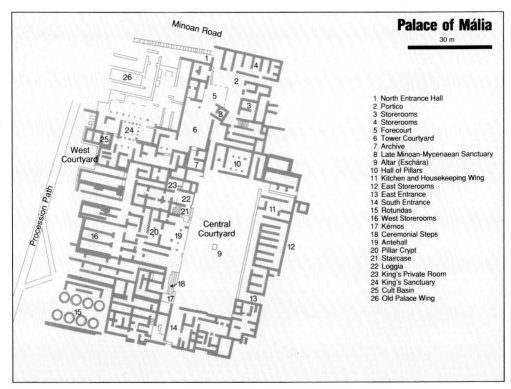

Palace of Mália

30 m

1 North Entrance Hall
2 Portico
3 Storerooms
4 Storerooms
5 Forecourt
6 Tower Courtyard
7 Archive
8 Late Minoan-Mycenaean Sanctuary
9 Altar (Eschára)
10 Hall of Pillars
11 Kitchen and Housekeeping Wing
12 East Storerooms
13 East Entrance
14 South Entrance
15 Rotundas
16 West Storerooms
17 Kérnos
18 Ceremonial Steps
19 Antehall
20 Pillar Crypt
21 Staircase
22 Loggia
23 King's Private Room
24 King's Sanctuary
25 Cult Basin
26 Old Palace Wing

has lost none of its natural beauty, this rapid development has meant that it is always congested.

Three km to the east and you reach the Palace of Mália, the third largest of the Minoan palaces. According to the myth, this was the palace of King Sarpedon, brother of Minos and Rhadamanthys. It was built around 2000 BC, renovated in about 1650 BC and finally destroyed in 1450 BC. Like the other palaces, it has a rectangular courtyard which lies in a north-south direction (50 metres by 22 metres) and comprises sacral rooms, storerooms, pillared rooms and royal apartments as well as kitchen quarters.

In the so-called "Loggia" a sceptre and a sword were found (AMI, IV, 47, 52) but no frescoes were discovered. Near the southwest side of the courtyard on a paved gallery, there is the famous **Kérnos**, a round stone (diameter 90 centimetres), which has been the subject of various interpretations.

The stone has 34 evenly-spaced small hollows around the edge and a large hollow in the centre. It was thought for a while to be a kind of gaming board, but that theory has now been discounted. Some say it is more likely to have been a sacrificial stone. But none of the interpretations is certain, and as the stone still lies in its usual place, you can form your own impressions.

The Palace of Mália is not as impressive as that of Knossós, but its location on the seashore provides a new perspective on the Minoans and their lifestyle.

Later, when you have visited Festós and Káto Zákros, the question uppermost in your mind may well be: which is the more pronounced – the differences between the palaces, or their similarities? It is fascinating to compare and contrast these historic sites when, as an amateur archaeologist, you explore the relics of ancient but advanced Minoan civilisation on Crete.

Luxurious hotels line the coast of Mália.

133

FROM IRÁKLION TO THE SEA OF LIBYA

The village of **Agía Varvára** with its open spaces and wide streets, lies almost 29 km from Iráklion. During the months of June and July, even before you reach the village, you will be greeted by an interesting sight. You will see the local children holding up strange-looking clusters for sale. These are bunches of cherries, beautifully bound on sticks. As Cretan cherries are very popular, and because the sellers take no heed of road safety while plying their wares, traffic jams often build up. Nevertheless, do try one of these delicious cherry sticks before driving on.

The square in front of the small Church of Elias at the entrance of the village, is taken to be the geographical centre of the island, thus the navel of the Cretan world, so to speak. In fact, that's its name, Omphalos, the navel. And that's really all that there is worth mentioning about Agía Varvára.

A small road which branches off to the left, almost back in the direction of Iráklion, leads to **Priniás**, which is about 6.5 km away, and the site of ancient **Rizinia**. There was a settlement here in Minoan times, and its most important period was during the 6th and 7th centuries BC. It was the work of two Italian archaeologists in particular which revealed the ruins of two temples, the famous knight fresco in the style of Daedalus, many sculptures (Briómartis among others) as well as many other artefacts (AMI, XIX).

After this detour, it's back to Agía Varvára, where the right fork leads the visitor in the direction of **Panasós** and **Gérgeri**. Whereas Panasós is beautiful to look at, Gérgeri, with its hordes of happy children, makes a livelier impression. There is a 15th-century Panagia Church in the village cemetery.

Unfortunately not much of the fresco decoration remains. The church was built in Byzantine style, and the church tower, set at a distance from the church itself, looks quite incongruous. Behind Gérgeri there are huge octopus-like agaves, or century trees, some of which reach a height of 10 metres, their graceful, sturdy limbs curving delicately upwards, loaded with seed pods.

The contrasts continue, and after the restraint of **Nivritos**, you come to **Zarós,** which is large and noisy, with about 2,000 inhabitants. The spring water here is so exquisite that even in olden times, the city of Górtis went to the expense of building an aqueduct to obtain it. There is one *tavérna* next to another along the short stretch of main road you drive along, and they certainly don't just sell water. Just before you leave the village the road forks, and you go to the right.

The Monastery of Vrondissi: Just 4 km

Left, church bells ring on the way to the Sea of Libya. Right, baking for Easter.

after Gérgeri, also on the right, there is a road up into the mountains. One km on, and you will find yourself in front of the Monastery of **Vrondissi**. The forecourt alone would have made the journey worthwhile, but it is merely an introduction. On each side of the entrance to the monastery is an enormous plane tree.

The trunk of one was once apparently hit by lightning, and is now hollow. There is room inside for a small one-man kitchen from which coffee is served. In the corner, behind this Plane Tree Café, the Venetian fountain can be seen. Adam and Eve stand over the four sources of paradise, symbolised by four bearded heads. Unfortunately, the sculptures have been badly damaged, and one can only guess at the former beauty of the fountain. But it is lovely nevertheless.

On the right side of the square, under the other plane tree, long tables and benches have been set up, looking for all the world as if the feeding of the 5,000 was about to take place. But they are simply there for the Feast of St Thomas, which is celebrated on the first Sunday after Easter, and then there are only just enough seats for everyone. There is, however, a large guesthouse opposite the entrance to the monastery, which can give hospitality to anyone unable to find space under the trees.

It is not known exactly when the Monastery of Vrondissi was built. Although the dates 1630–39 are inscribed in the building, they may be not be correct. According to experts, the monastery must have been at least 250 years older, and could have belonged to the monastery at Valsamónero, which is much larger.

One nave of the church is dedicated to St Anthony, and one to St Thomas. In front of the church stands a bell tower in Venetian style. The inside, particularly

Evening calm by the beach at Iráklion.

the southern nave, is decorated with frescoes and icons. In fact these icons are from the church in Agios Fanoúrios, which is all that is left of the enormous monastery complex of Valsamónero. The works of art were brought here for reasons of safety, as there has been a considerable increase in church robberies in recent times. The six Cretan icons by the painter Damaskinós, for which the monastery of Vrondissi was so famous, have, since 1800, been kept in the Ekateríni Church in Iráklion. They were brought there to be saved from the ravages of the Turks. The decision proved to be the right one as in 1821 the Turks destroyed everything they could find in the monastery, including the extensive library.

A glorious gateway leads to a beautifully paved inner courtyard. Yet a strange odour emits from a shed at the far end of the yard. It is the smell of cheese being produced in the time honoured method, using a goat or sheep skin. But the other side of the yard is fragrant with the scent of pines, palms and orange trees, and the view of the valley from there is glorious.

The right hand corner near the entrance, under a pergola, is where the solitary monk who still lives here has his home. The monastery is an impressive sight, particularly when the sky is overcast or in rainy weather. Take your time here and try the excellent coffee made by the man in the Plane Tree Café.

As you go on to **Vorizia**, down on the left, below the road you will see a row of dilapidated houses. This is all that remains of the village of Vorizia, destroyed during World War II by the Germans. A row of houses built very close, as if for comfort, became the new village of Vorizia.

At the end of the village, a 3-km-long road leads to the Monastery of **Valsamónero**. The keys for the church of

Tentacles hung out to dry.

Agios Fanoúrios have to be procured from the Greek Orthodox priest or the custodian, the *Filakás,* in Vorizia. The Byzantine frescoes here show a specifically Cretan style of representation, and it is even suggested that they may have been the work of El Greco or of Mikhail Damaskinós. Although this theory is not supported by art historians, it is difficult to see how either of the two masters of art could have improved upon the beautiful originals.

The Kamáres Cave: The small village of **Kamáres** lies 3 km past Vorizia, and is a good starting point for walks in the Ida Mountains or for climbing Mount Psilorítis. Mountain guides are available on request. And if you are interested in more than just climbing mountains, one of the main cultural attractions of the island is on the doorstep: but it is a good 4-hour climb up to the famous **Kamáres Cave**.

The cave is 1,525 metres up, and has a depth of about 80 metres. The huge entrance, about 40 metres wide and 20 metres high, can be seen from a long way off, even from as far away as Festós. In Minoan times the cave was used for living as well as burial purposes, and the Goddess of Fertility was worshipped here.

The clay vessels, the Kamáres ceramics found in the cave, were produced in the workshops of the palaces of Festós and Agía Triáda. It was not until Kamáres ceramics were found in graves of the Middle Empire of Ancient Egypt, that the dates could be accurately assessed. A selection of pottery may be admired in the Archaeological Museum in Iráklion, room III. They are characteristically thin, and brightly coloured, particularly in white, yellow and orange on a dark background.

Just a few kilometres further on from Agía Varvára is the **Vourvoulitis Pass**. There, from a height of 620 metres, you

Steps at the Temple of Apollo Pythios in Górtis.

will have your first view over the Messará Plain right to the Asteroúsia Mountains, which are in the south, between the plain and the Sea of Libya. Even in summer, when lorries full of melons and tomatoes pass by, a cold north wind can make one hurry on.

Agii Déka: About 44 km from Iráklion, 15 km to the south of Agiá Varvára, is the village of **Agii Déka**, or the "Saintly 10". Here 10 Cretan bishops were put to death by the sword under rule of the Roman Caesar Gaius Decius (249–251). All of them had refused to take part in the consecration of a heathen temple. The stone which served as execution block has been preserved in the church. The 10 martyrs, later canonised, have been buried in a chapel on the western edge of the village.

Deep in thought.

Górtis: Only 1 km west of Agii Déka is the extensive site of ancient Górtis. From the road the imposing grandeur of the **Basilica of Titus**, one of the most impressive buildings on Crete, is clearly visible. It was built in the 6th century in memory of Titus, pupil of St Paul and later the first bishop of Crete. The church had to be renovated in the 10th and 14th centuries. The three-naved church which we see today is mainly the result of work undertaken at the beginning of this century. The only service held in the basilica these days is in memory of St Titus, and it takes place on 23 December. It is not easy to imagine the former glory of this place, as the traffic thunders past on the Mires road only about 20 metres away while the noisy spades do their worst.

Near the Odeon one takes in more sense of history. It is reached from the basilica, over the Agorá and then a little to the north. The **Odeon** is a 1st-century Roman rotunda. The famous inscription of Greek law is at the rear of the pillared entrance. For the Romans, who hardly understood the dialect, it served

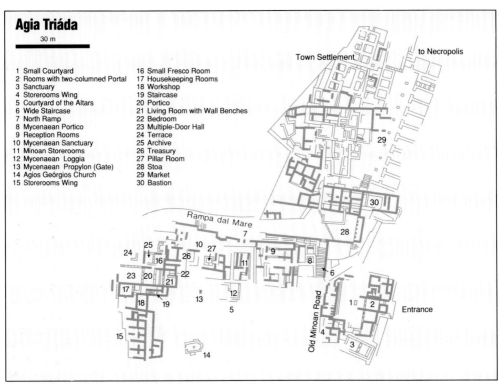

Agia Triáda

30 m

1 Small Courtyard
2 Rooms with two-columned Portal
3 Sanctuary
4 Storerooms Wing
5 Courtyard of the Altars
6 Wide Staircase
7 North Ramp
8 Mycenaean Portico
9 Reception Rooms
10 Mycenaean Sanctuary
11 Minoan Storerooms
12 Mycenaean Loggia
13 Mycenaean Propylon (Gate)
14 Agios Geórgios Church
15 Storerooms Wing
16 Small Fresco Room
17 Housekeeping Rooms
18 Workshop
19 Staircase
20 Portico
21 Living Room with Wall Benches
22 Bedroom
23 Multiple-Door Hall
24 Terrace
25 Archive
26 Treasury
27 Pillar Room
28 Stoa
29 Market
30 Bastion

Town Settlement
to Necropolis

Rampa dal Mare

Old Minoan Road

Entrance

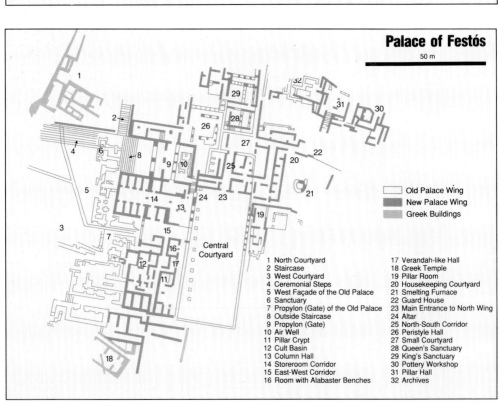

Palace of Festós

50 m

Old Palace Wing
New Palace Wing
Greek Buildings

Central Courtyard

1 North Courtyard
2 Staircase
3 West Courtyard
4 Ceremonial Steps
5 West Façade of the Old Palace
6 Sanctuary
7 Propylon (Gate) of the Old Palace
8 Outside Staircase
9 Propylon (Gate)
10 Air Well
11 Pillar Crypt
12 Cult Basin
13 Column Hall
14 Storeroom Corridor
15 East-West Corridor
16 Room with Alabaster Benches
17 Verandah-like Hall
18 Greek Temple
19 Pillar Room
20 Housekeeping Courtyard
21 Smelting Furnace
22 Guard House
23 Main Entrance to North Wing
24 Altar
25 North-South Corridor
26 Peristyle Hall
27 Small Courtyard
28 Queen's Sanctuary
29 King's Sanctuary
30 Pottery Workshop
31 Pillar Hall
32 Archives

no civic function, but was left there untouched for decoration. Opposite the Odeon is a small theatre.

One could enjoy a wonderful view of the whole Górtis area from the hill where an **Acropolis** once stood, but unfortunately the olive groves are too thick. However one can clearly see the aqueduct, by means of which water was brought here from Zarós, 15 km away.

To explore the southern and larger part of historical Górtis, cross the main road and carry on along the asphalt road for about 250 metres, then turn off to the left. Here, close to each other, are a small theatre and the **Temple of Apollo Pythios**, which was built on the site of a Minoan building. On the outer walls there are inscriptions of Greek law which are older than the famed inscription of Górtis.

A little further to the north is the somewhat surprising temple in honour of Egyptian gods. They were worshipped on Crete for a while after the conquest of Egypt (AMI, XX). The highlight is the **Praetorium**, an extensive building complex which formed the palace from which the Roman Governor, the Praetor of Crete and Cyrene ruled. Everything in this imposing building seems to have been organised for efficiency. Even the ruins seem to reflect the builders' will to dominate. Minoan architecture, in contrast, seems ornate and harmonious, in keeping with its peaceful, matriarchal culture.

Further south are the thermal springs, the amphitheatre, the cemetery and the stadium where chariot races were held. From a cultural and historical point of view this southern part of Górtis is considered rather unimportant. But whatever the experts say, for the visitor who really wants to understand life in a classical city, this site in Górtis is unique.

Down the steps of the Palace of Festós.

Just by walking around and keeping one's eyes open, where everything is "historical", one can learn so much more than from reading books or visit-

ing a museum. Much of the ground is covered with fragments and potsherds which one is prohibited by Greek law from taking away. The visitor may find it hard to believe that this was once a centre of power, pride and battle. Nowadays the atmosphere is peaceful and one can spend many happy hours just exploring and simply enjoying the atmosphere of the place and absorbing the sense of history.

Festós: On the way to Festós one passes **Mires**, with more than 3,000 inhabitants, the largest town of the Messará Plain. On Saturdays there is a big market here, a colourful, lively event. Mires is still comparatively untouched by tourism, as people do not seem to have realised the favourable location of the place. It is easy to reach Festós or Agía Triáda for example, and the whole of the glorious Messará Plain opens up in the direction of Hárakas and Pirgos. Apart from *tavérnes,* cafés and

shops, there is a chemist, post office, OTE and even a branch of the Greek National Health Insurance.

The **Palace of Festós** is almost 7 km from Mires (62 km from Iráklion). Five km along the road, a signpost points to the excavation site, and soon afterwards the palace itself is reached.

Festós is most impressive but not, like Knossós, because of its reconstruction. Here it is the site which is spectacular. The palace was built on a hill, 70 metres high, the summit of which was flattened to facilitate construction of the first palace. The panorama is breathtaking in any season, mountains to the north and south, the sea on the western horizon, and the seemingly endless fertile plain to the east.

This is a particularly beautiful place in spring, with its wonderful colours, and in autumn too. But in summer, the heat can be unbearable, when the temperature is above 50 degrees, and one wonders what on earth made the Minoans choose such a place – an anvil in the sun. Their choice was certainly not based on climatic criteria. For them the focal point was indeed something quite different. In the Ida Mountains to the north, to the right of a twin summit is a dark hole. It is the Kamáres Cave. The north-south axis of the palace points directly to this cave. Fragments of pottery found in the cave underscore this relationship, for some of the wares at least were made in the palace.

In Festós one comes across another member of the mythological family of Zeus, Europa and her children. Rhadamanthys, the brother of Minos, is said to have ruled here, before being elected judge of the underworld.

Festós is mentioned in the *Iliad* too, King Idomeneus set out from here with his troops to support the Achaians in their struggle against Troy. As scientific research makes it seem ever more likely that the Trojan War actually did take place, mythology and history seem inextricably linked.

The site of Festós has been shown to have been inhabited from Neolithic times onward. The first palace was built in about 2000 BC, and it must have been heavily damaged by three strong earthquakes and fires. At the height of Minoan civilisation, the period between 1600 and 1500 BC, a new palace was built on the foundations of the old one. This palace too was completely destroyed soon afterwards in the catastrophe of 1450 BC.

Finds from the Geometric period and Hellenistic Epoch indicate that the area around the palace was also inhabited in post Minoan times. The prophet Epimenides was born in Festós in the 6th century BC. His most famous saying is, no doubt, "All Cretans are liars." But despite this artful paradox, it must not be forgotten that he was a serious thinker, who was even cited by Aristotle. In the 3rd century, before our time

Left, a flutist's way of welcoming visitors to Festós. Right, the palace ruins.

reckoning, Festós was forced to cede its position of superiority to Górtin.

The Palace of Festós is somewhat smaller than that of Knossós, but similar in layout. The separate sections, used for a variety of purposes, are grouped around a central courtyard (46 metres long by 22 metres wide). Stone masons' marks found in both Knossós and Festós indicate that some of the same craftsmen were at work in both palaces. There is also a great deal of evidence pointing to a close relationship between the two places as political and religious centres. The exact nature of the ties is, however, still not quite clear.

The famous Festós Disc, copies of which may be seen at every souvenir stall on the island, was not found inside the palace itself, but in the so-called archives to the north of the site. It is not at all certain though whether the room was in fact used as the archives. It may have been a storeroom for the palace guards.

This makes even a rough interpretation of the clay disc impossible

On Crete a brochure on sale gives an interpretation of the disc as merely a list of goods for export to the various countries with which Crete traded at the time. This interpretation dates from 1982, and despite its overwhelming simplicity, it is not entirely convincing to many people. It is completely discounted by the experts (AMI, III, cabinet 41).

In the cult basin, various ceramic vessels were found, among them the beaked can with grasses. They are exhibited in the Archaeological Museum of Iráklion (Room IV, cabinet 49). The melting furnace in the so-called production yard is one of the oldest such installations to be found in the whole of Greece. It is not true to say that the Italian excavators F. Halbherr (from 1900) and D. Levi (from 1952) did no reconstruction in the Palace of Festós. This impression is simply a result of

Festós, where the beautiful countryside beckons.

144

comparing their work with that done at Knossós. Parts of the palace were rebuilt, but the work was less ambitious, undertaken cautiously, and restricted to what was absolutely necessary.

Rooms are available in the tourist summer house at Festós, and it can be an unforgettable experience to spend the evening and the night in proximity to such an ancient palace. This encounter is definitely more interesting than the more usual tourist attractions.

Agía Triáda: In front of the car park in Festós there is a road which leads directly to the west, to the **Palace of Agía Triáda**. The route is a rather unusual one. You must proceed back onto the main road, then 2 km further towards Timbáki, and then towards the left once at the signpost.

A few metres on, you will find yourself at the Geropótamos River, and depending on the time of year and the water level, you have to decide whether or not to cross. There is no bridge. In summer, this proves to be no problem. But if the water level is high, you might not want to risk it. Once across the river, you should turn left at the next crossroads in the country lane, and on through the olive groves to the car park in Agía Triáda (Holy Trinity).

Since no name survived this place, it was given the name of the 14th-century church not far away, which is all that remains of a village named for Father, Son and Holy Spirit.

Agía Triáda is not strictly speaking a palace, as it does not possess the main feature of all other Cretan palaces, a central courtyard. The rooms are set in two wings which are almost at right angles to each other. The label Royal Villa would have been more appropriate for this structure.

There is much evidence to suggest that Agía Triáda belonged to the Palace of Festós; it may have been the summer

Agía Triáda, another scenic sight near Festós.

residence of the rulers. In Festós no frescoes or cult objects were found, whereas there was a surfeit in Agía Triáda. The palace and villa were linked by a paved road. The question then arises as to why, if the Minoan ruler wanted sea breezes, he or she didn't build nearer the shore. The answer to that was provided by the Italian archaeologists, who felt there was enough evidence to indicate that about 3,500 years ago, the sea was much nearer Agía Triáda than it is now.

Of all the precious finds, the most important are: the Harvester's Vase (AMI, VII), octopus and dolphin frescoes (AMI, XIV), steatite vases (AMI, IV), and the "Talents", 19 bronze bars, each weighing 29 kilos, from the sarcophagus of Agía Triáda (AMI, XIV) (see chapter on Cretan history).

Kómmos: If you return to Festós and from there go on through **Agios Ioánnis** (St John) in the direction of Mátala, you will reach the excavation site of **Kómmos**. Just about 1 km after the village of Pitsidia, take a right turn onto a road which leads to the church. You have to continue for only another 500 metres along the shore to the north, to reach the site.

Kómmos, which was a port of Festós, has only been excavated since 1976, by Canadian archaeologists. The place was inhabited at the beginning of the middle Minoan period, around 1800 BC, and like Festós reached the height of its importance in the late Minoan epoch. The excavations are not yet far enough advanced for any extensive conclusions to be reached.

If the theory that the sea lay nearer Agía Triáda in those days is correct, then there must have been a bay here, with Kómmos being established on the southern side. Thus the western part of the Messará Plain must have been alluvial land. But don't let all this theorising

Home to the hippies in the 1960s: the Mátala caves.

stop you from enjoying the excellent bathing on this lovely beach.

Mátala: The fishing village of **Mátala** is only 7 km from Festós. Well-known during the 1960s for the invasion of the hippies, it now offers a surprise of its own. It is so famous that one would imagine it to be overcrowded and the beach totally overrun with tourists. Wrong. The fact is that Mátala has hardly changed at all. Of course it has spruced itself up a bit, has a few more *tavérnes* than it used to, but it has not lost its character.

The houses still make a strange matt impression in daylight. They look like a collection of old, temporarily inhabited gold prospectors' huts. There's still a whiff of the freedom of the 1960s and 70s in the air, reminiscent of the old days of the flower children. The atmosphere is relaxed, and no one pressures you to rent a room. There are still plenty of young people here, all enjoying the

Mátala has one of the finest beaches on Crete.

ambience of this laid back village. The place itself is beautiful, and the houses are grouped around the natural harbour and the steep cliffs.

It is true that the caves were barred up a few years ago, but there are always climbers and they can be seen clambering up on the narrow cornices. These caves, inhabited in Neolithic times, were taken over as living quarters again in the 1960s, when they provided comfortable homes for the hippies. Later, backpackers and hikers wanted to take up permanent residence, but they were evicted, mainly for reasons of hygiene. Many a crocodile tear was shed for this last bastion of freedom.

In the evening if you sit in one of the restaurants opposite the cliff of caves, Mátala looks just like a ship about to set sail. It is a great place to relax as well as a good starting point for exploring the region and its towns, Kómmos, Festós, Agía Triáda and Górtis.

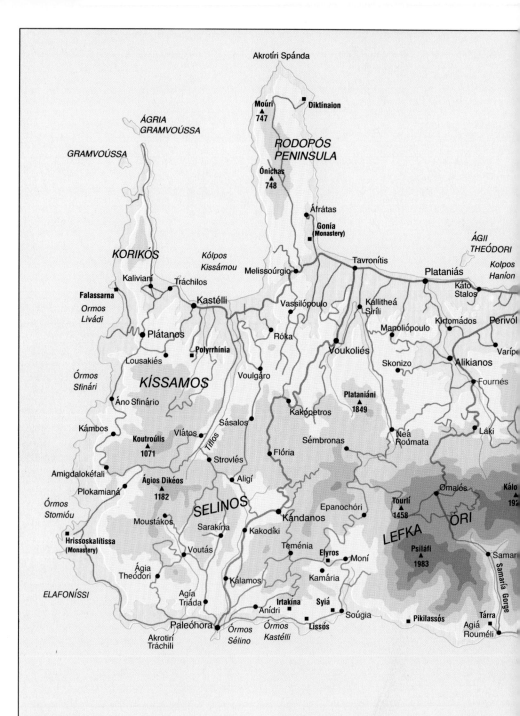

Akrotíri Spánda

Moúri ■ Diktínaion
▲
747

RODOPÓS
PENINSULA

Ónichas
▲
748

ÁGRIA
GRAMVOÚSSA

GRAMVOÚSSA

Áfrátas

Gonía
(Monastery)

ÁGII
THEÓDORI

KORIKÓS

Kólpos
Kissámou   Melissoúrgio   Tavronítis   Plataniás   Kolpos
Hioón
Kaliviani   Tráchilos   Káto
Stalos
Falassarna ■
Ormos   Kastélli   Vassilópoulo   Kállitheá   Kirtomádos   Perivól
Livádi   Síríli
Manoliópoulo
Plátanos   Róka   Varípe
Polyrrhínia   Voukoliés
Lousakiés   Skonizo   Alikianos
Órmos   KÍSSAMOS   Voulgáro   Fournés
Sfinári
Áno Sfinário   Plataniáni
▲
1849
Kámbos   Vlátos   Sásalos   Sémbronas   Neá   Láki
Koutroúlis   Roúmata
▲   Strovlés   Flória
1071
Amigdalokéfali   Ágios Dikéos   Aligí   Ómalós   Kálo
Plokamianá   ▲   Tourlí   192
1182   Epanochóri   ▲   ÓRI
Órmos   SELINOS   Kándanos   1458   LEFKA
Stomíou   Moustákos   Sarakína   Kakodíki   Psiláfi   Samar
Voutás   ▲
Hrissoskalítissa ■   Teménia   Elyros   Moní   1983
(Monastery)   ■
Ágia   Kálamos   Kamária
ELAFONÍSSI   Theódori   Agía   Irtakína   Syiá   Soúgia   Tárra
Triáda   Anídri   Lissós   Pikilassós   Agiá
Paleóhora   Órmos   Órmos   Rouméli
Akrotíri   Sélino   Kastélli
Tráchili

Sea   of   Libya

152

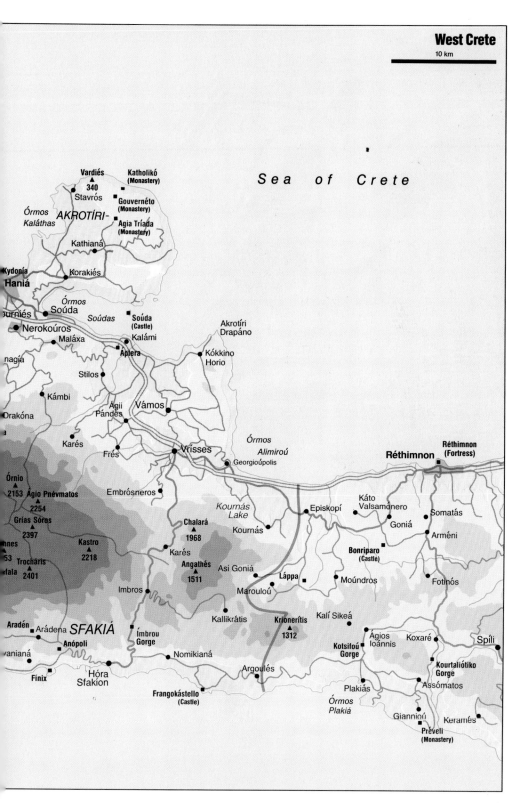

Sea   of   Crete

Vardiés
▲ 340
Stavrós
Katholikó
(Monastery)

Órmos
Kaláthas
AKROTÍRI-
Gouvernéto
(Monastery)
Agia Tríada
(Monastery)

Kathianá

Kydonía
Korakiés

Haniá

Órmos
Soúda
Soúdas
Soúda
(Castle)

Akrotíri
Drápano

ournés
Nerokoúros
Maláxa
Kalámi

nagía
Áptera
Kókkino
Horio

Stilos

Kámbi

Drakóna
Agii
Pándes
Vámos

Karés
Frés
Vrísses
Órmos
Alimiroú
Georgioúpolis

Réthimnon
Réthimnon
(Fortress)

Órnio
▲ 2153 Ágio Pnévmatos
Embrósneros

Kournás
Lake
Episkopí
Káto
Valsamónero
Somatás

▲ 2254
Grías Sóros
Chalará
▲ 1968
Kournás
Goniá
Arméni

▲ 2397
nes
Kastro
▲ 2218
Karés
Bonriparo
(Castle)

53 Trocháris
fala ▲ 2401
Angathés
▲ 1511
Así Goniá
Láppa
Moúndros
Fotinós

Imbros
Marouloú

Aradén
Arádena **SFAKIÁ**
Ímbrou
Gorge
Kallikrátis
Krionerítis
▲ 1312
Kalí Sikeá
Ágios
Ioánnis
Koxaré
Spíli

vanianá
Anópoli
Kotsifoú
Gorge

Fínix
Hóra
Sfakíon
Nomikianá
Argoulés
Kourtaliótiko
Gorge
Assómatos

Frangokástello
(Castle)
Plakiás
Órmos
Plakiá

Giannioú
Keramés

Préveli
(Monastery)

RÉTHIMNON AND SURROUNDINGS

The suburbs of Réthimnon are disappointing, with the usual boredom of concrete blocks. But if you leave the main road, and turn towards the sea, you will find yourself in the fascinating old part of the city of Réthimnon. The most interesting way in is through the beautiful Large Gate (Megáli Pórta) on the Square of the Four Martyrs. Many visitors are moved by this place, and as one of them, you could feel yourself transported back to the Middle Ages.

Réthimnon is a city of many contrasts, which is a result of the turbulent course of its history. There is the Fortezza and the Venetian harbour and lighthouse, as a reminder of the days of Venetian rule. Memories of the Turkish occupation linger in the mosques and minarets, two of which you can visit. To the east are the new parts of the city, with hotels and restaurants in profusion, and the many interesting small shops selling everything from Cretan boats to lace. There is much to keep the visitor occupied in this fascinating city.

The area around Réthimnon was probably settled as early as the Late Minoan Era. A rock grave was found in the suburb of **Mastrabas**, and various archaeological finds are displayed in the Archaeological Museum of Réthimnon. However, no actual settlement of this period has so far been discovered. During the 3rd and 4th centuries BC a town named Réthimna flourished here. It was autonomous and had the right to mint its own coins. Where today the Fortezza stands, was once the site of the Acropolis of Réthimnon with the Temple of Artemis and a shrine to the goddess Athena.

After Constantinople was conquered by the Crusaders, Crete fell to the Genoese Bonifatius of Monferat, who

later sold the island to the Venetians. With or without the treaty of sale, it took the Venetians a further five years to rid themselves of the Genoese, who had established extensive trading contacts. Near the present day village of Monopári one can still see the remains of the Genoese Fort of **Bonriparo**. In 1229 the Venetians finally made the city more secure, concentrating on the western side of the little harbour. The more important fortifications were constructed during the period 1540–70, and the outer wall, parallel to today's Dimakópoulou Street and part of the "Great Gate", can still be seen. The architect was Michele Sanmicheli.

In 1573 work was begun on the "city within the city," as the Fortezza was often described. New buildings sprang up, and others were completed, such as the Rimondi Fountain, the churches of St Mary, St Mary Magdalene, St Francis and the Loggia, in which the

Preceding pages: sunset over the hills; the face of Réthimnon emerging from the shadows. Left, Turkish part of the old city of Réthimnon. Right, the towering minaret.

155

Archaeological Museum is housed nowadays (Arkadíou Street 220). The **Rimondi Fountain**, among other renovated fountains and wells, helped solve the city's water problems. The spelling Arimondi, which is often seen, is simply the result of adding the A of the first name Alvise to that of Rimondi. The lions' heads between the Corinthian pillars have unfortunately been ravaged by time, but the water still flows.

When the attacking Turks appeared outside the city in 1646, the inhabitants hesitated for too long before taking refuge in the unpopular Fortezza. Eventually they were forced to enter, but it soon became obvious that the fort could not withstand the Turkish onslaught. After a siege lasting 22 days, Husein Pasha took the city as well as the fort.

Réthimnon retained its position as administrative centre under the Turks, but its appearance was radically changed. All the Christian churches were given minarets and new names, thereby turning them into mosques. Thus St Mary's Church became the **Neratzés Pasha Mosque**, and St Mary Magdalene's became the **Angebút Pasha Mosque**, but which today is the Orthodox Church of **Kiría Ton Angélon** (Our Lady of the Angels). Even the Venetian **Loggia** was not spared, and was changed into a mosque as well. The Rimondi Fountain was given a traditional Turkish domed roof. Thus the Turkish rulers put their stamp on the way the city looked, a clear indication of their dominance.

The Turks wanted to change the Greek Orthodox inhabitants of Crete in the same way. They forced as many Cretans as they could to become Muslims. Some did convert, for reasons of practicality, but others remained steadfast despite reprisals. As a warning to others, four of those who resisted were hanged on the square which is today

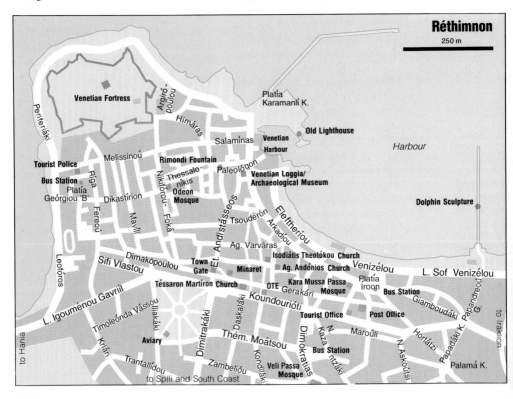

known as Platía Tessáron Martíron (Square of the Four Martyrs).

Tension between the two peoples came to a head in 1821, when the Turks unleashed a bloodbath among the Christians, and in 1828 there was even fighting outside the gates of the city. In 1866, by which time Greece had long since attained independence, the Turks took possession of the Monastery of Arkádi. Thousands of resistance fighters, women and children had taken shelter there behind the walls of the monastery. On 8 November 1866, realising the hopelessness of their position and determined not to fall into Turkish hands, they blew themselves up. It was not until 1898, long after the tragedy of Arkádi, that Réthimnon was finally freed from Turkish rule. The city was not spared during World War II either. In May 1941, Réthimnon was attacked by German parachutists and it then became an occupied city.

Harbour sights at Réthimnon.

A visit to the **Fortezza** is an absolute must for everyone. It is open all year round, and the view alone is an experience. You look out over the city, the mountains in the distance and the whole expanse of countryside reaching the sea. The Fortezza was built between 1573 and 1586 on the site of the old fortifications. The total circumference is 1,307 metres. There are four bastions, and the building follows the natural contours of the hill. The main gate in the east was the only link with the town, and was therefore built high and wide. The north and west gates were used for delivering supplies and for leaving the fort in the direction of the sea. Apart from barracks, warehouses, administrative buildings in the southern part of the fort and the powder and food stores in the northern part, the most interesting feature is the Venetian Cathedral, which is at the centre of the edifice.

Here was yet another indication of

the supposed unpopularity of the Fortezza. In 1585 the cathedral was to have become the seat of the bishop, but Bishop Carrara with many a feeble excuse, refused to move there. It was briefly taken over by the Turks, who converted it and named it after Sultan Ibrahim. Apparently a minaret was added, but it later disappeared.

These days the summer months see an enormous influx of visitors, and the city of Réthimnon is completely geared up for tourism. The beach is right at the edge of the old city and extends to the east, and there is an open-air pool too. Bathing is better further away from the city, however. In March and April, a flower festival is held in the city park, which is just outside the old city. More well-known, however, is the flower market. People come from miles around to stock up on seeds and cuttings as this is an area of the island where there are many greenhouses for propagation. The

Wine Festival takes place in mid July. During this lively festival, the low entrance fee will give you free wine for the evening. Following that there is the Music Week where dancers and groups from all over Greece come to perform. The proceeds of these events are used by the city administration to pay for necessary maintenance work.

The city and immediate environs make a prosperous impression, but in fact Réthimnon is actually the poorest of the four administrative regions in Crete. Unfortunately, the outlook for the city is not rosy either. The goal of a link to Athens (Piraeus) by ship is not attainable, nor is it possible for the city to participate in the trade and passenger transport between Soúda and Iráklion. It thus loses out on a very profitable link. A wrongly designed breakwater has led to the silting up of the harbour, and as a result the big ships cannot berth there. About a third of the city popula-

"Fancy a coach tour?"

tion is dependent on seasonal earnings related to tourism. That, of course, is problematic in itself. But the real problem stems from the land itself. This is the most mountainous region in Crete, which makes life very difficult indeed for the farmers. The Amari Valley and the Nida Plain are fertile and prosperous, but olive growing, animal husbandry, milk production and flower and vegetable cultivation, mainly undertaken in green houses, are not very profitable at all.

It is not merely since the founding of the **Faculty of Philosophy** in 1977 that Réthimnon has had the reputation of being an intellectual city, although not much was possible under the constraints of military dictatorship. Many rich Cretans in the 14th and 15th centuries sent their offspring to Padua to study. They returned with new ideas, and it is thus that the ideas of the Italian Renaissance came to Crete. The "Cre-

The Fortezza has much to offer to explorers.

tan Renaissance" which followed in the 15th and 16th centuries produced literature of a high standard, and artists and intellectuals of Réthimnon played a prominent part. They included writers such as Geórgios Hortátzis with *Erophili*, M.T. Bounialís with *The Cretan War*, and probably the most admired of all, Vinzéntos Kornáros with the verse drama *Erotókritos*. Emánuel Tzánes Bounialís, one of the most highly regarded of all icon painters came from Crete. Such cultural expressions were forcibly interrupted for a long time by Turkish rule. Once again, in the 20th century, there is a great name in the literary world which is associated with the city, that of Pantelis Prevelákis.

Trips into the Surrounding Area: To reach **Argiroúpoli**, you can turn off the Réthimnon-Haniá motorway (at km 14) towards Episkopí. The village of Argiroúpoli, which is to the south of Episkopí, is of interest because it was

built on the ruins of the Dorian settlement of **Láppa**. Láppa was completely destroyed by the Romans in 67 BC but rebuilt shortly afterwards by Octavius, later Augustus Caesar, who held the first census in the Roman world.

Near Argiroúpoli peasants found a burial site composed of five chambers. They believed it to have been the burial place of the five holy women who died as Christian martyrs during the Roman occupation. But archaeological research has indicated that the grave was older. Two children and two adults lie buried around a central room, which appears to have been used for sacrifices. The two statues found nearby, of Artemis and Aphrodite, are displayed in the Archaeological Museum of Haniá. Some mansions from Venetian times have also survived.

Argiroúpoli, as a centre of resistance, must have incurred the particular wrath of the Turks, for in 1867 it was sub-

jected to an especially brutal campaign of revenge. Houses were razed to the ground, orange and olive trees felled, and even the graves were disturbed and the remains of the dead strewn about.

Today, although seldom visited by tourists, the village is relatively prosperous. It lies between two rivers, and the water enables olives, maize, cereal and citrus fruits to grow well, while cattle graze in the lush meadows.

The village of **Miriokéfala** lies at a height of 500 metres, up in the Lefká Ori. The "Monastery of the Panagía," founded in the year 1000 by John the Hermit, was burned down by the Turks in 1821. Only the church, with frescoes from the 11th and 12th centuries withstood the fire. Miriokéfala is a good starting point for more ambitious tours of the Lefká Ori range, as the best mountain guides live here.

Agía Iríni (St Irene) is another destination in the immediate vicinity of Réthimnon. On the way south, you pass the dilapidated houses of the former settlement of **Mikrá Anógia**, which was once a fortress. Just before arriving in Agía Iríni, you will see the ruins of a monastery. There is a basilica, with three naves, and a reservoir hewn in the rocks. The next village is **Roussospíti**, where there are some well preserved Venetian houses, a fountain and 15th-century murals in the church.

Kapedianá is next, from which one can set out to climb the **Vríssinas** (858 metres), to the south. In a wonderful position right at the summit is the Church of the Holy Spirit, **Agios Pnévmatos**. Every year at Whitsun, mass is celebrated here, drawing believers from all over the region. In 1938 clay idols were found, indicating that there was a sanctuary here in Minoan times. In 1973 pictures of bulls, eagles and goats were found in clefts of the rocks.

If you are interested in murals, return to Réthimnon via **Hromonastíri**. Near there is the Church of **Agios Eftíhios**

Getting food ready for the lunch crowd.

with 11th-century murals, which are among the oldest in Crete, but unfortunately not very well preserved.

The road continues through the Gorge of **Míli**, with an abandoned village of the same name located in the middle. It is then only a stone's throw to **Missíria**, from where the bus for Réthimnon leaves.

There is another gorge near the village of **Prassés** on the way to Amari. You can only walk through the **Prassanó Gorge** in summer, as there is a gushing torrent a metre high in winter and in spring. The gorge was formed by the river **Plataniás** which flows into the sea east of Réthimnon. The walk through the gorge takes the visitor a good five hours. At their highest, the cliff walls just reach 150 metres, nothing like the height of the imposing Samariá Gorge.

The beauty of the gorge lies in its lush vegetation – carob trees, plane trees and oleander grow here – as well as in its peaceful atmosphere, despite the proximity of Réthimnon. There has as yet been little here in the way of development. The turning to **Mírthios**, where there are a couple of ruined houses dating from the 7th and 8th centuries, leads on to **Sellí** and **Karé**, in which are the remains of a basilica with a lovely mosaic floor. Then it's back again to Réthimnon via Arméni.

Along the Coast: Réthimnon has been blessed with beautiful beaches. Nowadays this means one thing – the building of new hotels and the advent of the masses. So often this spoils the character of a place. **Missíria** and **Adele**, on the longest sandy beach of Crete, stretching more than 15 km have, however, managed to preserve a friendly atmosphere and a touch of elegance but not much individuality.

Platanés and **Stavroménos** have retained more of their original character. Behind Stavroménos you drive through the fertile delta of the **Mi-**

lopótamos, a lush area of fruit and vegetable cultivation. The village of **Pánormos** has no beach and is thus quite unable to compete with its neighbours. It has visibly deteriorated since Byzantine times when, as the port of **Eléftherna,** it was known as Panormos. All that remains of its former days of glory are ruins of the old harbour walls and parts of the Byzantine basilica. Of the enormous Venetian castle, which one would have expected to survive the ravages of time, only the name has survived: Milopótamos.

To the east of Pánormos is the little village of **Balí**, which lies behind the great beach in a bay, and is considered by many the most beautiful on Crete. The motorway has, of course, robbed Balí of some of its isolated charm. It is still a glorious spot, however.

Experts think this was the site of another ancient city, **Astáli**, the port of the city of **Axós**. The small village of

No longer deserted: the beach at Balí.

Balí is on the way to becoming the Kritsá of fishing villages. Despite the threateningly large streams of tourists who visit, the infrastructure has managed to cope, and so far no high-rise hotels have been built. But the place is too lovely to remain that way. The rather shabby gravel beach will not put people off much longer.

The Monastery of Agios Ioánnis must not be overlooked. It is situated in the northern foothills of the **Kouloúkonas** mountain.

Arméni: If you enjoy walking at leisure and come prepared for the sun, you can reach **Arméni** in about two hours. Leave the town in a southerly direction through the villages of Gállou and Somatás and you will come to the late Minoan necropolis of Arméni. It mainly comprises underground beehive and chamber tombs hacked out of the rocks. The larger ones can be reached by steps.

Many of the finds unearthed in this cemetery, dated at between 1350 and 1200 BC, are displayed in the Archaeological Museum of Haniá. There are clay idols and ceramic pots, but also tools, weapons and sarcophagi. They are richly decorated with religious motifs and among some of the most valuable finds on the whole island. They also indicate the spread of Minoan culture to the west of Crete.

One of the most impressive of the larger graves is probably that of a Minoan duke or king. The impressive entrance area, 13 metres long, leads down 7 metres to the grave itself, which is about 4.5 square metres in area. The scarabs on the steps are reminiscent of Egypt. The burial chamber, despite the technical capabilities of the time, is not symmetrical. Nor was it designed according to any geometrical principles.

It is also quite impossible to fit the graves themselves into any kind of pattern or systematic arrangement. It has been maintained that the graves had some kind of alignment, either north-south or some other formation, but none of these criteria accords with the facts. It seems that some completely different way of thinking underlay the arrangement here. There was also a settlement near the burial site, but that has not yet been found.

Strange insects fly around the area, which cannot readily be identified as any known species. They are about 2 centimetres long, seemingly multi-winged with greenish yellow bodies which are thick and roundish. From their heads protrude large beak-like probisces which, apart from stinging and sucking, seem to be used for some kind of work.

One way to return to Réthimnon is by way of **Methóhi Risváni**. This is a settlement where the house of Irfan Bey may be seen as well as some ruined churches. Perhaps the best view of Réthimnon, from anywhere, is from the hill of Evliyiás.

Below, still life in a *tavérna*. Right, peasant woman on her way to the Ida Mountains.

FROM RÉTHIMNON TO THE IDA MOUNTAINS

If you take the road southwards from Réthimnon, you reach the intersection at **Koxaré** and then the **Kourtaliótiko Gorge**. The motorway goes part of the way through the gorge, and it really is a good idea to stop here for a while. This gives you the opportunity to enjoy the island atmosphere. You just listen to the sound of water splashing, of birds singing and frogs croaking. A shepherd whistles to his goats while nimbly climbing up the steep slopes of the hills. The source of the river water is just near the entrance to the gorge. High up in the rocks there are five holes from which the water springs.

This is a miraculous phenomenon ascribed to Agios Nikólaos (St Nicholas). The five holes are said to symbolise the five fingers which he laid on the rock. The strange fact is that the river never dries up, not even in the hottest summer. A narrow path leads to a little chapel erected to commemorate the spring, which is known locally as "the Blessing of the Lord."

Just down the road, there is a dilapidated settlement. Although it does not look impressive, it is worth a visit. Above one of the doors is a plaque with the date 1795 on it. There is a stable too, with room for over 20 cattle, quite a few smaller rooms, most of them quite well kept, and some with murals. A well house with a dome, dated 1865, has been constructed over the spring. Finally, on the church wall is a plaque commemorating the destruction of the village by the Turks in 1821.

These ruins are in fact all that remains of the Lower Monastery of Préveli, **Káto Préveli**. What is inconceivable is that the monastery was actually built here in the first place. Strategically, it is very badly positioned, and location was always an important consideration for those building a monastery on Crete. It is possible that the mountain used to look different, or that the construction of the road altered the place.

Whatever the case may be, the fact is that Upper Préveli, or **Písso Préveli**, was the more important structure, and this is what is generally meant when the Monastery of Préveli is mentioned. Its location is quite superb, 170 metres above sea level, facing southeast. It is not known when the monastery was built. And as the old monastery church, where one might have expected to find clues, was abruptly demolished in 1853 when the new one was built, there seems little chance of finding out any more now. Some chroniclers believe that circumstantial evidence points to a date of construction of about 980.

The whole place has a friendly atmosphere, in fact almost merry. There is a

television antenna on the abbot's roof, and soft drinks are kept cool in a plastic bag in the inner room of the church, all of which adds to this light-hearted impression. But one must not be misled, for particularly during the years of oppression, Préveli was a centre of solidarity and national strength.

Although not of the same political significance as Arkádi, it was far more important in economic terms. In its heyday, the monastery was incredibly rich. Gifts, generous donations and transfers by means of which rich Cretans kept their possessions out of Turkish hands, brought huge areas of land under the protection of the monastery. The olive harvest brought in about 130,000 litres of oil per year. Then there were 80 tons of cereals, 120 tons of carob, as well as large amounts of fruit and vegetables. About 2,000 goats and sheep grazed in the meadows, and there were pigs, cattle and mules.

In addition, the monks kept bees and silk worms. Préveli was like a prosperous estate which invested in community projects and social progress. Churches, schools, hospitals and many other establishments were founded or aided with the money from Préveli. It is thus no wonder that one finds valuable icons here as well as an interesting library and an extensive museum.

The most important item in the monastery is a gold cross set with diamonds, in which a splinter of the cross of Jesus is reputed to be kept. It was a donation of the former abbot, Ephraim Prévelis (1755–75), a direct descendant of the founder of the monastery, Akákis Prévelis. The cross is said to heal eye disorders, and is even supposed to have given the blind their sight. There are many tales concerning the powers of this miraculous cross.

One tale relates to the German occupation during World War II. The Ger-

Mountain road from Préveli to Plakiás.

mans had heard of the conspiracies and resistance activities centred on Préveli. Many Britons and New Zealanders hid here and later managed to escape in Allied ships. As punishment for such opposition, the Germans wanted to weaken the economic power of the monastery. They chased animals away and robbed the monastery of its treasure. Among the articles stolen was the miraculous cross.

Three times the Germans attempted to take the cross to Germany, but each time they put it on board an aircraft, the engines, which up to then had been in perfect working order, failed. In the end the Germans did not merely give up, they actually returned the cross to the place where it belonged.

A little further westwards is the small palm-fringed beach of Préveli. As you come away from the monastery, turn right into a country lane about a kilometre down the road. It is easy to find but not marked. In season, others are bound to be looking for the place too, and if in doubt one can always ask the locals. The reward is that after a detour of about a quarter of an hour one arrives in a real tropical paradise.

From Koxaré to the West: Apart from the Monastery of Préveli, there are a few other interesting villages in the region of **Agios Valiléos** (St Basil). They can be reached either on the broad road from **Koxaré** or from Préveli by way of **Lefkógia**. Further to the west at the crossroads of Préveli-Réthimnon-Frangokástello is the village of **Selliá** at an altitude of 300 metres. To the north it is protected by the massif of **Psílis** and to the south the countryside stretches away to the Sea of Libya.

The far more well-known former fishing village of **Plakiás** belongs to the same municipality. Its mild climate and wonderful beach and the proximity of the gorges of **Kotsifoú** and **Kourta-**

A sheltered cove below the Monastery of Préveli.

Liótiko make it a great attraction for the tourists. Plakiás is a typical example of just what happens when a place turns to tourism as its main source of revenue. It used to be an insignificant little village, and due to its natural beauty, particularly the fine beach, it has experienced what could be referred to as an economic upsurge. In other words, it is bursting at the seams.

Further west, almost in the rural district of Sfakiá, renowned for its fighting men, are the villages of **Ano Rodákino** and **Káto Rodákino**. Long ago the feuding families Papadópouli and Páteri lived here. For years violent acts of vengeance perpetrated by these families in their long, drawn out vendetta led to the deaths of so many family members that finally the people in the five villages concerned came together and effected a peace treaty between the two clans. As so much has been written about the islanders' thirst for vengeance and violent characters, here at least is one example of Cretan good sense.

East of Koxaré: Spíli is a lovely place in a bad position. People are always on the way through, usually on the way to Préveli, Agía Galíni, Mátala or Festós. Yet Spíli has far more to offer than just the water with which one refreshes oneself for the rest of the journey. The fountains are one of the main attractions of the town, but the old churches and comfortable *tavérnes* are not to be overlooked. Stop and sit a while.

Arriving in **Agía Galíni** in the evening, which is the loveliest time, is like wandering into a dreamland. A terrace of coloured lights seems to hang in the velvet sky. From the breakwater in the harbour one can see the lights of Mátala twinkling in the distance.

The car park on the harbour is full of cars and the narrow streets are crowded with people. One huge restaurant takes up a whole street. It doesn't sound very

Spíli is one spot where you can drink spring water from the mouths of "lions".

cosy, but in Agía Galíni it seems just fine. Next day, in the cold morning light, the place loses some of its glamour, but is still pretty.

It is evident what tourists come here: at the newspaper kiosk there are only a couple of English but over two dozen German papers. There are visitors of all age groups here. The inhabitants of Agía Galíni – the name means "Holy Peace of the Sea," in fact – are said to have been successful smugglers before they turned their attention to tourism. That may well be true, for there is no denying a certain rather charming rakishness in their expressions. Agía Galíni, permeated by the latest hits and yet so attractive a seaside town, is definitely a place to come back to.

The Valley of Amári: This incomparably lush valley is reached by turning south at Missíria. Even if you have passed all the other cultural points of interest, you should not exclude this place. The main crops are olives and fruit, and trees alternate with a profusion of wild flowers, of which there are a variety, including wood and prickly bindweed and yellow ox-tongue.

Mount Samítos (1,014 metres), standing right in the middle of the valley, has resulted in there being two ways through, one on each side of the mountain. One route takes you through **Apóstoli**, where in 249, the men now known as the 10 holy ones or Agii Déka, were put to death for their Christian faith. It takes about five hours to climb **Kédros** (1,777 metres) from **Gerakári**.

The other road goes from Apóstoli to the 17th-century **Assomáton Monastery**, which these days houses a School of Agriculture. **Monastiráki** is reached by way of the village of **Thrónos** in the northeast, where the 14th-century Panagiá Church is worth a visit to see the well preserved frescoes. Near Monastiráki a mid-Minoan settlement was

Caïques bob in the harbour of Agía Galíni.

discovered (approximately 2000–1800 BC).The storage jars from this settlement are exhibited in the Archaeological Museum of Haniá.

From here you go on to **Amári**, an exceptionally pretty village, at least 1,500 years old. It was the main village of the district of Amári even in Venetian times. Through the villages of **Fourfourás**, **Kouroútes** and **Níthavlis** one comes to **Apodoúlou**. There the 13th-century frescoes in the Agios Geórgios Church are worth seeing. Moreover a late Minoan mansion and a dome grave have been discovered and excavated at the southern side of the village. The four sarcophagi are housed in the Archaeological Museum of Réthimnon.

Moní Arkádi: There are many little villages on the way from Réthimnon via **Adele** (birthplace of Konstantin Gaboudákis) such as **Pigí**, **Loutró**, **Kiriánna** and **Amnátos**. The latter is almost 300 metres above sea level in a fertile region of great contrast, slopes and steep gorges. Her you will find gorse bushes and olive trees as well as Greek saffron, briers and the Greek strawberry tree.

The Monastery of **Arkádi** is a haven of peace, but that impression is at variance with its history. It has existed since the 14th century, but its appearance was completely altered in the 16th century. The fort-like arrangement extends for more than 5,200 sq. metres and has entrances on all four sides. Later additions make it difficult to visualise the original structure at the beginning of this century. The main entrance is in the west, rebuilt in 1872 after the damage of 1866. This leads to the Early Baroque facade of the church built in 1587. The bell tower still shows traces of the fighting in 1866. The interior of the church was renewed later. The altar wall was carved in 1927 out of cypress wood and includes parts of the original iconostasis

Below: left, the peaceful Monastery of Arkádi viewed from the outside; right, interior vaulted room, Arkádi.

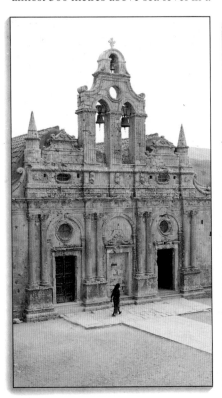

which withstood the fire. The west wing has two storeys and the galleries have bow-shaped openings into the courtyard. The monks' cells are almost exclusively on the second floor. In the northeast corner is the powder storeroom with a memorial tablet; in the north wing, the guesthouse and refectory surrounded by kitchen rooms. The museum is in the south wing. Apart from ecclesiastical manuscripts and religious relics, you can see memorabilia of 1866 and personal effects of the Abbot Gabriel. You also learn that the international arms trade began long ago – some of the Turks used Prussian arms.

The tragedy for which the monastery is famous took place on 8 and 9 November 1866. Earlier in May of that year, preparations for a rebellion were underway in Arkádi. Since as many as 15,000 Cretans had met here, it was not surprising that the scheme was discovered by the Turks. Abbot Gabriel was ordered to disband the revolutionary committee. When he refused, the Turks attacked Réthimnon, whereupon about 700 women and children fled to Arkádi and sought refuge there. When Abbot Gabriel refused a second ultimatum, the vastly superior troops of Mustapha Pasha attacked the monastery. Despite the small cache of weapons at their disposal, the Cretans managed to hold off the first onslaught. But by the next morning the rounds of ammunition had been expended. The survivors, mainly women and children, gathered in the powder storeroom. No one was to be taken alive by the Turks. Just as the Turks forced their way into the storeroom, Konstantín Giaboudákis, with the agreement of Abbot Gabriel, ignited the powder kegs, so that the explosion killed many Turkish soldiers too.

Thirty-six men survived, either because they didn't make it to the storeroom, or because they disagreed with

Greek Orthodox decoration in the Monastery of Arkádi.

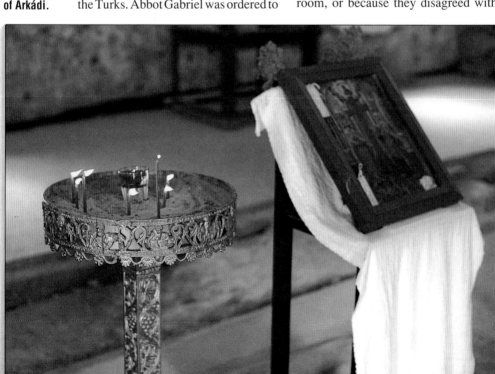

171

the suicide pact. They hid in the refectory, where they were later brutally murdered. Legend has it that an infant girl was blown into a tree, and survived; she later became a nun.

Shot marks and sword cuts can still be seen on the door of the refectory and on some of the tables. The monastery was set on fire. In the ossuary just outside the monastery, the skulls of the victims are laid, and an inscription honours the heroes. The news of the tragedy of the Arkádi Monastery was received with horror in the rest of Europe. The shock of the mass suicide and destruction of a monastery altered Cretan politics. Now 8 November is the "National Day" of Crete in memory of the victims.

Via Margarítes to the Nída Heights: Go along the coast a little further eastwards until you turn inland near the little village of **Stavroménos**, which is in the rural district of **Milopótamo**. Just south of **Aléxandrou** is the pottery village of **Margarítes**. The workshops are just above the village. Here, all kinds of pots are made, in particular the large storage *pithoi* which were known in Minoan times. In some places one can still see ovens made from oil barrels, used for firing smaller objects. Next to these are the walled ovens, several metres high, for the *pithoi*.

As you wander through the lovely village, stop to have a look in the former monastery church of Agios Ioánnis Prodrómos (John the Baptist). The architecture of the church and the well preserved 12th-century frescoes are most interesting. In the nearby church of Agios Geórgios there is a most expressive painting of the Virgin Mary.

If you cross the road to the southwest, you reach **Prinés**. To the west are the ruins of the Dorian city of **Eléftherna**, important right up to the Byzantine era, then destroyed by the Saracens.

Then it's back to Aléxandrou via

Below and right, striking painting conjunction of colours on the facades of houses in Margarítes.

Margarítes, and from there a wide road leads to Anogia. At **Pérama** is the **Melidóni Cave** where long ago Hermes was worshipped in hollows filled with stalactites. The altar there now is a reminder of more recent history. In 1824 several hundred Cretans had hidden here. The Turks lit a fire at the cave entrance, and all the Cretans suffocated.

Axós, mythology has it, was founded by Oaxon, a grandson of Minos, and was inhabited from late Minoan times. Ruins of an acropolis indicate a period of glory in the past, and later historical indications are reflected in various Byzantine churches. In the 13th century the inhabitants were driven out for their resistance to the Venetians. They moved southeast and founded **Anógia**.

The village was set 800 metres up in the Ida Mountains in terrace form, reflecting the resistance mentality of its founders. The Turks destroyed it in 1821 and 1866, but it was rebuilt each time. One of the worst periods in the history of the village was during World War II, when on 15 August 1944, following the abduction of the German General Kreipe, all the males in the village were shot, and the place completely destroyed. But despite, or maybe because of that, the character of Anógia has remained unique. The people here are very friendly and inquisitive. It is easy to meet them, but not so easy to understand what they are saying, as they speak an old dialect which has only survived here. But one doesn't need to speak to buy the beautiful crafts made here, and speech is completely superfluous to the appreciation of the wonderful music and dance performed here in traditional costume.

Anógia is a good point from which to set off into the Ida Mountains. There is a 20-km path to the **Nída Plateau** at 1,370 metres. In summer the shepherds of Anógia gather up here. At the edge of the plateau, in a rugged, wild landscape lies the **Ida Cave**, believed to be Zeus'

childhood home. In this extraordinary vault (35 metres wide, 40 metres deep and 60 metres high), bronze shields, gold jewellery, hand drums and many other objects were found. An altar was discovered too, making this one of the oldest places of worship on Crete.

The landscape and climate – perhaps the people too – have hardly changed since mythical times. The shepherds still keep bees on the Nída Plateau and live in stone houses called *mitáta* built on the same principles as the Minoan dome graves. The plateau is a good place to start out on longer tours of the Ida Mountains.

Inexperienced climbers are strongly advised to avail themselves of a guide. The **Tímios Stavrós** at 2,456 metres is the highest peak of the Psilorítis range, and the ascent takes about five hours. Then, from the roof of Crete, so to speak, the visitor has a magnificent view of almost the whole of the island.

HANIÁ AND SURROUNDINGS

Haniá, the capital city in the administrative district of the same name, has about 62,000 inhabitants, making it the second largest city on Crete. Regular flights and shipping links to Athens, and the expansion of the charter business have given it a cosmopolitan air. Although the newer parts of the city are cold and functional, the old city, especially around the Venetian Harbour, has retained its unique charm, and is home to many foreign expatriates.

The history of Haniá is particularly interesting as the attention of Crete's conquerors has always been focussed here. There are, of course, traces of the Byzantines, Venetians, Turks and Germans. Linear-B Tablets found in ancient workshops indicate that Haniá was the site of the Minoan city of Kydonía. Homer describes West Crete as the home of the Kydonians. The name originated from their king, Kydon, who is sometimes said to be the son of Minos, and at other times his grandson. Kydon was renowned for his immense hospitality. Perhaps Kydon's prestige contributed to the fact that in late antiquity, Crete and Kydonía were one and the same.

It was not surprising that nearby states coveted this strategically important island, and there were many attempts to invade. In 429 BC, Athens failed in its attempt to overrun the island. The Romans, after a long siege, finally added Crete to their empire in 67 BC. In the ensuing period, many splendid buildings were built on the island, especially during the time of Caesar Hadrian, who visited Crete in AD 123.

Onorio Belli, a Venetian, who lived in what later became Canea, reported that even after 1583, remains of a Roman theatre could be seen. As the

Venetians then began using the ancient site as a quarry, there is nothing to be seen there today. Some underground burial sites and fragments of beautiful floor mosaics can only give an indication of those glorious times.

During the first Byzantine Epoch from AD 352, Crete remained a military base in the Mediterranean. The Byzantines reinforced the city wall of Kydonía to ward off attacks by pirates. However, these fortifications were not enough to repel the stronger attacks of the Saracens, and Kydonía eventually fell in 826. Much of the city was destroyed, and it lost its former importance. For a long time it was even known as "City of Rubbish". Nikefóros Fokas, later Emperor, reconquered Crete and settled many noble and military families from Constantinople in Kydonía, but the city never regained its former greatness.

After the Crusaders had taken Con-

Preceding pages: marines in Haniá; stopping by the waterfront. Left, another towering minaret overlooks the town. Right, just waiting for visitors.

179

stantinople, Crete was given to Bonifatius II, the Margrave of Monferrat, who in turn sold the island to the Venetians. In the expectation of lucrative trading connections, many merchants moved from Venice to the city which was then known as La Canea. The Venetians renewed the city wall and fortified the Byzantine castle, known as "Kastéli". La Canea prospered.

By 1537 the Venetians had to admit that their defences were inadequate, for Chaireddin Barbarossa easily took the city and plundered it. The specialist in fortifications, Michele Sanmicheli, was summoned all the way from Verona, and he was responsible for the forts built at La Canea and Cándia/Iráklion. These took almost 20 years to complete, and two bastions, the shipyards and part of the sea wall can still be seen. These works marked a peak in the history of La Canea, which was then referred to as "The Venice of the East." The monasteries of San Francesco (St Francis), San Nicolo (St Nicholas) and San Salvatore had by then been founded outside the town.

The fortifications were adequate to repulse several attempted Ottoman invasions, but finally in 1645, after 55 days of siege, the Turkish army under Yussuf Pasha conquered the city. The Turks, as was their custom, quickly altered the appearance and character of the place. Churches and monasteries were turned into mosques.

Today the Archaeological Museum of Haniá is found in the San Francesco Basilica. In the inner courtyard the 12-sided Turkish fountain can still be seen. The dramatic changes of history are particularly evident in the San Nicolo Church which has a minaret as well as a campanile, and is now a Greek Orthodox Church called Agios Nikólaos.

In 1692 an attempt by the Venetians to retake La Canea failed. The Turks

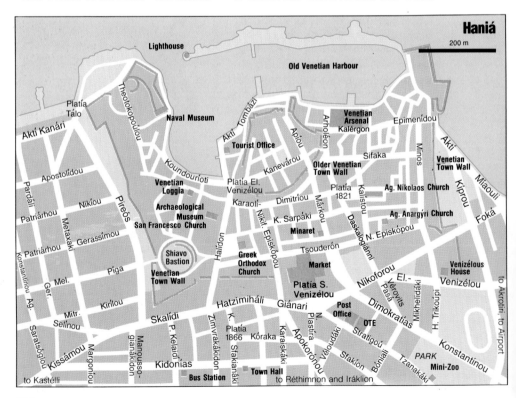

Haniá

200 m

Lighthouse

Old Venetian Harbour

Platía Tálo

Theotokopoúlou

Naval Museum

Akti Kanári

Akti Tombázi

Apíou

Artholeon

Venetian Arsenal
Kalérgon

Epimenídou

Tourist Office

Koundourioti

Kanevárou

Older Venetian Town Wall

Sifaka

Mínos

Akti

Venetian Town Wall

Míaouli

Apostolídou

Venetian Loggia

Platía El. Venizélou

Platía 1821

Kalistou

Ag. Nikolaos Church

Kíprou

Foká

Pardáli

Nikíou

Pireós

Karaolí-

Dimitríou

Márkou

Nikit. Episkópou

Daskalogiánni

Ag. Anargýri Church

Patriárhou

Metaxaki

Archaeological Museum
San Francesco Church

Halídon

K. Sarpáki

Minaret

N. Episkópou

Gerassímou

Patriárhou

Píga

Shiavo Bastion

Venetian Town Wall

Greek Orthodox Church

Tsouderón

Market

Nikoforou

El.-

Vétovits

Mikhelidáki

Venizélous House

Venizélou

to Akrotíri, to Airport

Konstantínou Ag.

Ger.

Mel.

Kirílou

Platía S. Venizélou

Pasa

Dimokratías

H. Trikoúpi

Saratsóglou

Mitr.

Selínou

Skalídi

P. Kelaídi

Zimvrakákidon

Hatzimiháli

Giánari

Plastíra

Post Office

Veloudáki

Stratigoú

OTE

Konstantínou

Kissámou

Margoníou

Manousso-gianákidon

Kidonías

Platía 1866

Stakianáki

Kóraka

Karaiskáki

Apokorónou

Stakíon

Bóniali

Tzanakáki

PARK

Mini-Zoo

to Kastélli

Bus Station

Town Hall

to Réthimnon and Iráklion

180

established themselves on the island, and in 1850 Haniá became their seat of government. But there were still many uprisings against the Turks. In 1866, after the fall of Arkádi, these revolts reached such proportions that the Great Powers finally turned their attention to Crete. But it was not until 1898 that allied troops occupied Haniá, and Prince George of Greece took up his official post as High Commissioner.

In the so-called "Battle for Crete" in 1941, the city was badly damaged by German bombs, although many ancient monuments did escape the bombing. The Djamissi Mosque, better known as the **Janissary Mosque** at the Venetian Harbour (EOT nowadays), and the minaret of the **Aga Mosque** in Daskalo-giánni Street survived.

The Janissaries were often described as the "elite troops" of the Sultan. But it must not be forgotten that these were in **Haniá's hues.** fact abducted Christian children who,

by brutal methods, were "re-educated" and made into the worst enemies of their own people.

Some great buildings of the Venetian period remain, such as the Loggia, the Arsenal, the Archives and some palaces near the harbour, which are now hotels and guest houses. The Pacific Hotel was once the Renieri Palace. The area around the Venetian Harbour, although on the edge of the city, is actually the natural centre of activity. There are cafés and restaurants, and the whole place is always full of life. But it is not merely a tourist area. No local resident would miss an evening stroll around the harbour. One can walk out as far as the breakwater and look back on the city and in the distance to Lefká Ori. It is also a great place to get away from the loud disco music. Admire the harmony of the design of the lighthouse, and then decide whether it is of Venetian or Turkish origin. You are entitled to your own

opinion on that, as even the experts can't seem to agree.

Another aspect of foreign domination now completely accepted by the Cretans is the city park in Tzanakáki Street, which was originally a private garden belonging to Reouf Pasha. There is a quaint small zoo with an enclosure containing the rare kri-kri mountain goat. This place too is a favourite attraction for the people who live in the city. In summer there is an open-air cinema. Musical performances are also held here during this season, making the park a good alternative to the harbour.

Of course the loveliness of the garden cannot conceal evidence of the Turks' reign of terror. Their cruelty penetrated into all aspects of Cretan life. Traces of the persecution of the Christians at this time are particularly evident in what was then the capital city. Haniá retained its position of capital until 1972. In the once wholly Turkish part of town,

Splántzia, there is a memorial tablet to one of the leaders of the resistance to the oppressors, the murdered Bishop Melhisedék, and his fellow fighters.

The **Market Hall** of Haniá is very famous. Its layout is in the form of a cross, and it is situated on the old Turkish market place. But much of its fame is misplaced, as in fact it is no more than a copy of the market hall in Marseilles. But there is no denying that it brings prosperity to the town. In its crowded area, fish, meat, fruit and vegetables are traded. But one can also buy medicines, shoe soles and books. For hardened city dwellers this early form of buying, selling and bartering in a crowded and friendly atmosphere is a welcome change from the modern supermarkets and department stores.

Traditionally, the market place has been a meeting place for people interested in airing their political views. If you don't mind the noise, you can sit and relax in one of the restaurants. The food here is not particularly good, however, and a little more expensive than elsewhere.

There are so many people buying and selling in Haniá that the market stalls are never sufficient. Those who do not manage to get a stall set out their wares around the hall on certain days. Skrydlof Street is one of the tourists' favourite places, and because of the crowds it has been made into a pedestrian precinct. Here you can easily find leather articles as well as hand-made embroidery, ornamental jewellery and ceramics – all surrounded by heaps of kitsch. If you manage to grab a seat in the little *tavérna* in the middle of the street, you can watch the action over a glass of beer or oúzo and *souvláki*. Of course you can also have your shoes and boots made to measure. You can even watch the cobbler at work. Otherwise, you can just place your order and pay in advance. Service in terms of quality and quick delivery are guaranteed and the

Left, Cretan boots are world-famous. Right, handmade lace for sale.

Cretans are internationally famous for their buff-coloured boots.

The museums of Haniá are most interesting. Details of the resistance of the Cretans to the various foreign occupations are documented in detail in the **Historical Museum**. In the **Nautical Museum** there are many models of ships, while the **Archaeological Museum** has a collection of artefacts from the whole region.

The administrative part of the city, **Halépa**, in the east, is worth seeing. These buildings were very cleverly put under a preservation order early on to protect the area from property speculators and attendant architectural alteration. The old government building today houses the administrative offices of the region (the Nomarchía).

The motorists of Haniá are probably the most impatient on the island. Their carelessness often becomes a hazard, and to recuperate from the traffic of Haniá, it is a good idea to take refuge in one of the many green parts of the town.

Even if the days of Kydon are over and in place of the legendary hospitality one finds the hotelier's routine, Haniá is still well worth a visit. There's merriment in the air, an international flair and a special warmth which remains with the traveller long after he has left.

Akrotíri: The Peninsula of **Akrotíri** lies northeast of Haniá. It is an easy place to get to, as buses leave every half hour to the different villages.

You should definitely not miss the Memorial to **Venizélos**, on the western slope of Akrotíri. On this historical spot, the father Elefthérios Venizélos (1864–1936) and his son Sophoklís (1896–1964) are buried. It was here that in 1897 the revolutionary committee met in the **Elías Monastery** under the leadership of E. Venizélos. Finally, in 1913 the demand for union with Greece was granted. All that remains of the

Soúda Bay, prohibited military area.

184

monastery today is the little St Elías Church. Nevertheless, the view overlooking Haniá and the Rodopós Peninsula is spectacular.

On the road to the airport there is a turning to the village of **Korakiés**, where the convent of the *Prodrómos*, the Forerunner, thus John the Baptist, is situated. This place played a particularly important role in the struggle against foreign oppression. In times of trouble it became an asylum for young women who wished to avoid being sent either to a Venetian brothel or to a Turkish harem.

Today, 20 nuns live here under the care of an astonishingly young mother superior, who sometimes serves coffee and biscuits to visitors. It is always interesting to see how nuns look after their convents, in contrast to how monasteries are kept (although it must be admitted that often there are only a couple of old men living in them). The

Checkpoint at the American base in Akrotíri.

monasteries have a neglected air about them. In a small room, the nuns sell their embroidery and hand painted icons.

After **Stavrós,** which you should see if you enjoyed the film *Zorba the Greek*, you come to the villages of **Profilías**, **Kounoupidianá** and **Horafákia**. All are equally well known for their excellent honey and mild Attic climate. But if the wind does blow, you'll certainly know about it. The bay and sandy beach of **Kalathá** are worth a detour, and from there you can make your way northwards to Stavrós.

Stavrós lies on the seaside, and is made up of small hotels, bungalows, the tiny harbour and the beautiful beach. Opposite is the slope on which the "Boss" cable car was erected for the film *Zorba the Greek*, and which was so photogenically caused to collapse. The place itself has nothing to offer today, apart from a *tavérna* ("Mama's Restaurant") and a new restaurant, the dimen-

sions of which, reminiscent of a gymnasium, give an indication of what it is like in the high season.

The highlight of Akrotíri is the 17th-century Monastery of **Agía Triáda**. Another name given to the monastery is Tzangaroli, which is the name of the Venetian merchant family who erected it. Currently, six monks live here and keep the surrounding land, with its olives and vineyards, in excellent order. Agía Triáda was always a rich monastery, due to the support of its own work force. In 1821 the Turks laid it to waste, but soon after rebuilding in 1830, it had regained its former wealth.

The massive, somewhat severe building is impressive, and houses a library of more than 700 volumes, some extremely old. Here you will find also several icons by the Byzantine painter Skordíli. Fortunately, many of the treasures were saved from destruction. However the only icons on view in the church nowadays are those from the 18th and 19th centuries.

About 4 km to the north of Agía Triáda is the 16th-century Monastery of **Gouvernéto**. The monks' cells, uninhabited now, are grouped around an inner courtyard. In the year of terror, 1821, most of the monks here were murdered, and the monastery itself was razed to the ground. The library and icon collection were completely destroyed by fire, so there are no treasures of art to attract the visitor here these days. However, there are sculptures, some on the church portal, where strange creatures, half man half mythical beast, have been carved, seemingly by a soul mate of Hieronymus Bosch. Unfortunately, the soft sandstone used by the sculptor is crumbling.

Further to the north, slightly downhill, the road leads to the so-called **Bear's Cave**. The name comes from a huge stalagmite, larger than a man, in

The deserted Monastery of Katholikó of Akrotíri.

the shape of a bear. Findings confirm that this cave was a place of worship in Neolithic and late Minoan times. There is a tiny Lady Chapel here now, just near the entrance under the overhanging rocks. It was built during the 16th and 17th centuries. On 6 and 7 October each year, processions and services are held here in memory of St John, who was killed by a huntsman's arrow on 6 October 1042.

Down a path which ends in a flight of steps in the rocks, you finally arrive at the **Cave of St John**. It apparently goes 135 metres back into the mountain and its rather complicated layout takes some time to figure out.

The legendary **Monastery of Katholikó,** which dates from the 10th and 11th centuries, is close by. The founder was none other than St John himself, and the monastery is possibly the oldest on Crete. The bell tower with its facade, the church, and other additions came into

being much later in the 16th century. Pirate attacks forced the monks to move to Gouvernéto.

Even without the monastery and cave, Akrotíri would still be worth visiting because the scenery here is outstandingly beautiful. However, enjoyment of this peaceful landscape is somewhat disrupted by the piercing noise of Greek military jets screeching across the sky.

A Trip to the South: The area around Haniá can easily be explored by bus, taxi or even on foot. **Mourniés**, for example, is only 6 km south of the city. Though a humble place today, Mourniés once played an important part, at great cost, in the history of the island. When the Turkish commander Mustapha Pasha raised the level of taxation beyond the endurance of the people, he caused an armed demonstration in Mourniés. During the course of the action, most of the Cretan peasants were

Six monks still live in the Agía Triáda Monastery.

captured by Turkish soldiers, then hanged on mulberry trees.

The village also suffered during the German occupation. When, after an attack on German headquarters, the culprits could not be found, "punitive action" was immediately taken: all males between the ages of 15 and 50 were assembled under an old plane tree, which is still the centre of the village, and shot. These gruesome events are still very much talked about by the locals, though no grudges are held.

Incidentally, the birthplace of Elefthérios Venizélos is here too. South of the village, built into a rock face, is the church of Agía Varvára. Nearby are the entrances to tunnels built by Cretan forced labour, and used by the German occupying forces as arms depots. The mines, used by the Germans to secure the tunnels, were still being used during the 1950s by fishermen, with mixed results. The seas around Crete appear to be quite lifeless now; after the so-called "dynamite fishing", the number of blind victims and amputees in the area is high.

Approximately 15 km from Haniá are the ruins of **Aptera**, the great ancient city in this part of the island, and undoubtedly one of the most prosperous of its day. It was inhabited from about 1000 BC, and its name was probably derived from Apteron, the Minoan king who ruled around 1800 BC. The city was situated on a plateau and surrounded by a wall almost 4 km long, of which about 600 metres survive. The city was destroyed by an earthquake in AD 700 and most of the survivors were forced to leave the area. As a result, it was not difficult for the Saracens to take the city in 823.

Sadly, Aptera was plundered by antique smugglers before being put under archaeological protection by the authorities. Statues, inscriptions, vessels and many coins minted in Aptera were simply sold. Since World War II, however, more statues, clay tablets and vessels have been found and these are now exhibited in the Archaeological Museum of Haniá. In the area of ancient Aptera, remains of a Doric and a Hellenic temple, Byzantine ruins, parts of a monastery, Roman cisterns, rock graves and a small theatre have been discovered. While in Aptera, don't miss the magnificent view of Soúda Bay.

There are other Minoan remains which can be seen in the nearby villages of **Stylos** and **Samonás**.

Térisso, 16 km from Haniá, is accessible through the gorge of the same name, also known as the Venizélos Gorge. Its strategic position (580 metres above sea level) made it an ideal base in the struggle against the Turks. In 1905 Venizélos and his revolutionary committee lived here. Today it is an ideal place from which to set out on tours to **Mesklá** and **Soúrva**, or for climbing the highest peak of the Lefká Ori, **Páchnes** (2,452 metres).

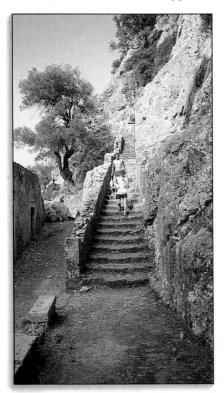

Left, down the steps of the Monastery of Katholikó. Right, detail of the wall at the Agía Triáda Monastery.

WEST CRETE

A bus leaves the long distance depot in Haniá every hour for **Omalos**. The picturesque journey takes you inland through lush gardens, eucalyptus woods and orange groves. Nine km from the city is the village of **Agiá**, which was founded under Arab rule (AD 800–1100). In this village you will also find a three-naved basilica which is built on the ruins of an ancient temple. Unusual pillars of red marble and granite survive from the earlier structure.

There are two interesting churches in the village of **Alikianós**. The older, Ai Kyr Jánnis, dedicated to John the Hermit, dates from the 10th and 11th centuries and has interesting murals and mosaics. In the Church of Agios Georgios (St George) of 1243, there are also some well preserved frescoes.

The road continues through **Fournés**. Not far from there is the cave of **Hiróspilios**. A turning leads to the village of Meskla with the ruins of the Dorian city of **Rizinía**. Archaeological finds indicate that the city of Rizinía reached a period of greatness around 400 BC. There are remains of a wall and an acropolis.

The road then winds its way up to almost 1,100 metres to the 25 sq. km Plateau of Omalós. Up here the soil is extremely fertile, and cereals, potatoes and tomatoes are grown. Sheep graze in between the crops. The tiny hamlet of Omalós is only inhabited in the summer, and if you intend to stay overnight here on the way to the **Samaria Gorge**, you must book your accommodation well in advance. There are two guesthouses for travellers.

In winter, the plateau, almost circular in shape, is flooded by water coming down from the surrounding mountains. Fortunately, the water can flow down the 2.5 km long **Tzanís Cave**. Legend has it that on moonless nights, a shepherd, enchanted by a water sprite, plays his lyre and sings of his sorrow at the mouth of the cave. The geographical position of the plateau made it ideal as a base for resistance to the Ottoman Turks, and on one of the hills is the grave of Hatzí Micháli Giannári.

Just before the descent to the Samaria Gorge there is a path leading to the Greek Mountaineers' Association Hut. It lies at an altitude of 1,650 metres and can serve as a starting point for mountain treks. You climb down into the gorge on a path still known as "Xilóskalo", which means wooden ladder. The name is a reminder of the days when the only access to the gorge was by ladders.

Botanically speaking, this is a fascinating place. Apart from cypresses and kermes oaks, pines and plane trees, the Greek yellow ox-tongue, Cretan corymb and the Cretan campanula grow here. Eagles and falcons soar above the steep rock faces. In earlier times, when there were fewer people about, one could often see the extremely shy mountain goat or "kri-kri" (*Agrími* in local parlance) as it climbed about on the mountainside.

Four km on, you reach the Church of Agios Nikólaos, and 2 km further up is the deserted settlement of Samariá with its Byzantine church of Osía Maria the Egyptian. This is the place which gave the gorge its name. There is a spring here, a refreshing spot for tired travellers. Just behind the village a stream, underground until here, emerges, and this will have to be crossed a few times as you continue on through the gorge.

The last 4 km are the most interesting as you go through high cliffs where all the sounds are magnified. When the wind howls through the narrow *Sideróportes* (Iron Gates) one can understand how tales of water sprites, demons and other strange creatures came about.

The last stretch is extremely narrow, only 3 metres wide with 500-metre-

The way West.

high vertical cliffs towering above. You look through the gap to a wide valley which stretches to the sea.

The little village of **Agía Rouméli**, still unspoiled despite the number of visitors to the gorge, is at the far end. The few inhabitants only make their living from tourism during the hiking period (April–October); the rest of the year they are busy with their cattle and bee-keeping. They also sell *Díktamos*, a very rare plant which grows in particularly inaccessible parts of the gorge and is used in herbal teas, especially in what the Greeks call "mountain tea".

Recently, a Samariá Round Tour has been organised. You arrive by ship in Agía Rouméli, take a few steps in the gorge, and then leave.

From Agía Rouméli to Frangokástello: Near what is now Agía Rouméli was once the Minoan city of **Tárra**. The few finds, which include a stone tablet inscribed with the double axe are dis-

played in the Archaeological Museum of Haniá. In mythology, Apollo is said to have come to Tárra. After conquering Crete, the Dorians erected a temple here to their revered Apollo. On this site, the Panagía Church was built in the 12th and 13th centuries.

The coins from Tárra show the head of a goat and a bee, very similar to coins from other towns in the Cretan League of Cities, to which Lissós, Elyros-Syia, Poikilássos and Irtakína also belonged, around 300 BC. The town also had a trading agreement with King Magas. In AD 66 an earthquake destroyed Tárra, and it was never rebuilt.

There are good connections from Agía Rouméli to **Loutró**, **Hóra Sfakíon**, **Soúgia** and **Paleóhara**. A walk to Loutró is recommended. It is not a difficult walk, although it does take about five hours and you are advised to arm yourself with hat and sun-block. From the turning to Agios Pávlos you can hitchhike to **Anópoli**. Then it is only 3 km south to Loutró.

There's nothing left in Loutró now of its former glory. Once known then as **Fínix**, the city was famous in ancient times as the rich port of Anópolis. Together the two towns probably had 60,000 inhabitants. West of the village are a few scattered ruins. The **Sotíros Christoú Chapel** with frescoes from the 14th and 15th centuries is lovely. In Byzantine times it was a bishopric.

There are hardly any fishermen left in Loutró. Up until the beginning of the 19th century there was a fleet of small trading ships, but that has now dwindled to a couple of boats. As in so many coastal villages, tourism is now the mainstay. Private houses and rooms are rented out to visitors, and there are several *tavérnes* to choose from. Formerly, the place could only be reached by boat, but a road is ensuring the survival of the village.

Anópoli lies north of Loutró, some 600 metres up, at the foot of Mount

Left and right, the Samaria Gorge.

Kástro (2,218 metres). Here one of the most famous of all freedom fighters was born: Joánnis Vláhos, whose wide education earned him the nickname of *Dhaskalojánnis*, "Teacher John". It was he who led the rebellion of 1770.

Anópoli was one of the most important of the ancient Cretan settlements. It was burned to the ground in 1365 for resisting the Venetians. In 1867 it suffered the same fate, but this time at the hands of the Turks.

Twelve km to the west is **Hóra Sfakíon**, the capital of the Sfakiá region which is famous for its fierce fighters. The buildings are arranged around the harbour in an amphitheatre. There is plenty to do here. There are many hotels, pensions and cosy *tavérnes*. A bus leaves every two hours for Haniá, and in summer there is a ship to Agía Rouméli every three hours. Twice a week you can go to Gávdos island and once a week to Agía Galíni.

Climate, food and lifestyle seem to be particularly beneficial here, as when you look at the inhabitants of this western part of Crete you will notice plenty of healthy-looking old folks, despite the embroilment of so many in feuds and vendettas over the years.

There are, in fact, quite a few centenarians. The inhabitants of Sfakiá have the reputation of being strong, traditionalist and belligerent. During the long years of foreign rule, they never gave in to oppressors, whether Venetians, Turks, Saracens or Germans. The message is clear – resistance keeps you young, as long as you manage not to get killed. Some say the people of Sfakiá are fanatics for justice; others feel that they simply like violence. Evidence of the latter was the "Omalós Vendetta" which claimed 63 victims between 1947 and 1960. Visitors to the area still take locally made knives away with them as souvenirs – mementoes of

Below: left, you need good shoes to traverse the rugged Samaria Gorge; right, so many villages to explore!

western Crete's mountain men and their ready daggers.

Frangokástello is reached via **Patsianós** (Agía Galíni bus). This Venetian castle, built in 1340, was originally named after the neighbouring church of Agios Nikíta. But to stress its foreign nature, the Cretans christened it Frangokástello – Castle of the Franks, modern Greece's generic term for "foreigners from Europe". On 18 May 1828 there was a battle here between 700 Cretans led by Hatzimicháli Daliánis, and 800 Turks under Mustafa Bey.

On a morning between 17 and 30 May each year a strange phenomenon is said to take place, an event immortalised in legend and guidebooks of the 19th century. Just before sunrise a shadowy procession leaves the ruins of the Church of Agios Harálambos, and for about 10 minutes columns of armed black figures march along the castle walls. The locals believe that these ghosts who return each year are the unredeemed souls of the dead. Due to their appearance in the damp early morning air, they are known as *Drosoulítes*, or "dew men". Scientists have looked into the matter and their conclusion is that the whole phenomenon is merely a mirage from Libya, perhaps brought about by an unusual refraction of light.

If you want to see the dew men, you will need quantities of luck and patience. Luck, because the sea must be calm and the humidity just right, and patience, because no one, apart from the scientists, knows exactly where the procession appears from and when, and there are only 10 minutes when conditions are right for the phenomenon. Thus, it may take a few years to catch a glimpse of the dew men. Nevertheless, the sandy beach and cosy *tavérnes* are inviting anyway.

North of Hóra Sfakíon, high on a plateau (780 metres) is the village of **Imbros**. It is only inhabited in the summer, and apparently the first people

to live there were outlaws. This is where one of Crete's wildest and most beautiful gorges begins, the **Imbrou**. It is just 7 km long, and its walls reaching a height of up to 300 metres close in to a gap of no more than 2 metres at the narrowest point. There are hardly any tourists here, but the Imbrou Gorge is an excellent alternative to the Samariá Gorge, if one doesn't have the time for both. From Imbros the road leads on towards Haniá through the fertile plain of **Askyfou** (800 metres), where there are lush vineyards, and potatoes, fruits and nuts are cultivated.

After **Krapi** the so-called "Wild West" of Crete is at an end. Overall, this region gives the impression of being one vast battlefield of history. Almost every village was involved in fighting the Venetians, Turks or the Germans in World War II.

In **Vrísses**, a friendly village, you can fortify yourself for the 33-km journey to

The Venetian Castle of Frango-kástello.

Haniá with sheep's yogurt and honey.

Paleóhora: The little town of Paleóhora, with about 900 inhabitants, lies on a peninsula jutting out into the Sea of Libya. This geographic situation means that there are two beaches, a long sandy beach to the southwest, and a pebbly stretch in the east. Sometimes, this pebbly beach offers a very welcome alternative, as the sandy one is often too windy to enjoy. Both have showers and restaurants nearby, making them ideal for holiday-makers.

Paleóhora has two ports, of which only one has been used to date. It is only suitable for small boats and links the place daily to Agía Rouméli at the Samaria Gorge, and weekly to Elafoníssi. A projected new harbour will be able to accommodate large car ferries and facilitate motor access to some of the interesting villages in the area which are still difficult or even impossible to reach by bus.

The new houses which have replaced the old in recent years have fortunately not spoiled the centre of the village of Paleóhora. Behind the breakwater of the harbour the little streets are still much as they were before the advent of the tourists. Here, in the evening, only a few metres from the bustle in the centre, the old women still sit with their needlework and chat. They look as if progress has completely passed them by. But tourism has changed even these people. Much of the traditional Cretan hospitality has been lost as a result of the tourist invasion. Nowadays, bus loads of foreigners descend half naked (that's how conservative Cretans view visitors dressed in shorts) and mill about taking pictures of the old folk. Yet the people are friendly and you can win their affection – but to do that you must first learn to speak a little Greek.

Go through the old part of the town bordering on the Panagiá Church with

Overlooking the Paleóhora peninsula.

its resonating bell tower, and you will come to the ruins of a Venetian castle, built in 1282, called **Sélinou**. Nowadays, this is the name given to the whole region. Don't miss the Festival of the Virgin Mary held in March, when three Orthodox priests and two local singers demonstrate their musical prowess at the *paneyíri*, or Name Day feast..

Paleóhora is definitely the most important town on the southwestern coast. There is a medical station, and several doctors and dentists practise here. Since 1988, a pharmacy has been added to this service. There is also a post office, telephone exchange, a police station, a kindergarten, a junior and senior school and two travel agencies. Children are transported from the surrounding area by specially laid on buses. Most people here manage to make a living from fishing and raising cattle, and supplement their income in the summer with the profits of tourism. During winter they grow vegetables (tomatoes and cucumbers) in greenhouses. The vegetable season in **Kondoúra**, a village to the west of Paleóhora, starts in September and goes on until the May–June of the following year.

Paleóhora earned a reputation as a hippy hangout in the 1960s, but that's all over, and the tourists these days are quite tame, although they are still predominantly young. In the summer season the main street is closed to traffic after six in the evening, and it is then that the evening siesta begins. In the cafés, restaurants and *tavérnes*, tourists and locals mingle until the early hours. This is a lively spot and if you don't enjoy the fun here, you have probably only yourself to blame.

Asogirés and Soúgia: There are several interesting trips which you can make from Paleóhora. One is to the village of **Anídri**, which lies just 5 km to the northeast. Here stands the beautiful

Misty morning: sunrise over Lefká Ori.

Agios Nikólaos Church, which was decorated with paintings by Joánnis Pagoménos in 1323.

Only 2.5 km further is **Asogirés**. Here the population has shrunk from 400 (1971) to 40. Just outside the village, next to the oil press, there is an enormous plane tree, the leaves of which remain green even in winter. Legend has it that the tree was planted by the 99 Holy Fathers. Scientific examinations have so far failed to come up with any explanation of this wonder of nature. The church, dedicated to the Holy Fathers (Agii Páteres) of 1864, is built into a rock face, just outside the village. A tour of the church and the little folk museum is conducted by a friendly custodian. You have to ask for him in one of the *tavérnes* and he will then take you around. Weapons, pots, books, clothing and other objects provide visitors with a lively picture of life on Crete in the 19th century.

The road to the **Cave of Souré** in which the 99 Holy Fathers lived winds its way up into the open countryside. Through a small door in the wire fence (right fork at the top), you reach a path which leads downhill first, then up again. A black cross marked on a rock indicates the entrance to the cave. There are three iron ladders to enable you to get down about 15 metres to the floor of the sacred cave. It is quite cold down there and you get a strong feeling of the ascetic environment of the hermit's life. You have to feel your way forward with the help of a rope. The cave goes back about 70 metres, slightly uphill into the mountain. Further up the cave, the path becomes oppressively narrow. If you want to go right to the far end, you need a reliable torch.

Then it's on to **Teménia** (17 km from Paleóhora), a village which supplies the whole of West Crete with mineral water. Nearby are the ruins of the ancient city of **Irtakína**, which was an important autonomous city in the Hellenic period. Fountains and parts of buildings can still be found between plants growing wild. Irtakína, like the other towns in the League of Cities, minted its own coins. The dolphin and stars depicted on these coins indicated the seafaring tradition. For years, no one bothered about this place; people just took the debris from the ruins to finish building their own houses. However, no one ever found any use for a 3rd-4th century BC headless statue of Pan, so it is now displayed in the Archaeological Museum of Haniá.

According to the records made available by the private archaeologist Dr. Paterakis, the city of Lissós, to the west of present day Soúgia, was founded by old men who had been driven out of Irtakína because of famine there. Irtakína did not benefit, but Lissós soon became so rich that it was able to send supplies to Irtakína as well.

If you stop a while in the village of

A familiar relic to remind visitors of the port of yesteryear.

Rodováni do try the delicious black bread which is still made from a traditional recipe. East of Rodováni are the ruins of the Dorian city of **Elyros** with a view of the harbour of Soúgia. Pictures of goats and bees on coins which have been found there indicate that the people of Elyros were hunters and beekeepers. Ruins of a Byzantine church show that the place was later a bishopric. All appearances indicate that the place was eventually destroyed by the Saracens. Also east of Rodováni is the little **Cave of Skotiní** in which ceramic remains from the Classical epoch (550–67 BC) have been found.

The road then goes on towards Haniá through **Agía Iríni**, the last village before the Omalós Plateau. It would of course be possible to begin a walk through the Samaria Gorge from here. About 11 km south of Rodováni, you come to **Soúgia**, a village with a broad pebble beach, which is now definitely

on the tourist map. Here lay ancient Elyros-Syia, and in the church built in 1875 there is a beautiful mosaic floor which originally belonged to a 6th-century basilica.

From an archaeological point of view the ruins of **Lissós** are more interesting. During its heyday in the Roman epoch, the town was so rich that it could afford to mint coins in gold. Only Irtakína was comparably wealthy. Lissós also became famous for its mineral springs. Remains of bath chambers show that this place was a spa in ancient times. Most impressive of all is the Asklepios Shrine. Everywhere you look are ruins of houses, theatres and public buildings, a fascinating sight. Various statues are exhibited in the Archaeological Museum of Haniá.

From Paleóhora to Hrissoskalítissa: Most of the way the road is asphalted, and the few gravel stretches do not pose any problems. You drive in the direction of Haniá through **Plemenianá** to **Drís** and **Strovlés**, villages set among the chestnut groves. The next stop is **Elos**, which is a larger village where a chestnut festival is held every year in October. Cretan visitors rave about the excellent chestnut cake baked at this time and the traditional music.

The last stage of the journey is through **Váthi**. The Convent of Hrissoskalítissa, set 35 metres up on a cliff on the west coast unfortunately does not shimmer as brightly in the distance as it used to up until a few years ago. The sky-blue roof which was the building's hallmark had rotted and so had to be repainted with a darker but more durable paint. The name of the convent means "Virgin of the Golden Step," and thereby hangs a tale.

The 90 steps leading up to the convent are said to have been fashioned from gold which can only be seen by a pure, sinless person. So you can find out for yourself how virtuous you are. Perhaps you will see the "elusive" gold. The

Sacrificial lamb.

place is really well worth a visit. It is a very isolated place, but when asked recently if she finds the solitude extreme at times, the abbess merely replied that she could not even begin to imagine living anywhere else.

Elafoníssi and Gávdos: The island of **Elafoníssi** is about 6 km to the south of the convent. But the road is so bad that it seems much further. In a certain light the sand has a pink glow. Here you will find everything you need for a good holiday: sea, sun, fresh air, pines and hardly any people.

Easter of the year 1824 was a day of sorrow and tragedy on this island. A terrible slaughter took place. Many Cretan women and children had fled from Ibrahim Pasha Messez and his followers. They hid themselves here. In those days, the Turks had a simple strategy: if they couldn't seize the men, they would simply make off with the women and children. The Turks found their hiding place and killed 850 people. After the massacre, the soldiers prepared to plunder the convent, but beekeepers living there set upon the Ottomans and put them to flight. The convent was thus spared from destruction.

From 1 July to 15 September, a boat leaves twice a week for **Gávdos Island** – the southernmost point in Europe. The 37-km journey takes about three hours. When you arrive, you will find that you can camp overnight in the small harbour of **Karavé** with its sandy beach. It is an idyllic spot, but dramatically cut off from the main island, along with everything else. The loveliest beach there is **Sarakíniko**, to the north of the harbour, and there is a pension there too, where visitors love to stay to get away from it all. In spring and autumn, however, the sudden and unpredictable storms can cause one to be stranded for several weeks on Gávdos.

Despite the advent of electricity, the **Snow-capped Lefká Ori.**

island is really only for those who are prepared to rough it. Compared to Crete, Gávdos is tiny, but it still takes two days to walk round the 37-sq. km island. The path is rough but not dangerous; so as long as you are careful, it should not present any problems. Settlements on Gávdos remain as yet unexcavated. Apparently it was densely populated in the Byzantine epoch, with some estimates putting the number as high as 8,000 inhabitants. In those days it even had its own bishop. There is a headless statue of a woman dating from this period, but to see it one needs to go to England. In Venetian times Gávdos was above all a Corsair hide-out. During the period of Turkish domination it became one of the most important refuges of the resistance fighters.

Today there are about 100 people on Gávdos, mainly in the principal town of **Kastrí** and in the villages of **Ambelos**, **Vatsianá** and **Metóhia**. On the island is

the cave where the nymph Calypso is supposed to have lived.

In another version the nymph lived on the Maltese island of Gozo. Whether on Gozo or Gávdos, it was she who was able to detain Odysseus for a period of seven years. The 99 Holy Fathers stopped here on their way from Egypt to Crete. There they intended to spread the Gospel among the Cretans. John the Hermit was among the group.

On the way to Kastrí from the harbour, you pass the Panagía Church, the bell of which once belonged to a ship. This ship was wrecked on the rocks near Gávdos during a storm. Later, one of the islanders saw the bell deep in the water, and with some help managed to dive down and salvage it. But diving to such depths caused him to lose his hearing so he became known as *Koufidákis*, the deaf one. There have been many attempts to remove the bell from the island but all were mysteriously

What all Greek men carry.

thwarted, and somehow it never left.

When, during World War II, German soldiers were stationed on Gávdos, a great deal of fighting took place against the British. The Germans mined the island, which led to numerous casualties among the civilian population. Many fishermen and farmers left their homes and moved to safety in Paleóhora on Crete.

Kándanos and Rodopós: On the way back to Haniá from Paleóhora one should stop at **Kándanos**. As this place has the highest rainfall in Crete, the vegetation is lush, with olives, chestnuts, fruit trees and vineyards growing in profusion. The rich meadows are ideal for cattle. The river Kándanos is narrow but has the great advantage that it does not dry up in summer. With its post office, telephone exchange, doctors, dentists and ambulance as well as a police station and several cafés and restaurants, Kándanos has become a centre for the 15 surrounding villages.

The history of the place goes back a long way. A little to the south lay the ancient city of **Kantánou**, which was situated on a hill, and split in two by an earthquake. Later, rich Venetian families lived here, and when the Turks took over the city, the Venetians converted to Islam. Kándanos then became an administrative centre for the region, with a high concentration of military installations. There were many bloody confrontations and battles leading to a high number of casualties.

The area is rich in old churches with good examples of Byzantine art, such as that in the **Panagía Tsivremiana Church**. There is nothing left of old Kándanos. After the Germans landed in **Máleme** on 20 May 1941, they got as far as Kándanos. The Cretans managed to kill 25, which led to heavy reprisals: the village was bombed on 25 May and almost destroyed. Very few inhabitants

Seeking refuge in the olive grove.

survived the attack. A bilingual (Greek and German) tablet refers to this terrible day. On it is written this stark message: "Here Kándanos once existed…"

The return journey takes you through the village of **Voukoliés**, where a market has been held on Saturdays for hundreds of years. Every year in August a week-long concert festival is organised, to which the best known Cretan musicians are invited. This is a great attraction for locals and tourists alike.

Another plus: if you get a stomach upset in Voukoliés, consider yourself relatively fortunate. The sparkling mineral water here is famous for curing disorders of this nature.

If you go on further to the northwest, through **Tavronítis**, you will reach the **Peninsula of Rodopós**. This is one of the most beautiful parts of Crete, although it isn't easy to get to. The asphalt road ends suddenly at **Afrátas** and **Rodopós** and proceeding north by car

becomes very difficult. But it is definitely worth the effort, as you cannot possibly say you know Crete if you have not visited Rodopós.

Just by the river on this peninsula is **Kolimbári**, a peaceful, shady place with a hotel, restaurant and lovely long beach. North of the village, also on the waterside is the Monastery of **Goniá**. There is a pottery school here as well as a large library and a notable collection of icons. Goniá was always a well known centre of resistance. Behind the monastery is the Orthodox Academy of Crete. Seminars for priests are held here but, otherwise, things are really quite unorthodox. The exchanges from West to East are by no means limited to theological ideas. New methods of agriculture are tried out here too, all thanks to the Bishop Irenéos Galanákos who, from 1972 to 1980, was Greek Orthodox Metropolitan in Germany.

About 2 km north of Afrátas is the

Long and winding road to Hóra Sfakíon.

fascinating and unusual cave of **Ellinóspilios**. It is not only large (165 metres long) and very beautiful, but archaeologically important too. Human and animal remains were found here, as well as ceramic fragments. Some of these are from the early Neolithic period (about 10,000 BC) and one skull was dated at 20,000 to 25,000 BC, which makes the finds the oldest human artefacts in the Aegean.

In the north of the peninsula near Kap Skala is the **Diktínaion**. Originally there was a 7th-century Doric temple here, dedicated to the nymph Diktynna. The nymph, identified with the Cretan goddess Briómartis, is said to have leapt into the sea here to escape the attentions of King Minos. She was saved from drowning by fishermen with their nets. The Emperor Hadrian is reputed to have ordered a new temple to be built here after his visit to Crete. Ruins of the temple, which was built in the 2nd cen-

tury AD, can still be seen today. At least, during the Roman era, the importance of this religious centre extended beyond the boundaries of Crete.

From Rodopós there is a road leading north to the church of **Agios Ioánnis**. There are many turnings and no signposts, so remember to turn right at the cistern. Soon you reach a point where you can see the church lying deep in the valley. On 29 August thousands of believers come here to commemorate the beheading of St John.

Binoculars are a great asset on Rodopós, as there are so many birds of prey to watch. It is so peaceful here that a day on Rodopós is definitely preferable to a visit to the Samaria Gorge if one really wants to get away from it all.

Kastélli and Gramvoússa: Kastélli, the main town of the region of **Kíssamos** lies exactly halfway between the two peninsulas of Rodopós and **Gramvoússa**. The little harbour, from which

Whitewashed simplicity: Greek architecture in Georgioúpolis.

ships leave for Piraeus twice a week, has made the town a "trading centre" of West Crete. The inhabitants are fishermen and sailors and they also cultivate vineyards and olive groves. The favourable climate and the abundant supply of water here give rise to a wonderfully green environment. As there are also lovely beaches, and hotels, pensions and *tavérnes*, Kastélli is gradually becoming a tourist resort.

This area has been inhabited since very early times. There was a late Minoan settlement here called **Kíssamos**, which was the independent port city of ancient **Polyrrhínia**. Above the present-day Polyrrhínia village, 6 km from Kastélli, are the ruins of the city of that name, founded in 8 BC and destroyed by the Saracens in the 9th century. Once again it was the typical set up of a Dorian double settlement: a well fortified city in the hills within sight of a port. Apart from the remains of a

temple, cisterns and burial chambers there are also ruins of a fort which was in fact rebuilt in Byzantine times.

The ancient city of **Agníon**, famous for its temple of Apollo, lay on the west side of the Gramvoússa Peninsula. Now the peninsula is uninhabited, and is a good place for walking and watching birds of prey, and vultures. You can take a boat to the island of Imeri Gramvoússa, one of the oldest pirate islands in the Mediterranean. The Venetian castle (1579–1582) is well preserved in parts. Built 137 metres up, it proved invincible, even to the Turks.

From Kastélli one can take a bus or taxi to **Plátanos**. This is a lovely quiet village. In the church are some interesting icons, among them one depicting the 99 Holy Fathers. From here one can visit the ancient city of **Falássarna**, which served Polyrrhínia as port. There is not much left of ancient Falássarna. The port now lies 6 metres up, and far

Bringing in the catch.

from the sea. For a long time it was assumed that the island rose in the west (Falássarna) as it dipped in the east (Eloúnda), but this theory is no longer deemed tenable.

One can ponder this question and other mysteries of Crete at leisure on the deserted beaches of Falássarna. There are a couple of *tavérnes* to take care of one's creature comforts, and it is possible to rent rooms.

Georgioúpolis and Kournás: The road follows the coast through countryside thick with reeds, through Tavronítis, and numerous small villages and newly built modern hotels.

Then you go on past **Máleme** where a large beehive tomb was discovered. But the place became known for other reasons. In World War II, Haniá Airport was located here. In 1941, after heavy fighting, it was captured by German airborne troops. There are 4,465 graves in the German Cemetery of Máleme,

mainly of very young men. Most of them lost their lives on 20 May 1941 on the night they landed. Their remains were kept in the Monastery of Goniá until the cemetery was founded in 1973.

The road carries on through Soúda Bay towards Réthimnon. There is no shortage of lovely places to stay on this stretch. In **Vámos**, for example, sporting events are held in winter and musical festivals in summer in beautiful surroundings with friendly people.

Even nicer is the pretty fishing village of **Georgioúpolis**, with its extra large village green. This was the site of the ancient city of **Amfímalla**, one of the ports of Láppa. But nothing remains of it now. The beach slopes gently to the sea and is ideal for families with young children and, although narrow, it makes up for that in stretching several kilometres towards Réthimnon. The place was named after the former high commissioner, Prince George. Although once infested with malaria, it is now a tourist resort. But it retains a gentle and dreamy atmosphere.

It is then 7 km to the **Kournás Lake**. This freshwater lake, which is about 1 sq. km in area, is almost circular in shape and is set 200 metres up in a landscape reminiscent of the Alpine foothills. For some time plans were underway to fill in the lake, because of the swarms of mosquitoes which bred there every year. But since the fertility of the surrounding countryside depended on the lake, the decision was taken to clean it twice a year instead. There is a legend which says that the lake was formed at the wish of a dishonoured maiden, and it is sometimes possible to see her out on the water at midday combing her hair.

Four and a half km beyond the lake is the **Cave of Kournás**. It has a geological rarity: a stalagmite on which two stalactites form the shape of a cross. At the village of **Keratidés**, you can treat yourself to a panoramic view over the lake to the sea.

Left, knotted only for a solemn purpose. Right, "You stay a monk as long as you toll the bell."

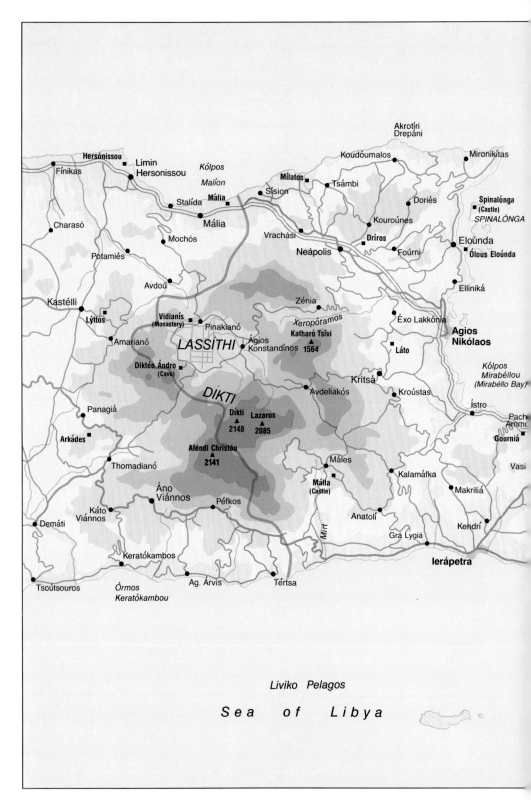

Fínikas
Hersónissou
Limin
Hersonissou

*Kólpos
Malíon*

Charasó

Stalída   Mália

Mochós

Mália

Akrotíri
Drepáni

Koudóumalos

Mílatos
Tsámbi

Sísion

Vrachási

Mironikítas

Doriés

Kouroúnes

Driros

Neápolis   Foúrni

Spinalónga
■ (Castle)
SPINALÓNGA

Eloúnda
Ólous Eloúnda

Potamiés

Avdoú

Kastélli

Lýttos

Amarianó

Vidianís
(Monastery)

Pinakianó

LASSÍTHI

Diktéo Ándro
(Cave)

Panagiá

Arkádes ■

Thomadianó

Káto
Viánnos

Demáti

Zénia

Xeropótamos

Ágios
Konstandínos

Katharó Tsívi
▲
1564

DÍKTI

Avdeliakós

Éxo Lakkónia

Láto

Kritsá

Agios
Nikólaos

*Kólpos
Mirabéllou
(Mirabéllo Bay)*

Kroústas

Ístro

Díkti
▲
2148

Lazaros
▲
2085

Aféndi Christóu
▲
2141

Áno
Viánnos

Péfkos

Elliniká

Máles

Málla
(Castle)

Anatolí

Grá Lygiá

Kalamáfka

Makriliá

Vasi

Kendrí

Pach
Ammo

Gourniá

Ierápetra

Keratókambos

Tsoútsouros

*Órmos
Keratókambou*

Ag. Árvis

Tértsa

Mírt

Liviko Pelagos

S e a   o f   L i b y a

212

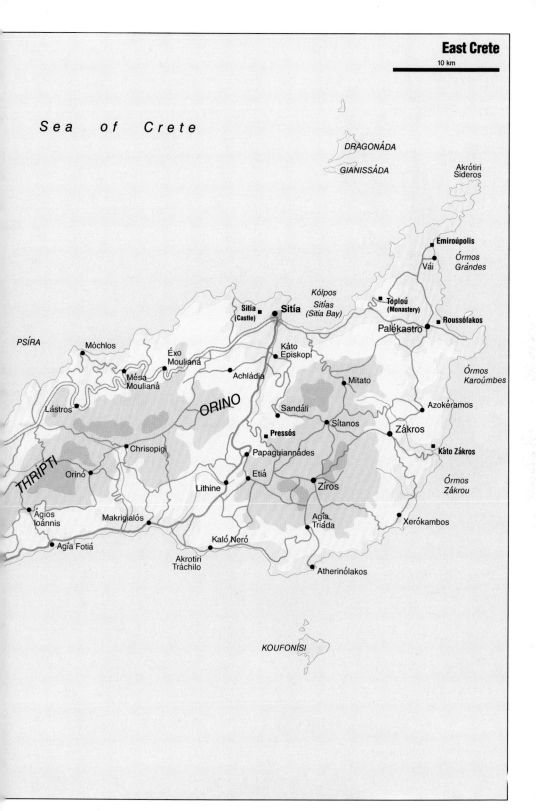

East Crete

10 km

Sea of Crete

DRAGONÁDA

GIANISSÁDA

Akrótiri
Sideros

Emiroúpolis

*Órmos
Grándes*

Vái

Kólpos
Sitía
Sitías
(Sitía Bay)

Sitía
(Castle)

Sitía

Toploú
(Monastery)

Roussólakos

Palékastro

PSÍRA

Móchlos

Éxo
Moulianá

Káto
Episkopí

Mitato

*Órmos
Karoúmbes*

Mésa
Moulianá

Achládia

ORINO

Sandáli

Azokéramos

Lástros

Pressós

Sítanos

Zákros

Chrisopigí

Papaguiannádes

Káto Zákros

THRÍPTI

Orinó

Etiá

Zíros

*Órmos
Zákrou*

Lithíne

Ágios
Ioánnis

Makrigialós

Agía
Triáda

Xerókambos

Agía Fotiá

Kaló Neró

Akrotiri
Tráchilo

Atherinólakos

KOUFONÍSI

AROUND AGIOS NIKÓLAOS

Agios Nikólaos, with its 8,500 inhabitants, is a very pleasant little city. It lies on a promontory and is bordered by sea along the eastern side. As its houses are also grouped around a hill, it is not always easy to get one's bearings here. Despite the natural beauty of the place, it is not immediately apparent why it has become such a popular tourist centre, as there is no particularly good beach here. Better bathing is to be found a few kilometres away, but even those places are no match for the best beaches of the island. It soon becomes clear, however, that water is not the main attraction of this area. Agios Nikólaos is quite simply a magnet for the trendiest of Crete's tourists – the one resort on the island which is reminiscent of Mykonos.

Agios Nikólaos is the ideal spot for people who want more than just a tan. It's a place for those who like the bustle of a town and who like crowds and enjoy wandering through the streets and going shopping. Nowhere on the island is the mix of nationalities more colourful. Nowhere, apart from Haniá, is it easier to get to know people. A respite from the noise may be found in the peaceful countryside, or in any of the many beautiful spots on Mirabéllo Bay.

One of the sights here is **Voulisméni Lake**. The lake is almost round, and has a diameter of about 75 metres. According to myth, the goddess Artemis bathed in this lake, which was said to be unfathomable. More recently it has been measured and found to be 64 metres deep. Whereas in earlier times it was famous for its "sweet" water – the water was supposed to come, or have come, from an underground spring – nowadays it is regarded as salty.

Culturally, Agios Nikólaos has not much to offer. The **Panagía Church** to the east of **Venizélos Square** is worth a visit to see the 14th-century frescoes.

More important is the **Agios Nikólaos Chapel** a little further out, behind the Minos Beach Hotel. This is one of the oldest churches on Crete but, if you compare the ages usually given for the church and its frescoes, you come to the illogical conclusion that the frescoes came first.

The oldest parts of the fresco are interesting, for following the iconoclasm of Leo III (726–843), no figures were to be represented, only ornamentation. This makes the Agios Nikólaos Chapel unique on Crete. The name of the town was taken from the chapel.

On no account should you miss the Archaeological Museum, if you are at all interested in the Minoan Epoch. Although the most spectacular items are housed in Iráklion, important exhibits can be found here too, such as the "Goddess of Mirtos", the skull of a

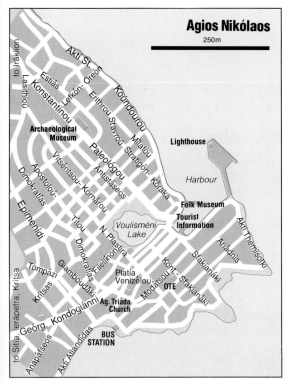

Agios Nikólaos

250m

Cretan contest victor, various vessels and containers such as a small cosmetic box, wine goblets, weapons, double axes, sarcophagi and idols.

It is true that there is nothing particularly sensational in the way of rare artefacts, but that has its advantages. As only finds from the east of the island are displayed here, the collection is more comprehensible than the more extensive exhibition in Iráklion, and you also get a good idea of Minoan culture.

In the eight rooms, there are exhibits dating from the Neolithic period, the Minoan and Post Minoan era right up to Roman times.

Not much is known about the historical development of the town of Agios Nikólaos. In Dorian times the port **Lató y Kamára** of the mountain town of **Lató** was situated here. Up on a hill where the city centre is today, remains of an acropolis were found. On the same site, the Venetians erected a castle,

Mirabello, of which hardly a trace remains. In the Turkish era, the place was almost uninhabited. It was not until 1870 that the present town of Agios Nikólaos was built.

Special mention should be made of Agios Nikólaos' unique climate: according to records, in summer the humidity level here is nil. For star-gazers and more serious astronomers, this is of great importance, as the stars can be seen exceptionally clearly.

Panagía i Kerá: The Church of **Panagía i Kerá** (Church of our Lady, Mother of God) is about 500 metres outside of Kritsá, on the right side of the road, in a grove of oaks, olives and cypresses. Some say that this is the most beautiful church on the island. In fact it would be difficult to find one which can compete from simply an architectural point of view.

What is interesting is that the aesthetic charm of the building, rather than

Still waters at the waterfront of Agios Nikólaos.

being a calculated effect in fact stems from the necessity of holding the vault together. The impression of size is modified somewhat when one looks at the interior. It is over 100 sq. metres in area. Its apparent unity would seem to indicate that it was built in a single phase. History, however, tells otherwise. The central nave is the oldest part, dating from the mid-13th century. The frescoes in the apse and on the walls of the tambour are from the same period. The south nave was built and painted between 1300 and 1340, and the north nave, 100 years later.

The central nave is dedicated to Mary, the Mother of God, and is decorated with pictures of the archangels, the prophets and evangelists and many well known biblical scenes, including Herod's massacre of the innocents and the raising of Lazarus.

The south nave is dedicated to St Anna and the north to St Anthony.

Photography inside the church is prohibited. Slides and books may be purchased in the small café next door.

Lató: The ruins of the Dorian city of **Lató** are easy to find, lying 3 km northwest of Kritsá. Just before the Kritsá signpost, a road suitable for vehicles leads off to the right, into the hills. For visitors wishing to walk from Kerá to Lató there is a path behind the café which is just along the road to Lató.

Lató was founded in the 7th and 8th centuries BC, and is a typical double settlement of a fortified town set between two hills within sight of the port. Its most important period was probably during the 4th and 3rd centuries BC, when it expanded in area as well as in population. A document from the year 193 BC gives the name of the hill city as **Lató y Etéra.**

One of the great advantages of Lató is that it still offers an accurate picture of a double settlement. The port of the

Heat wave at the harbour?

former hill city **Lató y Kamára** lay on the site of present-day Agios Nikólaos. Although originally the more important of the two, Lató y Etéra was eventually left deserted. One can only speculate as to why this happened. Most probably there was a long period of peace, when there was no need to take refuge in the hills. After that time the port took over all the necessary functions.

This Post Minoan place was also discovered by Arthur Evans towards the end of the 19th century, but was excavated by a French archaeologist.

The best way to approach Lató is from the city gates below. You can take the steps up to the centre which will give you a clear impression of just what an inhabitant of the city saw 2,500 years ago. This area, which one can enjoy walking through today, is only a small part of what was once the large expanse of the original city. If you have time, just take a look into the bushes to the side, and you will be amazed at how far the settlement extended, and just how much there is still to discover.

Kritsá: The village is 11 km from Agios Nikólaos, in the foothills of the Díkti Mountains. With 2,000 inhabitants, Kritsá is one of the largest villages on the island. As most visitors to Agios Nikólaos come here, it is usually crowded, so it's a good idea to leave the car in the car park at the entrance to the village. From there one can also go to the Katharó Plateau.

In the village, you are greeted by a bronze statue "The Maid of Kritsá," **Kritsotopoúla**. She is revered as a freedom fighter against Turkish oppressors. The Turkish Pasha Husein, who lived in **Houmeriáko**, a village north west of **Neápolis**, had chosen this daughter of the priest of Kritsá as his mistress. On the very first night, she stabbed the pasha, dressed herself as a man and joined the freedom fighters on the

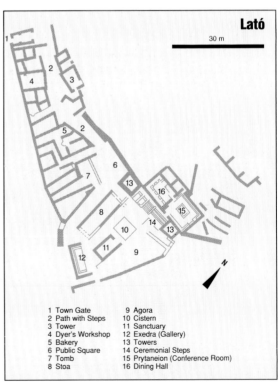

Brush fire near Agios Nikólaos.

Lató

30 m

1 Town Gate
2 Path with Steps
3 Tower
4 Dyer's Workshop
5 Bakery
6 Public Square
7 Tomb
8 Stoa
9 Agora
10 Cistern
11 Sanctuary
12 Exedra (Gallery)
13 Towers
14 Ceremonial Steps
15 Prytaneion (Conference Room)
16 Dining Hall

Lassíthi Plateau. It was not until she was wounded that her true identity became known to her comrades.

There are several churches worth seeing in Kritsá. Just at the entrance to the village, on the right, is the Cemetery Church of Agios Ioánnis with its late 14th-century frescoes. To the south is the **Agios Geórgios tou Kavousióti Church**, dating from the early 14th century with frescoes of the same date, and then the **Agios Konstantínos** Church with its frescoes of the mid-14th century, as well as the churches of Agíou Pnévma and Agía Paraskeví.

The main street is one huge, colourful bazaar, a mass of cloth, material and blankets. There is a wonderful selection of handicrafts here, although the label "Kritsá" doesn't indicate a low price. If you can manage it, do walk through the streets up to the lovely road lined with almond trees which runs along the hill above the village. From there you will have a glorious view over Kritsá and the valley, and Kerá shimmers white in the distance through the olives, oaks and groves of cypresses.

There's no doubt that Kritsá is a lovely place, especially its location. Then there are the weavers and potteries, but these are not the real reasons for its fame. It is the **Panagía i Kerá Church** on the way from Agios Nikólaos which is the main attraction.

In Kritsá the road to the **Katharó Plateau** branches off left from the main road. The road is asphalt for a short stretch, then gravel, although still passable. But the 16-km drive is well worth the effort, for the plateau, lying at 1,100 metres, has the most wonderful scenery imaginable. It is only inhabited and cultivated during summer, as it is usually snowed in during the winter. Potatoes, various vegetables and vineyards are the main crops up here.

Two km south of Kritsá on the road to

Street scene in Tzermiadon.

Kroústas is the Church of **Agios Ioánnis o Theológos**, which once belonged to the Monastery of **Toploú**. The iconostases in the three naves are exceptionally beautiful. After about 4 km you reach Kroústas. Then if you drive just as far again, you come to a left fork in the road which leads to another Church of Agios Ioánnis where the frescoes of 1347 are worth seeing.

Gourniá: Approximately 18 km southeast of Agios Nikólaos a road leads into the hills, to the Monastery of **Faneroméni**. Although the monastery seems very near, don't be misled: the road actually winds around for almost 8 km before you get there.

One km down the road you come to the Minoan city of **Gourniá**, which lies on a hill just outside **Pahía Ammos**. Gourniá is an archaeological godsend, as it is larger and better preserved than **Palékastro**, **Mírtos** or the surroundings of the Palace of **Káto Zákros**.

These sites, although interesting, do not give as clear an indication of a Minoan city planning. Findings in a necropolis on the edge of the city indicate that the period of habitation here was from about 3000 BC to 1100 BC. Most parts of the city which have been excavated are from about 1600 BC, the Late Minoan period. The great catastrophe of 1450 BC destroyed much of the settlement. It was then uninhabited for a long time, before being finally resettled in about 1300 BC.

On almost the highest point of the hill is a building which is generally thought to have been a Minoan palace. It lies in a north-south axis and the layout of the rooms around a central courtyard is reminiscent of the island's other great palaces. A governor of some kind probably ruled here, under the authority of either Knossós or Káto Zákros.

In the sanctum various cult objects were found, most of them ornamented **Cool cover.**

with snakes, as well as a sacrificial table, bulls' horns, double axes and a clay goddess whose outstretched arms are wound around with snakes.

More important than any theory, is the possibility afforded the visitor here, of wandering through the ancient streets at will, and being able to draw comparisons – perhaps with the Dorian city of Lató, for there are many similarities. It is amazing to see the little rooms in the residents' houses, and the remains of the stairs, which must have led to an upper storey. It is also fascinating to compare this city with present-day Cretan mountain villages. Many finds from the graves in Gourniá are displayed in the Archaeological Museum of Iráklion.

The little village of **Paheía Ammos** used to have an attractive harbour. The completion of the coastal road led to the stagnation of its growth, and it now relies on tourism for prosperity. This is

the narrowest point of the island, and this fact played an important part in the founding of Gourniá. Opposite the lilac-coloured hills is the wedge-shaped **Monastiráki Gorge**. If you make your way through the gorge you can reach the peak of the 1,476-metre high **Aféndis Stavroménos Mountain**, where there's a wonderful view of the island. The recommended route is through **Kavoússi** (coastal road from Agios Nikólaos at km 27), **Xerámpela** and the **Thrípti Alm** (850 metres).

Three km further south is the village of **Vassilikí** with its famous early Minoan excavation site. The black and red ceramic work has become known as the Vassilikí style. To locate the site, you should turn left at the signpost and then continue on for about 150 metres.

Another 3 km to the south is the friendly village of **Episkopí**, with its lovely little Agios Nikólaos Church in the shape of a cross.

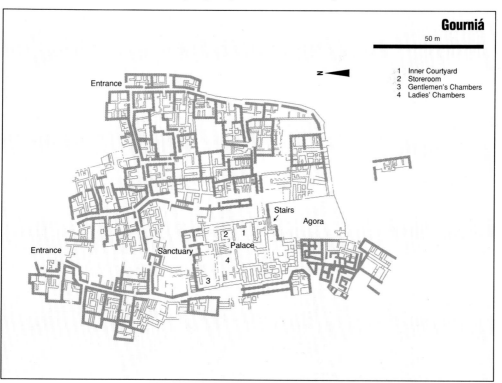

Gourniá

50 m

1 Inner Courtyard
2 Storeroom
3 Gentlemen's Chambers
4 Ladies' Chambers

Entrance

Entrance

Stairs
Agora
Sanctuary
Palace

The most eastern town on Crete is Sitía, 73 km from Agios Nikólaos. It is set in gentle mountain scenery and lush vineyards. The fertile soil makes the gardens of the 7,000 inhabitants gloriously colourful. A picturesque harbour links Sitía to the mainland and other islands. There are connections to Piraeus, Rhodes, Kárpathos, the Cyclades and the Aegean Islands.

Tourism is definitely booming. Whether it will grow too quickly and overwhelm the town as some observers fear is left to be seen within the next few years. The place has already made concessions to the industry – box-like hotels, promenade restaurants and beach discos abound these days – but, to date, it has still managed to keep its own laid-back character despite all that.

Burial findings indicate that the Bay of Sitía was inhabited in Minoan times. The ancient town of Itia or Etia or even Itis, with **Pressos** as its port, was probably not located on the site of present-day Sitía, but 1 kilometre inland on a hill.

According to Diogenes Laertius in his *Philosophical History of Greece*, Myson, one of the seven wise men of Greece, was born here. For Cretans today, Vinzentos Kornáros (1600–77) seems a more important figure. His *Erotókritos* is one of the most significant national poems of Greece.

In Byzantine times Crete was a bishopric. As this bay always attracted pirates and invaders, the Byzantines built a fort at the turn of the millennium, which soon encompassed almost the whole settlement. The Genoese, and later the Venetians fortified the walls, but very little of these works can be seen today. As the Turkish attacks increased after about 1648, the Venetians moved the people to places easier to defend. In earlier times the inhabitants had already

Left, the waterfront in Sitía.

223

had to cope with the loss of their homes. In 1303 and 1508, they were destroyed by earthquakes, and in 1538 by the ruthless Ottoman admiral Chaireddin Barbarossa. The fears of the Venetians proved well founded when, in 1651, a single attack by the Ottomans was enough to take their fort. The evacuated town fell into decay and was eventually brought back to life only on the initiative of the Turks in 1879.

If you are interested in the history of names, Sitía is a treasure trove, for there is a great variety of optional meanings to choose from. The name can be traced from a Linear-B inscription tablet, and was possibly included in Egyptian lists of place names. It may also be connected to "Lassíthi" (from or to La Sitía). A connection with the above-mentioned Itia or Etiá is also possible as, until recent times, there was a place called Etiá (or Ethiá, "Willow Tree") just 25 km south of Sitía. A hilltop sanctuary was discovered here during the 1950s.

A Franciscan monastery and a Venetian palace which once stood here were both destroyed. The fort is now the only building worth seeing in the town. The name **Kasárma** comes from *casa di arma* (House of Arms). Below the fort, about 50 metres to the east, are the remains of a horseshoe-shaped Roman fish pond with a diameter of about 6 or 7 metres. It is now located underwater and seems to indicate that East Crete has sunk. Strong doubts have been expressed by some geologists about the theory that there was a simultaneous rising of the western part of the island (Falássarna) as the east sank, a view once held by some scholars.

One of the sights of the town is the recently opened **Archaeological Museum**. There all the important finds from the area are beautifully displayed. In a small **Folklore Museum**, you can see, among other things, the simple equipment used to make the elaborate

Cretan national costume in earlier times. The kitchen utensils and living rooms of 100 years ago are interesting too, and give a fascinating insight into the Cretan lifestyle of the 19th century.

To the east of Sitía is a long beach, which is quite steep in places. As the currents are strong, particularly when it's windy, children must be supervised if they swim at all. It is not really a place recommended for family outings.

There are differing opinions about Sitía. While some see it as the typical although rather rough but vital Levantine trading city, others grumble that it is a provincial one-horse town. One thing is certain, though. There are few lovelier sights in the world than the lights of Sitía glimmering in the darkness as you drive towards the city along the coast from Toploú or Palékastro.

The village of **Agía Fotía** is 5 km east of Sitía. In 1971 an early Minoan necropolis was discovered here which,

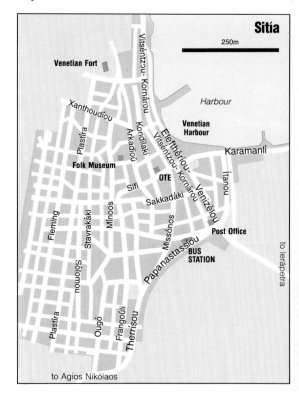

with its 250 graves, is one of the largest on the island.

Toploú and Vái: The landscape between Sitía and **Toploú** becomes more bizarre and surrealistic as you approach the Toploú Monastery. The steep road is asphalted these days. The clearly recognisable rock strata all around will bring joy to the heart of any geologist. After a while the monastery comes into sight between the mountain crests, its tall, Italianate belltower beckoning like the minaret of an isolated mosque.

Toploú is actually only the nickname of the monastery. It probably comes from the Turkish word *top,* meaning cannon ball. In Venetian times the monastery did possess a renowned cannon and in fact used it successfully against the numerous pirates in the area.

The monastery's real name is **Moní Panagía Akrotirianí**, Monastery of the Mother of God of the Foothills, also of the Cape. It was built in the 15th and

16th centuries on the ruins of the monastery of Agios Isodóros and then destroyed by a strong earthquake. It was during the subsequent rebuilding under the supervision of Abbot Gavríl Pantógalos that the monastery took on the appearance it has today. During Turkish rule, it was often attacked, as apparently secret revolutionary committees met here.

During World War II, it was a contact point for the Cretan partisans and the British. The Germans found out about this, and in retaliation shot the abbot and several monks. There is a memorial near the entrance to commemorate these events.

It may be better if you have not visited the monastery before and therefore do not remember the way it used to be. Then you will not be disappointed. The inner courtyard was once glorious, with white stone walkways, arcades and balustrades, but it is now unrecognisable.

Inviting palm beach at Vái.

The whole place has been filled with dark wooden scaffolding, which has been erected in order to make getting around easier: as a result the aesthetics have suffered.

In better days, 150 monks lived here, but now there are only two. The older monk, who only a few years ago posed proudly beside the wonderful icon – "Great are you, my God" – of Ioánnis Kornáros, now makes a sullen impression. And no wonder. He has seen his monastery taken apart and downgraded into a tourist attraction. But despite this, the Monastery of Toploú is still an impressive sight in the barren landscape of East Crete.

Northeast of Toploú, on the east coast of the island, is the palm-fringed, "tropical" beach of **Vái**. From Toploú, the quickest way to get there is via the direct road to the northeast; from Sitía it is easier to go via **Palékastro**.

The sandy beach of Vái lies in a small bay, like a lagoon, and is famous for its palm trees. The locals will tell you this date palm "forest" sprouted when Roman soldiers seeded the area – in passing – with date stones. It is a wonderful beach for children, as it slopes gently and the waves are not strong. The water is supposed to be slightly warmer here than elsewhere too. There is a restaurant, as well as showers, changing huts and lovely shady spots under the palm trees. You will find all you need for a delightful beach holiday. Campers overnighting in the past made such a mess of the little beach and the woods nearby that now camping and overnighting are forbidden. That is also the reason why the palm wood is fenced in nowadays and is a protected area.

The place is not, however, anything like the usual cliché of a tropical beach but is more reminiscent of the North African coast. But Vái would probably be just as famous if it had hazelnut

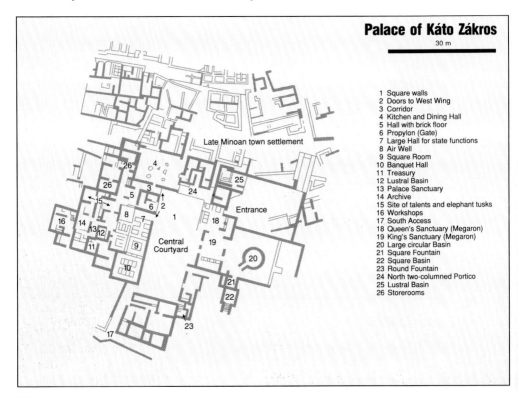

Palace of Káto Zákros
30 m

1 Square walls
2 Doors to West Wing
3 Corridor
4 Kitchen and Dining Hall
5 Hall with brick floor
6 Propylon (Gate)
7 Large Hall for state functions
8 Air Well
9 Square Room
10 Banquet Hall
11 Treasury
12 Lustral Basin
13 Palace Sanctuary
14 Archive
15 Site of talents and elephant tusks
16 Workshops
17 South Access
18 Queen's Sanctuary (Megaron)
19 King's Sanctuary (Megaron)
20 Large circular Basin
21 Square Fountain
22 Square Basin
23 Round Fountain
24 North two-columned Portico
25 Lustral Basin
26 Storerooms

Late Minoan town settlement

Entrance

Central Courtyard

bushes or oaks instead of palms, as its charm is really due to the contrast to the surrounding landscape.

Two km north of Vái is the little village of **Erimoúpolis**. This site on the cape was settled even during Minoan times. It was once the site of the powerful city of Itanos, from which regular trade was conducted with the Orient during Greek and Roman times. Below the acropolis, very little of which remains today, sections of streets as well as the ruins of an early Christian basilica have been discovered. More impressive than the excavations, however, is the view to the northeast of the rugged **Kap Síderos** with its lighthouse.

Káto Zákros and the Valley of the Dead: The most interesting way to reach the Palace of **Káto Zákros** is via Palékastro, for the roads are better and they take you through a fascinating mixture of lush countryside and totally barren landscapes. Beaches about a mile away,

Broken bones in the Valley of the Dead.

especially at the southern end of the bay, are worth visiting.

Palékastro is a delightful place, and also has an excavation site nearby. Two and a half km away to the east, at **Roussolákos**, are the remains of a Minoan port, second in importance only to Gourniá in terms of archaeological significance. As there is relatively little left to see here, the site receives far fewer visitors than the great palaces. In fact, Palékastro depends on the popularity of the monastery of Toploú and the beach at Vái for visitors.

Visitors to Káto Zákros and Zákros, also known as Ano Zákros or Epáno Eákros, to the south, find shops, *tavérnes*, hotels and rooms to let there. The scenery around Zákros is surprisingly green. This is because near the village there is a spring which provides water for the whole area.

Luckily the old days of dust and frazzled nerves on this stretch are over, and you can drive the 8 km to the excavation site of Káto Zákros on an excellent road. The last curvy and rather steep stretch is interesting as it leads through the most extraordinary scenery, rather like a moonscape. Yet the valley where the Palace of Káto Zákros is found, has lush vegetation. Spring water flows from Zákros, sometimes so strongly that parts of the palace area are flooded.

At the end of the motorway, the first place you come to is the lovely beach of Káto Zákros. In high season there is a lot going on here during the day, but the evenings are so quiet that you feel as if time has stood still and the Minoans could reappear at any moment. Also, this is one of the few places on the island where you can camp anywhere you wish. You can also spend the night in either of the two *tavérnes* which, with a couple of other houses, make up the village of Káto Zákros.

The Palace of Káto Zákros is one of the most significant excavations on Crete and certainly the most important

to be discovered since World War II. It is comparable to the palaces of Knossós, Festós and Mália in type and layout, although smaller in size. The reason for the importance of this palace, which dates from about 1600 BC, is not so much that it is the only one of its kind in East Crete. What is really fascinating is the fact that after the great catastrophe of 1450 BC, it was neither plundered nor altered in any way. Thus an extraordinary number of artefacts, over 10,000 individual articles, were found here. This "posthumous preservation" is also important in solving the mystery of the nature of the catastrophe which destroyed civilisation on Crete in 1450 BC. Evidence from Káto Zákros indicates that life was not wiped out by ashfall, but by tidal waves following the volcanic eruption on Santorini.

The entrance is from the northeast through the city settlement to the palace itself. The four chutes to the left of the path were once ventilating shafts in a metal melting works. In the northeast corner of the courtyard, which is on a north-south axis, is a stone square, possibly once the wall around a holy tree, but more likely an altar. Due to the absence of evidence, the specific functions of some of the palace rooms cannot be clearly defined. But one was probably a workshop as various kinds of stone, presumably for artistic work, were stored there. It can be assumed that the large hall with six pillars at the northern side of the courtyard was a dining room, as kitchen utensils were found in the small room next to it.

The archives were so named because of the clay tablets found there inscribed with Linear-A figures. But much remains unclear, such as use of the two basins, one round and the other square, found behind the so-called "Megaron of the King." In Room 8 of the Archaeological Museum of Iráklion the consid-

Ierápetra beach in winter.

erable finds from Káto Zákros are displayed, including elephant teeth, bronze talents, stone rhyta, ceramics, weapons and tools.

Past the palace site and the recently planted banana plantation, you come to the **Valley of the Dead**, named thus because it was here that the Minoans buried their dead. They placed them in caves or niches in the rocks of the gorge. Now and then a stray goat bleats here today, but apart from that the valley is completely silent, just as it must have been in ancient times.

Ierápetra and Mírtos: The best way back to Agios Nikólaos from Sitía is to take the inland road through **Piskokéfalo**, **Lithíne** and then drive along the south coast to **Ierápetra**. There is much of interest to see on the way: goats clambering up in the trees, and strange buildings which seem to merge the old with the new – they are concrete structures which encase the old houses

The art of improvising.

which, apparently, no one wanted to knock down.

The road runs on past **Férma** and **Agía Fotía**. Both places have lovely beaches and beautiful bays, which are mainly shadeless.

Iérapetra is probably the largest city in the Lassíthi district, and the southernmost in Europe. Estimates of the population vary astonishingly between 7,000 and 11,000 inhabitants. Ierápetra is like Sitía in that although one may like the place, it is difficult to recommend it to others, as there's not much to go on and the beach is not a great one.

It is a prosperous town, due to the cultivation of tomatoes, cucumbers and beans, grown mainly in greenhouses. This part of the island is known as the vegetable garden not only of Crete but of the whole of Greece, for it grows produce for the whole country. The olive harvest is considerable, as is that of oranges and mandarins. The reason

for much of this prosperity is the artificial lake north of the city, which has solved the water problems of the past.

The history of Iérapetra goes back to Minoan times. Its location on the narrowest part of the island made it an ideal place from which to trade with Libya and the islands of the Aegean. It is possible that there was an overland route from sea to sea. It is quite likely that the town of Gourniá was built on this route. Like the town itself, its name went through a series of metamorphoses: first it was called Kyrva, then in succession Pytna, Kamiros, Ierapytna and, finally, Iérapetra.

There are not many attractions in the town, and those that are can be found in the old part of the city. The Venetians built a castle towards the end of the 13th century to protect the harbour, but even then its best days of trade with Africa, in Roman times, were already a thing of the past. The famous house in which Napoleon spent the night on his way to the Egyptian campaign lies east of the Agio Nikólaos Church.

There are only a few Roman artefacts on display in the little Archaeological Museum, because it has recently moved. On the western edge of the old city is a dilapidated Turkish mosque. The minaret is damaged and this unfortunately means that one cannot go in. An octagonal fountain stands in front, and there is an inviting *tavérna* nearby. In the shadows of the tamarisks on the square, the men spend their time playing cards and *Tavli*.

Iérapetra lies on a latitude of 35 degrees, further south than much of the Mediterranean coast of Algeria and Tunisia. The sun shines almost all year round, making it an ideal place for an autumn holiday.

Fourteen km west of Iérapetra is the little village of **Mírtos**. On the way there you can visit two excavation sites. The first is **Foúrni Korífi** at km 12. Just by the sign "Nea Mírtos" is a hill on the right. Here traces were found of a huge family made up of more than 100 members who lived and worked in a many-roomed communal building. There, they manufactured various products in an almost industrial way in 2400 BC. Then there is **Pírgos**, a hill just outside Mírtos, with a Minoan mansion of the 16th century BC.

The little fishing village of Mírtos has adapted well to foreigners. But despite the concrete promenade stretching along the sea front, the place has not lost its former charm.

Then you drive back towards Iérapetra, and turn off at **Grá Lygiá** to **Kalamáfka**. Just behind Kalamáfka is the one spot on the island where you can see the Sea of Crete and the Sea of Libya. The place is not marked, but easy to find. Just climb a small hill on the right, and the wonderful panorama opens out. Even the artificial lake of Iérapetra can clearly be seen.

A modest harvest.

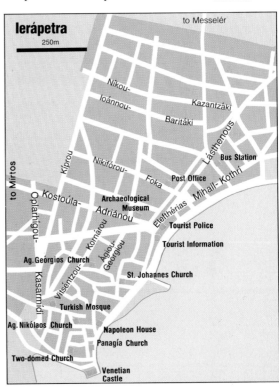

Ierápetra

250m

to Messelér

Níkou-
Ioánnou-
Kazantzáki
Baritáki
Kíprou
Nikifórou-
Làsthenous
Bus Station
to Mírtos
Oplárhigou-
Kostoúla-
Adriánou
Foka
Post Office
Mihaíl- Kothrí
Archaeological Museum
Eleftherías
Tourist Police
Tourist Information
Ag. Geórgios Church
Ágiou-
Georgíou
Komárou
Vitséntzou-
St. Johannes Church
Kasarmídi
Turkish Mosque
Ag. Nikólaos Church
Napoleon House
Panagía Church
Two-domed Church
Venetian Castle

OLIVES

And he stayed yet another seven days; and again he sent forth the dove out of the ark;

And the dove came to him in the evening; and lo in her mouth was an olive leaf plucked off; so Noah knew that the waters were abated from off the earth. – Genesis, 8 : 10–11.

Even in the Old Testament, the olive tree was a symbol of life, so it is clear that it has long been known and treasured. On Crete, evidence shows that olive trees have been there since Mycenaean times. Locals call it the blessed tree because everything from it is precious: the fruit, the leaves and the wood.

As one can make use of its components for food, soap and medicaments, and the tree seems so tailor made for man, it is small wonder that it has taken on such a religious significance. According to Homer, the gods rubbed themselves with perfumed olive oil.

The olive tree propagates easily. A new tree will grow from an olive stone or a piece of root. To "domesticate" the tree is more difficult. The wild tree must be three years old before it is transplanted to a convenient place for cultivation. The first few years then mean nothing but hard work for the farmer: grafting, transplanting, digging, fertilising, watering and protecting the tree from parasites. The trees, spaced apart at about 10 to 12 metres, react quickly to these measures, but it is still 15 to 18 years before the olive tree is profitable.

Different Mediterranean countries utilise varying methods of cultivation. In Spain three trunks are grown, whereas in Greece a single tall trunk is preferred. The tree flowers in April, and by May the first fruit is visible. It is a local belief that 20 May – Prophet **Respite from work in the olive grove.**

232

Elias's Day – is when the oil is formed.

Olive trees do need water, and in winter ditches are dug around the trees to catch every drop. In the hot Cretan summer, wells, ditches, pumps and hoses, expensive ways of watering, have to be used. Olive groves have to be watered at least once a week. On watering days, the trees have absolute priority. Houses set in the groves have no running water – however hot it is. Man and beast must give way. The harvest varies from year to year. A good harvest exhausts the tree, so that in the following year it will not yield much. In October, nets are spread out under the trees; from the beginning of November onwards, the ripe olives fall. Every three weeks the fruit is collected and sold in the market, or taken to the oil mill. Some types are harvested directly from the trees, using monstrous comb-like implements or compressed-air machines.

As in all Mediterranean countries, people in Crete cook with plenty of olive oil. The best grade oil is from the first pressing; middle grade oil from the second hot pressing is used for soap, creams and fuel. Oil presses used to be enormous vats in which a round stone was turned by hand. Nowadays, the olives are pulverised by machine, and the oil extracted from hydraulic presses.

There are no black and green olives; green olives are simply unripe black ones. However, there are different kinds of olives, and they are quite easy to tell apart. The large, almost round *Koroliá-Aetoniholiá* yield about 125 per kilo. The longer sort, *Ladoliá*, which are rich in oil, take about 1,000 to make up a kilo. There are some 500 other species of this dicotyledonous *Oleanceae* family, among them ash, jasmine, privet and in a few corners of southern Europe and East Asia, forsythia and elder. Of all the "souvenirs" available on Crete, pure olive oil in tins is one of the finest finds.

The harvest after the labour.

Spinalónga and Lassíthi

The village of **Eloúnda** lies about 12 km north of Agios Nikólaos in a long bay formed by the off-shore **Peninsula of Spinalónga**. This bay would be a perfect harbour had the depth in certain places not been merely three metres. This of course makes it quite impossible for large ships to berth. On the seaward side is the famous fortified island also known as **Spinalónga**.

Eloúnda spreads out over the hillside and the town is divided into various areas. **Shísma**, with its harbour installation is actually the centre. The square near the harbour is particularly popular, and there you can sit in one of the lovely cafés or restaurants and simply watch the world go by. In contrast to Agios Nikólaos, which always seems overcrowded, Eloúnda is much more pleasant and relaxing, as the tourists who come here spread out more.

In ancient times this was the site of **Oloús**, one of the most important and richest of all the cities on Crete. It is highly probable that Oloús was the port city of the Dorian city of **Dreros**. This was founded in the 6th and 7th centuries BC and lay in the hills west of Oloús. The strong tectonic activity in the 4th century AD led to most of Oloús sinking into the water.

A road, suitable for vehicles, leads across a narrow piece of land, split by a canal, to the Peninsula of Spinalónga. On the way you will pass salt production basins, set up by the Venetians and used until recently. After a bridge, you can see of three windmills, and an excavation site. The foundations of an early Christian basilica can be examined on foot, the main attraction being an exceptionally beautiful mosaic floor decorated with fish motifs.

If you drive on a little further, you will come to the spot where, on a calm day, you can see the remains of Oloú beneath the water. Not much is known about this ancient city. It was mentioned in certain documents of the 2nd century BC and in travel records by the Roman "travel writer" Pausanius in the 2nd century AD. According to him, Briómartis, a Cretan Artemis, was worshipped here.

In the city there were once apparently all kinds of treasures, including a statue of the goddess Briómartis fashioned by the artful Daedalus. Of course many present-day divers would love to explore the sunken city, but for obvious reasons, diving with compressed-air cylinders is forbidden on Crete. The island has simply lost too many artefacts in the past and now intends to preserve its ancient heritage. Bathing, on the other hand, is excellent in any of the lovely little bays of the peninsula.

Eloúnda is in one of the more sophisticated parts of the island. Of the eight luxury hotels currently on the island,

Left and below, toiling in the sun is a way of life for these Cretans.

235

three are to be found in Agios Nikólaos, three in Eloúnda and one more further south of Agios Nikólaos at **Kálo Horió**, making a total of seven in the Mirabello Bay. The Elounda Beach hotels host impressive art and other cultural events in season.

The Island of Spinalónga: This rocky island is about 400 metres long and no more than 200 metres in width. There are various points from which one can take a boat to reach it. The distance from Agios Nikólaos is greatest, making this the most expensive way. The usual way is from Eloúnda, but the shortest is from **Pláka**, a little fishing village north of Eloúnda.

The days when taking people across to the island afforded a good second income for the people of Pláka are over. Things are more organised these days but Pláka is still the best place to embark. If the captain is happy with the price, he will take a turn around the whole island, which gives the visitor another insight into the fascinating history of the place.

Just what the island looked like in antiquity is not clear. There was probably a fort named **Kalydon** which protected the harbour town of Oloú. As the island later served the Christians as a refuge from the Saracens, there must have been some fortifications, as flight to a barren island would not have served much purpose.

Its greatest importance was under the Venetians, who in 1579 transformed the place into one great fort. This strategic measure was intended to provide security for the military port near present-day Eloúnda. It seems that the Venetians, whose decline was beginning to become apparent to them, decided to change tactics. As they realised the approaching Turks would probably prove stronger in the long run, they concentrated on fortifying selected

"What's in store for me?"

bases. By doing this they hoped to maintain some degree of superiority at sea. In fact Spinalónga did in the end prove invincible. In 1669, when they conquered Iráklion, the Turks nominally took Crete, but they were forced to hoist the white flag before this little island and its 35 Venetian cannons. The same thing happened at Soúda and Imere Gramvoússa, which were equally well fortified. Forty-six years later, the problem resolved itself. Venice had become so weak that all three of its forts had to capitulate.

For a long time the Turks left Spinalónga unchanged. It was not until the 19th century when tension with the Christian population of Crete increased, that Turkish families began to settle on the island. By 1881 there were over 1,000 Turks living here. When Crete became "autonomous under the rule of the Sultan" in 1898, most of the Turks left. Those living on Spinalónga,

Spinalónga – the former leper colony.

who had become successful traders, were among the few who chose to stay. They were tolerated by the rest of the population until 1903. Then parliament under Prince George decided to turn Spinalónga into a leper colony. This was the final move, and it was not long before the Turks were gone for good.

Whether this was a political manoeuvre or whether there had indeed been previous plans for establishing a leper colony, is not clear. The fact that the sick were left isolated for four years would seem to argue for the first supposition. A strange thing did happen on the "Island of Dreams", however. In time a real feeling of community was born of the enforced communal living there. But the leper colony was finally closed in 1957 and little remains to be seen.

The Lassíthi Plateau: On the way to the **Lassíthi Plateau** you pass through **Neápolis**. The place was founded in the 16th century under the name of **Neo-**

horió (New Village). In 1870 the Turkish prefect Kostis Pasha moved the district administration and bishopric here. Then the name was no longer adequate and it was changed from New Village to New Town: Neápolis. But today, apart from the district court and the bishopric, all the important offices are in Agios Nikólaos, on the coast.

The road winds its way up through the villages of **Vrísses**, **Amigali**, **Zénia** and **Exo Potámi**, behind which there is a wood. At one point where the road widens, perched on the side of the cliff is a tiny *tavérna* and souvenir shop. Behind **Mésa Potámi** there is a pass at about 1,000 metres above sea level. After scaling the heights, the road gently leads down to the plain of Lassíthi, lying at about 850 metres.

This basin, which has an area of about 40 sq. km, is enclosed by the Díkti Mountains, and is one of the most fertile areas of Crete. Potatoes, fruits and cereals are the main crops grown here. There is no trace now of the windmills which pumped the underground water up here.

The Lassíthi Plateau was inhabited as early as Neolithic times. Remains of fortifications at entrance points to the plain indicate that it was a place of refuge for the Minoans. The tradition was retained by the Cretans as they fled here from the Venetians. This led to all the inhabitants of the plateau being banished in 1263. All forms of land cultivation were forbidden then. As nothing changed for almost 200 years, the plain fell into obscurity. It was not until a period of food shortages that the Venetians remembered the place at all. Then the land was recultivated and rented to the people.

After the victory of the Turks on Crete the place once again became a centre of resistance. The result was that in 1866 revenge was taken, and during the great uprising, the plain was com-

A shepherd of Oros Díkti ponders.

pletely laid to waste by 30,000 Turkish soldiers. Of the 21 villages encircling the plain, **Tzermiádo** and **Psichró** are particularly noteworthy. North of Tzermiádo, the capital of the plateau, is the **Cave of Trapéza**. Arthur Evans discovered it and Pendlebury explored it. The latter was able to ascertain that it was used as a burial place in Neolithic times. Over 100 burial niches and similar finds dating from all epochs were discovered in the cave.

Of greater importance, however, is the **Díkti Cave** near Psichró. The popularity of this cave is reflected in the crowds that make their way here every day. A large car park has been constructed behind the village to cope with the traffic. There are more mountain and tourist guides here than anywhere else on the island, so it's best to decide before you arrive, whether you would like a guide or not. The descent into the cave and some spots inside are a bit

Snow over Oros Díkti.

slippery, and engaging a knowledgeable guide might be a good idea. Their charges are quite reasonable.

The cave can be reached in about 15 minutes if you enter from the southwest. Its importance stems from the fact that it is generally regarded as the birthplace of Zeus. Those interested in mythology will note that Zeus is the late Greek form of a Minoan boy god. He was the son of the fertility goddess who was worshipped in the cave. There is a small rock chamber called "The Cradle of Zeus" and a large stalactite named "The Coat of Zeus." The many idols and votive offerings found in the cave are now displayed in the Archaeological Museum of Iráklion in Rooms 7 and 13.

Where else on the island could you find a more appropriate place to complete your trip? Here, at the end of your own 20th-century journey, you find yourself back at the beginning of Greek mythology.

TRAVEL TIPS

GETTING THERE

BY AIR

There are three ways to get to Crete by air:
1. Direct Flight to Crete.
2. Flight to Athens, change to connecting flight to Crete.
3. Flight to Athens, then by boat to Crete.

The first way is the quickest and the most comfortable. There is a choice between the standard airlines and charter flights. To compete with the charter flights, some major airlines, including Olympic Airways, have introduced special economy flights. But as conditions vary according to the season, it is advisable to check with the travel agent. Charter flights to Crete sell like hot cakes, so early booking is a must. These flights must be combined with another "tourist service", such as hotel accommodation, car hire, camping activity etc. The maximum period of stay is six weeks.

The second possibility is a little less convenient, for in Athens one not only has to change planes, but also airports. The advantage is that one can choose to land either in Iráklion or in Haniá, which is usually impossible on a charter flight. The ticket for the second flight is slightly cheaper if purchased in Athens, but more nerve-wrecking, so it is advisable to buy both tickets at the same time.

The third possibility is an ingenious combination of time-saving with "real" travelling. Crete is an island after all, and should thus be approached by sea.

Piraeus: At least two daily ferries ply to Iráklion (6 p.m. and 7 p.m.) and one to Haniá (7 p.m.). On certain days (enquire!) there is an early morning ferry to Iráklion and Haniá at 8 a.m. and at least once a week there is a ship to Agios Nikólaos and Sitía. The journey to Iráklion and Haniá takes 21 hours, to Agios Nikólaos and Sitía 14 hours.

BY SEA

The main ports with connections to Crete are in Italy: Venice, Ancona, Bari, Brindisi and Otranto . The further north the journey begins, the more expensive it is. The ships, all car ferries, leave at different times to various ports, some directly to Iráklion, some only to Patras, from Piraeus. Any established travel agent will have information on the various possible combinations.

BY ROAD

The overland route from northwestern Europe to Greece is a long one—some 1,900 miles from London to Athens. It is an arduous and impractical travel option if you're just trying to get to Athens for a brief vacation, but it can be an interesting trip if you make the journey a part of your vacation. By car there is an E route that runs through the interior of Yugoslavia, entering Greece just above Thessaloniki. There are also inexpensive bus services, along the lines of the famous Magic Bus, which connect Athens and Thessaloniki with many European cities—a three and a half day trip from London. The various trains that you can take from northwest Europe will take about as long as the bus, will cost considerably more, but may get you to Greece feeling more intact. Hitching to Greece is also a possibility, though hitching through Yugoslavia is reported to be difficult.

If you're travelling to Greece from Asia you'll pass through Istanbul and cross into Greece at the Evros River. The recommended route is by car or bus. The road is good and the journey from Istanbul to Thessaloniki takes approximately 15 hours; various bus companies run the route. The train has the mythic appeal of running the route of the old Orient Express, but unless you're a great train fan the travel may be prohibitive; some 25 hours from Thessaloniki to Istanbul. This trip crosses the fascinating region of Thrace; a fine adventure if you have the time and the spirit for it.

TRAVEL ESSENTIALS

VISAS & PASSPORTS

No visa is necessary for citizens of Western Europe, the U.S., Canada, Australia and New Zealand, for entry into Crete, and for a stay of up to three months. The addresses below will help you to extend your stay over three months:

Piraeus: Aliens Department, 37 Iroon Polytechniou Street, 18510 Piraeus, Tel: 41 22 501, 41 28 607. Opening hours 8 a.m. to 2.30 p.m.

Athens: Aliens Department, 173 Alexandras Avenue, 11522 Athens, Tel: 64 68 103, 77 05 711, Ext. 379.

In order to avoid difficulties on arrival, your passport should not contain an entry stamp to the Turkish part of Cyprus.

MONEY MATTERS

The Greek unit of money is the Drachma, plural Drachmas, abbreviation Drs, comprising 100 Lepta. A foreigner is entitled to bring in 25,000 Drs. There is no limit to the amount of foreign currency a visitor may bring in, nor to the amount of cheques (Euro, Travellers, etc.) provided they are made out in the name of the traveller.

Sums exceeding $1,000 per person, must be declared on arrival so that unused sums may be taken out of the country again. The exchange rate is far more favourable inside Greece than elsewhere, thus it is advisable only to exchange enough to start off with. Money can be changed in banks and post offices in Greece. Eurocheques are to be made out in Drachmas and not in any other currency.

Credit cards are accepted in most tourist centres. It is possible to obtain telegraphic credit at Cretan post offices.

At the time of going to press, the exchange rate was:

Sterling Pound: 298 Drs.
U.S. Dollar: 154 Drs.
Australian Dollar: 118 Drs.
Japanese Yen: 1.15 Drs.
German Mark: 103 Drs.

HEALTH

For tourists from European countries there are no special precautions necessary. If you arrive from a country stricken by an epidemic, you will need to show proof of the necessary inoculations.

There are two things to watch out for on Crete: the sun and the olive oil. Even in the summer there is usually a pleasant breeze which veils the heat of the sun, and the first few days of a vacation can easily be ruined by sunburn. It is a good idea to use creams or oils with a high shield factor, at least at the beginning of a visit. Stomach upsets due to too much olive oil are not rare. However, this inconvenience can be cleared up within a few days, and avoided if the visitor accustoms himself/herself to Cretan-style food before arrival. If the stomach upset is accompanied by a high fever and a lot of pain, it could be salmonella poisoning, and a doctor's opinion should be sought immediately. Of course it is unwise to drink ice cold beverages in the heat. Fruits and vegetables should be washed before being eaten.

Definitely recommended is Cretan water, whether from the tap or at the roadside. It is not merely potable but also refreshingly cool.

Do not drink from any place with stagnant water, e.g. ponds, pools, lakes, cisterns etc.

Mosquito bites are a nuisance but not dangerous, as are scorpion stings, which are rare. If there is an allergy to a wasp or hornet sting, a doctor must be consulted.

Cretan chemists are aware of the problems experienced by tourists and are well equipped to deal with them. As medicines are relatively cheap on Crete, it is not worth bringing your own along.

WHAT TO WEAR

What you bring along to wear is dependent on the time of the holiday and your plans. In the summer, light clothing is fine. But as it gets quite cool in the evenings, a jacket or jumper is also useful. If you are invited to meet locals, casual clothes are adequate.

Occasions requiring formal evening wear do not (as yet) take place on Crete, and suits and ties are seldom seen.

ANIMALS QUARANTINE

Dogs and cats require an international inoculation certificate or an official Certificate of Health in English or French. The document must declare that the inoculation was undertaken no longer than six months from the date of arrival for cats, and 12 for dogs. The certificate must be issued not more than 12 months in the case of dogs and six months in the case of cats and at least 15 days prior to arrival.

CUSTOMS

Visitors of at least 18 years of age, from EEC countries are entitled to bring in duty free:
–   300 cigarettes or 75 cigars or 150 cigarillos or 400 grams of tobacco
–   1.5 litres of alcoholic drink (22 percent) or 4 litres of wine, sparkling wine or similar beverages under 22 percent
–   75 grams of perfume and 3/8 litres Eau de Cologne
–   1 kg coffee or 375 grams coffee extract
–   200 grams tea or 75 grams tea extract
–   gifts to the value of 55,500 Drs or one gift to the value of 44,500 Drs.
For visitors from other countries the following is applicable:
–   200 cigarettes/50 cigars/100 cigarillos/250 grams tobacco
–   1 litre high percentage alcohol or 2 litres low percentage alcohol
–   50 grams perfume and ¼ litres Eau de Cologne
–   500 grams coffee or 200 grams coffee extract
–   100 grams tea or 40 grams tea extract
–   gifts of value 7,000 Drs.
Import of any plants, radios or electronic devices is forbidden.
Personal belongings are duty free. If these are particularly valuable and there is the possibility that they may be sold, the items must be listed in the passport. Examples of such items are surfboards, bicycles, video cameras etc.
On leaving the country, provisions for the journey to the value of $50 may be taken.

Souvenirs below a value of $150 are also duty-free. Antiques, including pieces of ceramics, are not to be taken out of the country.

RESERVATIONS

Reservations should be made before travel in the high season, which falls between June and September and during easter. It is advisable to make reservations for the main tourist areas at any time of the year.

GETTING ACQUAINTED

GOVERNMENT & ECONOMY

Crete is one of 10 administrative districts. Greece has a centralised, non-federal political structure, and the districts are ruled from Athens. Crete sends official representatives to parliament in Athens; branches in the administrative districts represent the various ministeries.

The four administrative districts referred to in the introduction to this book, are again divided into 20 rural districts, each with its own capital. These rural districts are made up of 572 communities, most comprising several villages – a total of 14,590 villages, and 11 larger towns.

Economy: Distribution of agricultural acreage on Crete according to official Greek statistics, in Stremmas.
(1 Stremma = ¼ hectare).

Cultivated Land	3,228,586
Pasture	4,370,700
Woods	396,900
Water	84,500
Roads, built up and unbuilt up land	349,500
Total	8,430,186

The cultivated land is further divided into:

Olives	1,348,201
Vineyards	453,133
Garden Vegetables	87,809
Citrus Fruits	51,999

Other cultivation   119,631
                          2,096,773

Expressed as a percentage of the total cultivated land:

Olives	42.87 percent
Vineyards	14.03 percent
Garden Vegetables	2.71 percent
Citrus Fruits	1.61 percent
Others	3.70 percent

TIME ZONE

Greece is on East European time, one hour ahead of Middle European Time. Like the rest of the Common Market, the clock is advanced one hour during summer to give extended daylight hours.

CLIMATE

The north coast of Crete has a typical Mediterranean climate. The following statistics apply to Iráklion, those for Haniá will be slightly lower. In the summer, which lasts for seven months here, the average temperature rises from 17° in April to as high as 26° in July and August. In November it falls to 17° and can go down to 12.3° in January.

Daytime temperatures in summer are between 26° and 32°. As the humidity is about 60 percent, the heat is quite tolerable, particularly as the *meltémia* winds often blow. These can however become strong and cause greater problems than the heat.

On the south coast the weather is subtropical to desert type climate. The average temperature in January in Ierápetra is 13°, yet the annual average is over 20°! Temperatures as high as 40° are not rare on the south coast, e.g in Arvi. But as the humidity is only about 30 percent, even this heat is bearable. The difference in temperature between day and night can be as much as 20°. Cooling breezes are rare in summer. A strong sirocco sometimes blows at the end of the rainy season. If it turns out to be part of an African sandstorm, it is called a *Chamsín*.

The climate up in the mountains is much rougher. In the summer, the temperatures rise to the Mediterranean heights of the north coast, but the summer only lasts four months. The rains set in as early as October, and last until May. The rainfall of 1,000 mm is double that of the north coast.

While frost is unknown on the plains and lower levels, the mountains are not immune. Above the snow level of 600 metres, the mountains remain white until April.

CULTURE & CUSTOM

Nude bathing is forbidden, punishable by fines or arrest. If you are determined to bathe nude, then be sure it is far from where locals might be offended. There is no shortage of smaller, isolated bays and beaches. If you are fortunate enough to experience *philoxenia*, the traditional hospitality of the Cretans, and assuming you can communicate, you will probably be amazed at just how interested the people are in every bit of detail of your life.

Shorts and short skirts are not acceptable attire for visiting churches and monasteries. Although the priests and monks do not actually voice their objections, one look can speak volumes.

TIPPING

Tip as you normally would for services. In restaurants, tavérnes, bars etc., a tip of 10 to 15 percent is customary.

The landlord gets no tip. Guests who have spent some time in the same hotel, and who have been served by the same waitress or chamber maid should leave something to show their appreciation at the end of their stay. One's own satisfaction is the best gauge of how much to give.

WEIGHTS & MEASURES

Weights and measures are generally standard, as in the rest of Europe. Areas are still measured in Stremmas, which can be easily converted, as 4 Stremmas=1 Hectare.

Liquids such as oil, wine etc., are measured not in litres but in kilograms (0.5 litres wine: *missó kiló krassí*).

ELECTRICITY

Hotels, pensions etc. have 220-Volt outlets. Ships occasionally have the old 110-Volt connections. An adaptor, available in Haniá or Iráklion, can be very useful. Torches are necessary, not just for visiting caves; in some regions there are frequent power failures. In Paléohora it happens, on average, once a night. Usually the power returns after a few minutes. Candles can be used during longer cuts.

BUSINESS HOURS

Shops are open during summer weekdays from 8 a.m. to 1.30 p.m. and then from 5 p.m. to 8 p.m. Photo shops in larger towns are usually open until 11 p.m. Many kiosks and souvenir shops are open continuously from 8 a.m. to 9 p.m., including Sundays. Exchange bureaux operate at all hours, and their rates are only slightly less favourable than those of the banks.

HOLIDAYS

On the following days, shops and offices remain closed:

1 January (New Year)
6 January (Epiphany)
25 March (The Annunciation, national holiday in memory of the uprising against the Turks of 1821)
Good Friday partially
Easter Saturday, offices are closed
Easter Sunday and Monday
1 May
15 August (Assumption of the Virgin Mary)
28 October (National Day,"*Ohi* Day", that is the refusal of Mussolini's ultimatum)
25-26 December (Christmas)

DIARY OF EVENTS

40 days before Easter: Shrove Monday
1st Sunday after Easter: Agios Thomas at the Monastery of Vrondíssi
50 days after Easter: Agios Pnevmatos
23 April: Agios Georgios
8 May: Agios Ioánnis at Préveli Monastery
20-27 May: Commemoration of Cretan resistance during World War II in Haniá
21 May: Agios Konstantínos in Pírgos
25 May: commemoration of the revolution of 1821 at Hóra Sfakíon
24 June: Ioánnis Prodrómos, John the Baptist, and Midsummer Festival
17 July: Agía Marína in Voní
20 July: Profítís Elías, especially on the Akrotíri Peninsula
26 July: Agía Paraskévi at the Skotinó Cave
6 August: Transfiguration of Christ on Mount

Joúchtas near Arhánes
25 August: Agios Títos
29 August: Beheading of John the Baptist on Rodopoú Peninsula
7 October: John the Hermit in the Monastery of Gouvernéto, Akrotíri
7-9 November: Commemoration in Arkádi Monastery
11 November: Agios Mínas in Iráklion
4 December: Agía Varvára in Agía Varvára

COMMUNICATIONS

MEDIA

Newspapers/Magazines: The more a place is geared up for tourists, the larger the selection of foreign papers and magazines. In all the big towns, daily newspapers are available in German, French, English and Dutch, although they are usually two or three days old. There is a wide range of magazines on sale. Some smaller but more central places often have a greater selection than, say, Haniá. A local "What's On" guide is avantres.

Radio: There are two state radio stations, ERT1 and ERT 2, which are divided into different "programmes". The First Programme (728 KHz) broadcasts news in English, French, German and Arabic every morning of the week. The BBC World Service offers news on the hour (plus other interesting programmes and features). The U.S. Armed Forces Radio (AFRS) operates 24 hours a day on 1594 KHz and 14844 KHz with news on the hour.

Television: Every day, after the Greek 6 p.m. news, there is a news broadcast in English.

POSTAL SERVICES

The bright yellow postboxes are sometimes hard to find, hidden among the flowers on tavérne or shop walls. Sellers of postcards sometimes have a licence to sell stamps, but often they only have 60/70 Drs stamps. Postage for a postcard costs only 40 Drs (to a European destination), and an additional 10 Drs is charged for each stamp. It is better to go to the *Tachidromío* or post office. It is usually open by 8 in the morning, and closed in the afternoon, so it is advisable to deal with mail in the mornings. Charges do sometimes vary, so it is a good idea to enquire first. Parcels must be wrapped in the post office, which means bringing string, paper etc. along with you. Letters can be sent *poste restante*, and you'll need your passport to collect them.

TELEPHONE & TELEX

The OTE (Organisationi Telefoniko Elleniko) is the place to phone or send telegrams or telexes. There is one in almost every major town. The opening times vary from place to place, but are usually from 8.30 a.m. to 6 p.m., sometimes right until 10 or 11 at night. Some kiosks and tavérnes also have telephones, although their charges are higher. Some hotels have telephone booths, and sometimes it is possible to telephone from your room. This, however, involves the porter connecting the line to your room, which can take a while. The dialling code from Greece to the UK is 0044, and from Greece to the USA or Canada, 001.

EMERGENCIES

SECURITY & CRIME

Although the days of leaving hotel room doors unlocked are over, there is no need to worry. There is very little crime on Crete, and what there is usually concerns personal property – campers and beach dwellers being robbed. If papers and official identification documents are missing, the consulate must be informed.

LOST & FOUND

There is no lost property office on Crete. The only way to find lost property is to go back to the place where the object was lost. Articles such as purses, cameras and pieces of luggage can often be recovered, if found by locals.

HEALTH SERVICES

There are many good doctors on the island who ensure excellent medical service. There are hospitals in the main cities:

Haniá: State Hospital, Dragoúmi 6-8, Tel: 27 231/5; First Aid, Tel:166

Iráklion: Venizélos Hospital near Knossós, Tel: 23 75 02; First Aid, Tel:166

Lassíthi: Agios Nikólaos, Lassíthithiou 2, Tel: 22 369

Ierápetra: Tel: 22 252

Sitía: Sifi 28, Tel: 22 231

Réthimnon: Trantallidou, Tel: 27 491

GETTING AROUND

MAPS

There are many different maps on sale. For general orientation, the map available at most kiosks for about 300 Drs is adequate. More detailed maps for walking are unfortunately not available. The best map available for hikers is the Nelles Map, (scale 1:200,000) which unfortunately is not on sale on the island.

FROM THE AIRPORT

The main airports are near Iráklion (5 km to the east) and Haniá (Stérnes on the Akrotíri Peninsula, 15 km to the east). The bus service only connects to Olympic Airways flights. There are taxis for passengers arriving on other airlines.

WATER TRANSPORT

Most of the boat routes have been superseded by roads nowadays. But in summer there are regular services between Agiá Rouméli, Loutró and Hóra Sfakíon. Boats also ply between the island of Gávdos and Paléohora and Agiá Rouméli, but are dependent on the weather. Some travel agents can arrange trips to the outlying islands around Crete.

DOMESTIC TRAVEL

The public bus system on Crete is reliable and economical. There are some adventurous drives, e.g from Haniá to Hóra Sfakíon. The buses serve not only the big cities, but also small hidden corners of the island. Each district has its own bus system. There are few connections across these districts. Frequency of service depends on demand, which can make journeys somewhat more complicated. As timetables change fre-

quently, it is a good idea to ask.

In Iráklion, Haniá and Réthimnon there are several bus stations, shown as numbers on the city maps. The red bus stations serve long distance travellers.

TAXIS

Taxis are cheap on Crete, but the price must be agreed upon with the driver before a long journey, since the meter will not be flagged on then. A consideration for the driver will also be whether he can expect a return fare from your destination. If you want to go from Haniá to Paléohora at night, you will have to pay the full fare of 4,500 Drs. This is 10 times the bus fare, but still it is not as expensive as the taxi fare in Europe. Although they drive like lunatics at times, the cabbies are friendly and like to chat with their passengers. In the bigger cities, however, some drivers have taken to retaining their own tips when returning the change. You'll need all your diplomatic talents in this situation.

PRIVATE CARS

Some cars have trouble adapting to Cretan petrol; the engine sounds strange, mileage is reduced etc. Tourists can get assistance from ELPA, the Automobile and Touring Club of Greece. Large yellow combi vans can be seen on the roads, with A.T.C.C. (ELPA) on them; they will assist in times of need. Small repairs can be undertaken immediately. You can find ELPA in:

Iráklion: Knossós Ave. & G. Papandreou St., tel: 081/28 94 40.

Haniá: 1 Apokoronou & Skoula St., tel: 0821/26 059.

CAR HIRE

The bigger the town, the greater the choice of car hire agencies. In Iráklion on 25th August St. is a street full of car hire agencies. In Haniá you find them near the Venetian Harbour.

For mopeds up to 50 cc there is no need for a driving licence. A licence is necessary for all other vehicles. For motor bikes and scooters over 250 cc a 1st class licence is required. Any vehicles hired should be checked out before you set off, as very few of them are in good condition.

TRAFFIC REGULATIONS

Traffic control and signals are basically the same as on the rest of the continent. But on Crete the first rule is, take care! The locals are not noted for their caution, and a red light is viewed more as a suggestion than as a rule.

Filling stations have switched from the English/American gallon measurements to litres, but tyre pressure is still measured in pounds/square inch.

ON FOOT

This is definitely the best way to get to know the real Crete, and the more remote parts of the island. But the walker should not forget that Crete is a mountainous place and there are some very steep areas. One should recognise one's own limitations; higher regions, where a guide may be needed, should not be attempted alone. Information can be obtained from the Greek Mountaineering Club: Iráklion – 74 Dikeonissis; Haniá – 3 Michelidaki.

HITCHHIKING

Hitching a ride is no easy matter on Crete. The locals have become wary after bad experiences, and Europeans are not keen on picking people up. It is easier to take the bus. Girls who hitchhike should dress conservatively, as on Crete scanty clothing indicates a certain lack of moral standards. There have been many misunderstandings and quarrels as a result of skimpy summer dressing.

WHERE TO STAY

HOTELS

To cope with the massive influx of tourists, new hotels have sprung up like mushrooms. It is advisable to book, even in pre and post high season. Only those with patience and plenty of flexibility should travel on spec.

The hotels are classified in categories from Luxury, A, B, C, D to E. Luxury hotels usually have their own beach, tennis courts, disco, air-conditioners etc.– in fact, total comfort. Hotels in categories A and B too are also of a very high standard. Hotels in category C, D and E, offer simpler accommodation. Category C, although with smaller rooms, still offers a shower or bath. Categories D and E are relatively lacking in comfort, provide shared baths etc. The classification indicates a minimum rate, so that a category A room will always cost more than a category B. Every hotel room must have a list showing the correct official rate.

In addition to the room rate there is a 15 percent service charge, 8 percent value-added tax, 4.4 percent local tax and 1.2 percent stamp duty. The price of a room can increase by as much as 10 percent, if the stay is only for one or two days. An extra bed is usually charged at 20 percent of the room rate. In the pre and post high season, reductions of up to 40 percent are possible. Visitors travelling alone should take note that almost 90 percent of all rooms are doubles. During the pre and post high season period it is possible that only one bed will be charged, but this is usually not the case in the high season, which makes the rooms more expensive.

In the list of hotels below, reference points are given for lesser known places. The numbers in brackets after the hotel names indicate the number of beds.

• **72200 Agía Fotia** (7 km east of Ierápetra), Area Code 0843

Category B:
Eva-Mare (130), tel: 61225
Mare Sol (40), tel: 28950

• 76056 Agía Galíni, Area Code 0832
Category C:
Acropolis (34), tel: 91234, 91264
Galini Mare (48), tel: 91358
Phaestos (16), tel: 91223
Category D:
Areti (63), tel: 91240, 91283
Chariclia (23), tel: 91257
Minos (23), tel: 91218
Pasiphai (19), tel: 91392

• Agía Marina (8 km east of Haniá), Area
Code 0821
Category B:
Santa Marina (120), tel: 68350, 68469,
68570, telex 291107
Category C:
Amalthia (78), tel: 68542, 68592
Ta Thodorou (14), tel: 68342, 68510

• Algía Pelagia (25 km west of Iráklion),
Area Code 081
Category A:
Capsis Beach (1090), tel: 811212, 811234,
811256
Peninsula, Psaronoura (301), tel:
289404–7
Category B:
Panorama (97), tel: 289401-3

• 72100 Agios Nikólaos, Area Code 0841
Luxury Category:
Minos Beach, Hotels and Bungalows (23)
Amoundi-Beach, tel: 22345-9, telex: 262214
Mirabello Village (251), on the beach, tel:
28401-5, 28806-10, telex: 262166
Category A:
Hermes (379), on the beach, tel: 28253-6,
telex: 262430

Category B:
Ariadni Beach (142), Gargadoros, tel:
22741-3, telex: 262196
Coral (323), Akti Koundourou, tel:
28363-6
Ormos (84), on the beach, tel: 24094,
28144
Category C:
Acropole (15), 45, Demokratias St., tel:
22998
Argyro (19), 1, Solonos St., tel: 28707

Creta (50), Kitroplatia, tel: 22518, 28893
Helena (77), 6, Minoos St., tel: 28189
Panorama (50), 2, Sarolidi St., tel: 28890

• 73008 Almirida (20 km east of Haniá),
Area Code 081
Category B:
Almirida Bay Hotel (93), tel: 31751, 31650

• 71110 Amnissos (7 km east of Iráklion),
Area Code 081
Category A:
Minoa Palace Holiday Resort (230), Post:
P.O. Box 1368, tel: 227802, 27824, 227846-
8, telex 262302
Category B:
Karteros (105), Post: P.O. Box 1150, tel:
228802, 228846

• 71500 Amoudara (4 km west of Iráklion),
Area Code 081
Category A:
Agapi Beach (391), tel: 250502, 250524,
250546, 250568, telex: 262266
Apollonia (593), tel: 821602
Category B:
Marilena (116), Post: P.O. Box 1450, tel:
254312
Category C:
Minoas (67), tel: 821557
Tsagaraki (83), tel: 251768

• 70100 Arhánes, Area Code 081
Category B:
Dias (55), tel: 751810, 751905

• 70004 Arvi (30 km west of Ierápetra)
Category C:
Ariadne (22), tel: 31200
San Giorgio, tel: 22190

• 73100 Daratso
(2 km west of Haniá), Area Code 0821
Category B:
Althea Village, Bungalows (78), tel:
31320, 31261

• 72053 Eloúnda, Area Code 0841
Luxury Category:
Astir Palace (551), on the beach, tel: 41580-
3, telex: 262215
Eloúnda Mare (150), tel: 41512, 41102/3,
telex: 262533
Category A:
Eloúnda Marmin (204), tel: 41535,

41513,41557, telex: 262438
Category B:
Driros Beach (32), tel: 41283
Category C:
Aristea (70), tel: 41301-3
Selena Village (64), tel: 41525

• **72200 Ferma** (12 km east of Ierápetra),
Area Code 0842
Category A:
Perma Beach, Hotel and Bungalows, (314),
tel: 61341, 28418, telex: 262252
Athen: 4, Veranzerou St., tel: 3617073
Petra Mare (422), tel: 23341-9
Category B:
Corina Village (69), tel: 61263, telex:
262508
Porto Belissario (85), tel: 61358-60, telex:
262538

• **Festós**, Area Code 0892
Category D:
Xenia (11), tel: 22836

• **73100 Galatas** (5 km southwest of Haniá)
Category A:
Panorama (309), tel: 54200-2, 31700-4,
telex: 291140
Category C:
Delfini (44), tel: 48467

• **73007 Georgioúpolis**, Area Code 0825
Category B:
Happy Days (160), tel: 61220, 61201-3,
telex: 291292
Category C:
Gorgona (70), tel: 22378, 61351
Phereniki (70), tel: 61297

• **71500 Gournes**, Area Code 081
Category B:
Royal (12), tel: 761231-5
• **Gouves**, Area Code 0897
Category A:
Grecotel Creta Sun, Hotel & Bungalows
(660), Post: P.O. Box 106, tel: 41103, telex:
262171
Aphrodite (446), tel: 41271-5, telex:
262321
Category C:
Calypso (68), tel: 41390
Mons Repos (90), tel: 41280-5
Sonia (35), tel: 41368

• **73100 Haniá**, Area Code 0821
Category A:
Kydon (195), Agoras Square, tel: 26190-
4, telex: 291146
Category B:
Arkadi (109), 1866 Square, tel: 28724,
telex: 291260
Doma (56), 124, El. Venizelou St., tel:
21772/3
Samaria (110), 1866 Square, tel: 5155,
telex: 291265
Category C:
Aptera Beach (92), 5, Voloudaki St., tel:
22636, 23973
Diktynna (66), 1, Betollo St., tel: 21101-3
Plaza (17), 1, Tobazi St., tel: 22540
Category D:
Ermis (16), 23, Hatzim, Giannari, tel:
22317
Nea Ionia (22), 3, Veronits Pasha, tel:
22706

• **71201 Iráklion**, Area Code 081
Category A:
Astoria Capsis (273), Eleftherías Square,
tel: 229002, telex: 262152
Galaxi (264), 67, Demokratias Ave., tel:
238812, 232157, telex: 262301
Xenia (156), 2, Sof. Venizelou St., tel:
284000-3
Category B:
Atrion (150), 9, K. Paléoulogou St., tel:
229225, 242830, telex: 262639,
Petra (59), 55, Dikeossinis St., tel: 229912
Category C:
Aretoussa (47), 15, Anthemiou St., tel:
285513
Athinaikon (77), 89, Eth. Antistasseos St.,
tel: 229312
Gortis (20), 4, Akrotiriou St., tel: 280613
Marin (87), 10, Beaufort St., tel: 220737,
226411
Selena (52), 7, Androgreo St., tel: 226377
Category D:
Arcadi (29), 235, Kalokerinou St., tel:
282077
Festos (41), 8, Tsakini St., tel: 283027
Minos (63), 24, Archiepisk. Makariou St.,
tel: 282256
Venetia (21), 189, Kalokerinou St., tel:
283239

• **72200 Ierápetra**, Area Code 0842
Category A:
Petra-Mare (422), on the beach, tel:

233419, telex: 262193
Category B:
Blue Sky (45), Peristera, tel: 28264, 25060/1, Telex: 262596
Category C:
Atlantis (134), Agios Andreas, tel: 28555
El Greco (19), 44, M Kothri St., tel: 284712
Lygia (29), Kyrba, tel: 28881/2

• **73100 Kalathas, Haniá/Akrotíri**, Area Code 0821
Category C:
Fereniki (18), tel: 28042
Tzanakaki Beach (68), tel: 64363-5
Zorbas (12), Stavros, tel: 22161

•**Kalo Horio** (12 km east of Agios Nikólaos), Area Code 0841
Luxury Category:
Istron Bay (197), tel: 61303
Category C:
Elpida (86), tel: 61403
Golden Bay (94), tel: 61202

• **71500 Karteros**, Area Code 081
Category B:
Amnissos (108), tel: 281332-5

•**Káto Stalos** (6 km west of Haniá), Area Code 0821
Category C:
Galaxy (20), tel: 21687
Grygoyiali (22), tel: 68239
Yamoukakis (20), tel: 68244

•**73400 Kastélli/Kissamos**, Area Code 0822
Category B:
Helena Beach (80), tel: 23300-5
Category C:
Castro Castel (21), tel: 22140
Kissamos (29), tel: 22086, 22861
Vai (45), Trahilas, tel: 22790

• **71500 Kokkini Hani** (12 km east of Iráklion), Area Code 081
Category A:
Arina Sand Hotel & Bungalows, tel: 761293, 761113, 761350, 761354, 761135, telex 262114
Knossós Beach, tel: 761000, 761310, telex 262206
Themis Beach, Pyrgos, tel: 761374, 761168, telex: 262359
Category C:

Akti, tel: 761260
Danae, tel: 761375, 761051

• **73007 Kournás**, Area Code 0825
Category C:
Happy Days Beach (69), tel: 22000, 61220
Manos Beach (29), tel: 61221
Category D:
Assimenia Ammoudia (15), tel: 61223

• **70014 Limin Hersonissou**, Area Code 0897
Luxury Category:
Creta Maris (1014), on the beach, tel: 22115, telex: 262233, telefax: 22130
Category A:
Belvedere (547), tel: 22371
Cretan Village (594), on the beach, tel: 229966/7, telex: 262583, telefax: 22295
Robinson Club Lyttos Beach (601), tel: 22575-8, 22676, telex: 262175
Category B:
Chrissi Amoudia (150), tel: 22971-3
Hersonissos (290), tel: 22501, 22588/9, telex: 262503
Lena-Mary (7), tel: 22907, 22984
Sergios (194), El. Venizelou Avenue, tel: 22583-5, telex: 262501
Category C:
Adamakis (32), tel: 22447
Armava (76), Gourgouthia, tel: 22544
Ilios (92), 1, El. Venizelou St., tel: 22500
Nefeli (53), tel: 22391
Regina (22), tel: 22007

• **Linoperamata** (5 km west of Iráklion), Area Code 081
Category A:
Apollonia (585), tel: 821602
Zeus Beach (717), tel: 821568

• **Makrigialos** (20 km east of Ierápetra), Area Code 0843
Category A:
Sunwing Crete (296), tel: 51621

• **73100 Máleme**, Area Code 0821
Category A:
Crete Chandris Hotel (767), tel: 62221-4, telex: 291100

• **70007 Mália**, Area Code 0897
Category A:
Ikaros Village (362), Mallia Peliados, tel: 31267-9, Telex: 262191, telefax: 31341

Kernos Beach (540), tel: 31421-5, telex 262255

Sirens Beach (479), tel: 31321-5, telex: 262194

Category B:
Alcionides (56), tel: 31558, 31526
Calypso (80), tel: 31012, telex: 262516
Malia-Beach (362), tel: 31301-3
Category C:
Amvrossia (30), tel: 31378
Efi (23), tel: 31640
Malia Holiday (157), tel: 31206

• **70200 Mátala**, Area Code 0892
Category C:
Bamboo Sand (30), tel: 42370
Matala Bay (104), tel: 22100
Zafiria (36), tel: 42366

• **Mohlos** (49 km east of Agios Nikólaos), Area Code 0843
Category B:
Aldiana Club (262), tel: 94211

• **73005 Omalos**, Area Code 0821
Category B:
Xenia (7), tel: 93237

• **73001 Paleóhora**, Area Code 0823
Category D:
Livykon (36), tel: 41250

• **Palékastro** (18 km east of Sitía), Area Code 0843
Category C:
Marina Village (54), Tel: 61284/5

• **Pánormos** (22 km east of Réthimnon), Area Code 0834
Category B:
Lavris (56), tel: 51226
Category C:
Panormos Beach (61), tel: 51321

• **73100 Plataniás** (9 km west of Haniá), Area Code 0821
Category B:
Filoxenia (18), tel: 48502
Villa Platanias (34), tel: 68339

• **74060 Plakiás**, Area Code 0832
Category A:
Kalypso Cretan Village (204), tel: 31210, 31296/7 (Réthimnon: P.O. Box 16, tel: 23392, telex: 291190)

Category B:
Alianthos Beach (124), tel: 31227, telex: 291103
Category C:
Lamon Hotel (46), tel: 31205
Livikon (27), tel: 31216
Sofia Beach Hotel (48), tel: 31251/2

• **74100 Réthimnon**, Area Code 0831
Category A:
Creta Star (625), 10 km east of Réthimnon, tel: 0834/93300, 93233, telex: 291186
Réthymo Bay (150), Missiria, tel: 27512/3, 21221
Theatemis Palace (335), tel: 27532, 23785, telex: 291322
Category B:
Adele Beach Bungalows (120), tel: 71081, 71069, telex: 291287
Brascos (158), 1, Daskalakis St., tel: 23721-3, telex: 291198
Nefeli Hotel (218), Platanes, tel: 21321, telex: 291288
Xenia (50), tel: 29111/2
Category C:
Astali (63), 172, Koundouriotou Avenue, tel: 24721-3
Golden Sun (64), tel: 71284
Katerin Beach, Adele, tel: 71270
Minos (145), Perivolia, tel: 28439, 29233, 24173
Valari (55), 78, Kountouriotou St., tel: 29368, 22236

• **72300 Sitía**, Area Code 0843
Category A:
Kappa Club Sitía/Satian Beach (310), on the beach, tel: 28821-4, 28827, telex: 262102 (Athen: 3, Metropolos St., tel: 3241828/9, telex: 218703)
Sunwing (600), Makrygiallos, P.O. Box 38, tel: 51621-5, telex: 262554, telefax: 51626
Category B:
Aldiana Club (270), Mochlos, on the beach, tel: 942122, telex: 262530
Maresol Bungalows (52), Agia Fotia, 5 km east, on the beach, tel: 28950, 28933, telex: 222922
Category C:
Alicc (69), 34, Papanastasiou St., tel: 28450, 28441
Castello (31), 21, Rousselaki St., tel: 23763
Helena (42), tel: 22681
Vaí (84), tel: 22528, 22288

• **70014 Stalis**, Area Code 0897
Category A:
Anthoussa Beach (314), tel: 31380-2
Category B:
Blue Sea (371), on the beach, tel: 31371,31373, telex: 262134
Palm Beach (48), tel: 31375
Zephyros Beach (145), tel: 31566, 31693, telex: 262139
Category C:
Heliotrope (140), tel: 31515-7

• **73100 Stalos** (5 km west of Haniá), Area Code 0821
Category C:
Dolphin, tel: 48467, 48507

• **Stavroménos** (14 km east of Réthimnon), Area Code 0834
Category B:
Cretan Star (401), tel: 22056
Marilena (377), tel: 93231

• **72300 Zákros**, Area Code 0843
Category C:
Zakros (30), Tel: 28479

• **70002 Zaros** (45 km south west of Iráklion), Area Code 0894
Category C:
Idi (40), tel: 31302

PENSIONS

There are signs to indicate rooms to let. All you have to do is ask. The pension employee does his/her best to find accommodation.

• **Agía Galíni**
Category B:
Stella (19), tel: 91357

• **Agios Nikólaos**
Category B:
Amalthia (38), 13, Pring. Georgiou St., tel: 28914/5
Diana (31), 28, Ethn. Atistaseos St., tel: 22694
Niki (26), 16, Idomeneos St., tel: 22095
Polydoros (11), on the beach, tel: 22623, 28792
Category C:
Atlantis (18), tel: 28964
Istron (16), Sarolodi St., tel: 23763
Perla (12), tel: 23323

• **Eloúnda**
Category B:
Korfos Beach, tel: 41591
Sophia, tel: 41482

• **Galatas**
Category B:
Ariadni (17), tel: 21084

• **Haniá**
Category A:
Captain Vassilis (13), 12, Theotokopou–lou St., tel: 51122
Contessa (14), 15, Theofanous St., tel: 23966, 57437, 55986
Category B:
Bikouvarakis (17), tel: 41904
El Greco (25), 47-49, Theotokopoulou St., tel: 22411
Pilikassos, tel: 51242
Category C:
Afroditi (20), 18, Ag. Deka St., tel: 57602
Manos (19), 17, Koundouriotou St., tel: 29493

• **73011 Hóra Sfakíon**, Area Code 0825
Category B:
Xenia (23), tel: 91202

• **Iráklion**
Category B:
Anna-Bella (14), Talon St., tel: 289728
Ares (30), 5, Agissilaou St., tel: 280646
Phaedra (41), 11, Satha Kamaraki, tel: 223950
Category C:
Atlas (35), 6, Kandanoleon St., tel: 288989
Knossós (46), 43, 25th August St., tel: 283247
Philippides (28), 27, Kapodistriou St., tel: 230141

• **Kalamaki**
(10 km west of Haniá), Area Code 0821
Category B:
Ariadni (17), tel: 21084
Castro, tel: 31882, 31995

• **Káto Stalos**
Category B:
Alkyon, tel: 48389

• **Kastélli/Kissamos**
Mady (20), tel: 22315

- **Kokkini Hani**
  Prima, tel: 761109, 711020

- **73100 Kounoupidiana Haniá/Akrotíri**,
  Area Code 0822
  Category B:
  Pyrgos (31), Tel: 64431

- **Limin Hersonissou**
  Category B:
  Adonis (18), 55, Venizelou St., tel: 22141
  Stella (21), 5, 28th October St., tel: 22561, 22650
  Zorbas 940), 1, Navarinou Nearchou St., tel: 22075

- **Palékastro**
  Category B:
  Hellas (24), tel: 61240

- **Paleóhora**
  Category B:
  Eliros (18), tel: 41348
  Lamboussakis, tel: 41221
  Category C:
  Lissos (21), tel: 41266

- **73100 Profitis Ilias Haniá/Akrotíri**,
  Area Code 0821
  Category B:
  Akrotíri (25), tel: 24669

- **Réthimnon**
  Category B:
  Leon (23), Arkádiou & 4, Vafe St., tel: 26197
  Zania (15), 3, Vlastou St., tel: 28169
  Zorbas Beach (24), 4, Alv. Svaitser St., tel: 28540, 28440

- **Sitía**
  Category B:
  Denis (25), tel: 28356, 22335

- **Stalis**
  Category B:
  Hera (35), tel: 31624

HOLIDAY APARTMENTS

- **Agía Fotia**
  Category C:
  Romantza (12), tel: 22394

- **Agía Pelagia**
  Category B:
  Perla (49), tel: 289408/9
  Villa Tsolaki (11), tel: 288556

- **Agios Nikólaos**
  Category A:
  Archodiko (20), tel: 23612
  Hera Village (88), Plevra, tel: 28971/2, telex: 262109
  Triton (22), tel: 22180
  Category B:
  Afroditi (20), tel: 28200
  Anagennissis (44), tel: 22125
  Lybritis (30), tel: 28880
  Madraki (14), tel: 22207
  Category C:
  Melas Apartments (31), tel: 28734
  Paradise Village (15), Koukounares, tel: 28031

- **Daratso**
  Category C:
  Agapi, Germaniko Pouli, tel: 27410

- **Eloúnda**
  Category A:
  Eloúnda Golf Villas (34), tel: 41279
  Category B:
  Nissos Eloúnda (23), tel: 41274
  Category C:
  Caterina (14), tel: 41484

- **Galatas**
  Category C:
  Creta Maria (29), tel: 51353, 24681, 22371
  Lotus (23), tel: 56660
  Villa Anastasia (20), tel: 20339

- **Gournes**
  Category A:
  Evina (50), tel: 761034, 761105, 761012
  Renata (24), tel: 761223

- **Gouves**
  Cristi Apartments (72), tel: 41359
  Marianna (48), tel: 4170

- **Haniá**
  Category B:
  Argyro (15), 11–13, Thcotokopoulou St., tel: 55019
  Category C:
  Kastro, tel: 48583, 27944

- **Ierápetra**
Category A:
Koutsounari Traditional Cottages (39), tel:
61291, telex: 262457
Kothris, tel: 24180

- **Karteros**
Xenios Dias, tel: 285694

- **Káto Stalos**
Category C:
Architect's Villas (12), tel: 68526
Villa Kistaki (22), tel: 68370
Villa Pavlaki (14), tel: 68309
Vlamakis (12), tel: 68526

- **Kastélli/Kissamos**
Category C:
Dimitris–Chryssanthi (28), tel: 23390

- **73100 Korakiés Haniá/Akrotíri**, Area
Code 0822
Category B:
Korakies Village (38), tel: 64584

- **73100 Kounoupidiana**, Area Code 0822
Category C:
Kourkounakis (18), tel: 64231

- **Limin Hersonissou**
Category A:
Kastri Village (44), tel: 22102, 22367
Category B:
Dédalos Village (46), Koutouloufari, tel:
22515
Koutouloufari Apartments (42), tel: 22688
Maria (32), tel: 22580
Category C:
Alecos (14), tel: 22110
Aloni (10), tel: 22562, 22594
Katerina (26), tel: 22304
Perakis 926), 3, Demokratias St., tel: 22534
Villa Ippokambi (20), tel: 22316

- **Mália**
Category C:
Ghianis–Maria (18), tel: 31313
Sun Beach (48), tel: 31428, 31557

- **Paleóhora**
Category B:
Elman (41), tel: 41412-4

- **Plataniás**
Category C:
Eleni (8), tel: 68218

- **Réthimnon**
Category B:
Anna, Missiria, tel: 22590
Elina Holiday, 157, Kountouriotou St.,
tel: 27395-7
Jason, 48, Yamboudaki St., tel: 22542,
27196
Category C:
Arsinia (28), Stavromenos, tel: 24295
Kantaras, Perivolia, tel: 25593
Stella, tel: 91357
Tryfon, Platania, tel: 24771-4

- **Stalis**
Category A:
Creta Solaris Aparthotel (30), tel: 31496,
31697, telex: 262310
Promavera (12), tel: 31591
Category B:
Amazones Villas (58), tel: 31488
Penelope (28), tel: 31370
Category C:
Alex (98), tel: 61324
Captain's Villa (28), tel: 31593

Villa Maria (22), tel: 31450
Cilla Ritsa (22), tel: 31492

- **Stavroménos**
Niki (22), tel: 71038
Pavlos (36), tel: 71304

CAMPGROUNDS

Camping sites in Greece are supervised by
the NTOG, National Tourist Organization
of Greece, which introduced categories to
the camping world. As with the hotels, the
categories do not give any fixed range of
rates.

The following is a list of camping sites on
Crete, complete with category (Cat.), location and relative distance from a city, administrative region (AR), telephone number,
area in sq metres, maximum number of oc-
cupants, number of places available at the
site, special facilities, type of beach. To aid
orientation, the sites are listed geographi-
cally: the north coast, from west to east, then
the south coast from west to east.

NORTH COAST

Mithimna: Cat. C; 6 km east of Kastelli, Kissamou; AR Haniá, Tel: 0822/31444/5, 31825; 10,384 sq metres; 162; 54; restaurant, bar, mini–market; pebble neach

Agía Marina: Cat. C; 10 km west of Haniá; AR Hanía; Tel: 0821/68555, 68565; 9,600 sq metres; 240; 80; restaurant, bar, mini-market; sandy beach

Haniá: Cat. C; bei Daratso; 4.5 km west of Haniá; AR Haniá; Tel: 0821/51090; 9,569 sq metres; 100; 33; restaurant, bar, minimarket; sandy beach two minutes away.

George Camping: no category given; 10 km east of Georgioupolis; AR Réthimnon; tavérne; pebble beach.

Elizabeth: no category given; near Missiria, 4.5 km east of Réthimnon: AR Réthimnon; Tel: 0831/28694; 2,500 sq metres; 492; 164; restaurant, mini-market, swimming pool; sandy beach.

Arcádia: Cat. C; near Missiria, 4.5 km east of Réthimnon; AR Réthimnon: Tel: 0831/28825, 22361; 7,500 sq metres; 150; 50; restaurant, bar, mini-market, tennis court, children's playground; sandy beach.

Iráklion Camping: Cat. A; near Amoudara, about 4 km west of Iráklion; AR Iráklion; Tel: 081/250986-8; 86,000 sq metres; 858; 283; restaurant, bar, mini-market, children's playground, swimming pool; sandy beach.

Creta Camping: Cat. A; near Gouves, 20 km east of Iráklion; AR Iráklion; Tel: 0897/41400; 16,300 sq metres; 270; 90; restaurant, bar, mini-market, pebble beach.

Caravan Camping: Cat. C; Plakias near Limin Hersonissou, 26 km east of Iráklion; AR Iráklion; Tel: 0897/22025, 5,500 sq metres; 108; 36; restaurant, mini-market; sandy beach nearby.

Sissi Camping: Actually Tzikas J. Camping, no category given; Sissi, 6 km east of Malia; AR Lassíthi; Tel: 081/281444, 283345; no area given; 120; 40; restaurant, bar, swimming pool; coast of cliffs.

Gournia Moon: Cat. C; 15 km east of Agios Nikólaos; AR Lassíthi; Tel: 0842/93243; 8,960 sq metres; 165; 55; restaurant, bar, mini-market, children's playground; pebble beach.

SOUTH COAST

Loupassis St. Camping: Cat. C; Paleóhora, 0.5 km northeast of Paléohora, AR Haniá; Tel: 0823/41225; 9,500 sqmetres; 120; 40; restaurant, bar, mini-market, disco; pebble beach; sandy beach just 10 minutes away.

Camping Plakias: no category given; in the south between Hóra Sfakíon and Agía Galini; AR Réthimnon; bar, mini-market; pebble/sandy beach.

Agía Galíni: Cat. C, east of the village; AR Réthimnon; Tel: 0832/91386; 9,866 sq miles; 135; 45; restaurant, bar; pebble beach nearby.

Pitsidia-Matala Community Camping: Cat D: Matala; AR Iráklion; Tel: 0892/42340; 25,327 sq metres; 300; 100; no facilities; sandy beach.

Koutsounari: Cat C; Rousa Skala bei Ag. Ioánnis, circa 7 km east of Ierápetra; AR Lassíthi; Tel: 0842/61213; 8,381 sq metres; 198; 66; restaurant; sandy beach.

Ierápetra Camping: no category given; bei Ag. Saranta, circa 10 km east of Ierápetra; AR Lassíthi; Tel: 0842/61351; 7,300 sq metres; 123; 41; restaurant, mini– market; sandy beach.

All camping sites are open from April to October; Haniá, Koutsounari and Mithimna are open till October (inclusive).

YOUTH HOSTELS

To stay in a hostel, an international Youth Hostel Membership card is required.

The hostels are located at:

Iráklion – 24, Handakos St.

Haniá – 33, Drakanianou St.

Réthimnon – 7, Pavlou–Vlastou–St.

Ag. Nikólaos – 5, Stratigou–Koraka–St.

Sitía – 4, Therisou St.

There are also youth hostels in Malia (on the eastern outskirts), in Mirtos and Plataniás.

FOOD DIGEST

WHAT TO EAT

Cretan cuisine is simple but good. No one remembers the reason why food is usually cooked in the morning and kept warm all day until eaten as the main meal in the evening. But, even now, this is the way a typical Cretan housewife prepares the meal. The dishes, although "cooked to death" are nevertheless delicious. One such typical dish is *stifádo*, stewed lean beef in onions and vegetables. If you like *stifádo*, you'll enjoy most Cretan cooking. Then there are the charcoal grilled *souvláki*, lamb brochettes, which are on sale everywhere. With chips these make a good economical meal. For *moussaká* aubergines, minced meat and either potatoes or noodles are layered, and then topped with a delicious golden egg and milk mixture. There are many different versions, and the secret of a good *moussaká* is in the spices. *Keftédes* are meat balls with a unique flavour. Other specialities are *pastítsio*, a mixture of noodles, minced meat and tomatoes; *brisóles* (pork chops), *kotópoulo* (chicken); stuffed tomatoes and peppers as well as vine leaves filled with rice, *dolmádes* or *dolmadákia*.

The garlic yoghurt *zazíki* is delicious, and the ubiquitous farmers' salad, *horiátiki* of tomatoes, cucumbers, lettuce, olives and *féta* (goat's cheese), served with bread of course. These ingredients can make a simple meal or a sophisticated culinary creation.

Fish is rare and very expensive. However a well prepared piece of swordfish, *xifías*, is always worth the price. It is only surpassed by the crabs and lobster, which when served with home-made mayonnaise are delectable. More common is red mullet, *barbunia*, and squid, *kalamaráki*, which are available everywhere. All the guest has to do is to indicate how he/she wants the fish cooked.

In smaller restaurants, however, it is still the custom to go into the kitchen and set the menu yourself.

Of the many desserts, the two best known are: *baklavá*, streudel leaves filled with nuts and honey, and *loukoumádes*, yeast balls fried in oil, served warm with honey poured over them. Both puddings are delicious.

WHERE TO EAT

Crete has many restaurants and tavérnes, most of which serve good food. Of course you won't find haute cuisine in the small towns. Omelettes, farmers' salad and possibly a piece of meat make a meal. The best restaurants apart from those in the luxury hotels are to be found in the big cities: in Iráklion, the "Knossós" and the restaurants in Dédalos Street. In Haniá the restaurants around the fishing harbour are most interesting: go past the Janitscharen Mosque on the right. But other cities too offer a good range of food; in Mátala on the seashore, in Sitía and Ierápetra. For some reason, waiters and waitresses in Crete only seem able to bring two dishes at a time. So it is probably better to order two dishes at a time. If you want chips in a restaurant on the island, then say "*tsips*", because no-one understands "chips".

DRINKING NOTES

The best thirst quencher is water. Unfortunately it is sometimes chlorinated these days. Though not as fresh as it used to be, it is still the most important drink in summer.

Despite Crete's being an island of vineyards, beer is often drunk, and even brewed on the island. One foreign beer the visitor should try is Henninger Bier.

Wines from the different vineyards are sold by the bottle, such as *Arhánes* or *Minnos*, *Gortys* and *Lató*. The house rosé wine from the barrel is excellent too, but very strong.

Although coffee is prepared in the Turkish style it is called *kafé ellinikó*, and there are many different ways of preparing it. For a start these variations will do: *kafé métrio*, fairly strong and sweet, *varí glikó*, very sweet, and *skéto* without sugar. A customary glass of water is served with the coffee.

CULTURE PLUS

MUSEUMS

The opening times and prices of entries listed here were correct at time of press.

• **Agios Nikólaos**
Archaeological Museum, Konstandinou Paleologou St.; Mondays, Wednesdays-Saturdays 8.45 a.m. to 3 p.m., Sundays and holidays: 9.30 a.m. to 2.30 p.m. (closed Tuesdays); 200 Drs.

• **Haniá**
Archaeological Museum, Halidon St., formerly San Francisco Church; Wednesdays-Saturdays 8 a.m. to 7 p.m., Sundays and holidays: 8 a.m. to 6 p.m. (closed Tuesdays); 300 Drs.;

Historical Museum, 20 Sfakianaki St., Mondays-Fridays: 8 a.m. to 1 p.m. (closed Saturdays, Sundays and holidays);

Nautical Museum, Akti Koundouriotou; Tuesdays-Sundays 10 a.m. to 7 p.m., Sat 7 p.m. to 9 p.m. (closed Mondays)

• **Iráklion**
Archaeological Museum, 2 Xanthoudidou St.; Tuesdays-Saturdays 8 a.m.to 7 p.m., Sundays and holidays 8 a.m. to 6 p.m. (closed Mondays); 500 Drs.;

Historical Museum, Kalokerinou St.; Mondays-Saturdays 9.30 a.m. to 1 p.m., and 3 p.m. to 5.30 p.m. (closed Sundays and holidays);

Icon Museum, Platia Ekaterinis; Mondays-Saturdays 9.30 a.m. to 1 p.m., and Tuesdays, Thursdays and Fridays 5 p.m. to 7 p.m. (closed Sundays and holidays);

Nikos Kazátzakis Museum, Mirtia, approx. 20 km south of Iráklion; 1 March to 31 Oct, daily 9 a.m. to 1 p.m., Mondays, Tuesdays, Saturdays, Sundays also 4 p.m. to 6 p.m. (closed Thursdays); Nov 1 to Feb 28, only Sundays 9 a.m. to 2 p.m.; 500 Drs.;

Harbour Castle *Koules*, Mondays-Saturdays 8.45 a.m. to 3 p.m.; Sundays and holidays 9.30 a.m. to 2.30 p.m.

• **Ierápetra**
Archaeological Museum Kostoula, Adrianou St.; Mondays, Wednesdays-Saturdays 8.45 a.m. to 3 p.m.; Sundays and holidays 9.30 a.m. to 2.30 p.m. (closed Tuesdays)

• **Réthimnon**
Archaeological Museum, 220 Arkádiou St. Paleologou Corner, formerly Venetian Loggia; Mondays, Wednesdays-Saturdays 8 a.m. to 3 p.m.; Sundays and holidays 8 a.m. to noon. (closed Tuesdays); 200 Drs.;

Venetian Castle – Pre and post high season 9 a.m. to 5 p.m.; season 8 a.m. to 8 p.m.

• **Sitía**
Archaeological Museum, El. Venizelou St., on the edge of the city; Mondays, Wednesdays-Saturdays 8.45 a.m. to 3 p.m.; Sundays and holidays 9.30 to 2.30 p.m. (closed Tuesdays);

Folkloric Museum of Sitía, Arkádiou St.; daily 9.30 a.m. to 3.30 p.m; 100 Drs.

IMPORTANT BUILDINGS

• **Agia Triada**
Mondays-Saturdays 8.45 a.m. to 3 p.m.; Sundays and holidays 9.30 a.m. to 2.30 p.m.; 200 Drs.

• **Festós**
Mondays-Saturdays 8 a.m. to 7 p.m.; Sundays and holidays 8 a.m. to 6 p.m.; 300 Drs.

• **Gortyn**
Daily 8.45 a.m. to 3 p.m.; 200 Drs.

• **Gournia**
Mondays-Saturdays 8.45 a.m. to 3 p.m. (closed Sundays and holidays)

• **Káto Zákros**
Mondays-Saturdays 9 a.m. to 7 p.m.; Sundays and holidays 10 a.m. to 5 p.m.; 300 Drs.

• **Knossós**
Mondays-Saturdays 8 a.m. to 7 p.m.; Sundays and holidays 8 a.m. to 6 p.m.; 500 Drs.

• **Mália**
Mondays-Saturdays 8.45 a.m. to 3 p.m.; Sundays and holidays 9 a.m. to 2.30 p.m.; 200 Drs.

• **Panagíai Kera Church**, near Kritsa
Mondays-Saturdays 8.45 a.m. to 3 p.m.; Sundays and holidays 9 a.m. to 2 p.m.; 200 Drs. Photography not allowed.

- **Tilissos**

Mondays-Saturdays 9 a.m. to 3 p.m.; Sundays and holidays 9 a.m. to 2 p.m.; 200 Drs.

- **Vathipetro** and **Fourni**

Officially Mondays, Fridays and Saturdays from 9 a.m. till evening.

Monasteries and Convents: Entry to monasteries and convents is free, although a visit to the inside rooms may cost a little, usually between 50 and 100 Drs. Overnighting in monasteries should never be counted upon. There are few monks nowadays and they are not prepared to receive visitors, although they will offer help in case of emergencies.

This list includes only the most important monasteries, but the opening hours of the others are similar to those given below.

- **Akrotíri Monastery**, Agía Triada, Gouverneto, Prodromou; 9 a.m. to 2 p.m. and 5 p.m. to 7 p.m.
- **Arkádi**, east of Réthimnon; 8 a.m. to 1 p.m. and 5 p.m. to 7 p.m.
- **Gonia**, at the end of the Rodopou Peninsula; 9 a.m. to 1 p.m. and 4 p.m. to 7 p.m.
- **Hrissoskalitissa**, south west coast; 9 a.m. to 1 p.m. and 4 p.m. to 7 p.m.
- **Préveli**, on the coast south of Réthimnon; 8 a.m. to 1 p.m. and 5 p.m. to 7 p.m.
- **Savathiana**, near Rogdia, west of Iráklion; 8 a.m. to noon and 4 p.m. to 7 p.m.
- **Toploú**, east of Sitía; 8 a.m. to 6 p.m. and 6.30 to 7.30 p.m.

CONCERTS/CINEMAS

On Crete there are no sophisticated cultural events like those in western Europe. Now and again you will come across placards advertising an exhibition of a local artist. Here and there, theatre performances are announced, sometimes in the Harbour Castle in Iráklion or in the forts of Réthimnon or Sitía. Ballet performances, operas and classical or rock concerts are not to be found on Crete. However, many towns do organise musical events which usually include dancing and can be enjoyable during holidays. The standard varies, rather like the flamenco performances of Spain, from classical to popular for the tourists. The so-called *Cretan Nights* are famous in Axós and Anógia,

where authentic Cretan folklore is on show.

There is a cinema in every larger town. These are often open-air, with single price tickets. Foreign films are shown in the original, with subtitles.

NIGHTLIFE

CAFES AND BARS

Greek bars are like Italian ones, rather like cafés, where snacks are also served. There are many of these, particularly in the centres of the larger cities. They are patronised mainly by Cretans, as tourists do not really seem to have discovered them yet. The prices are usually low and the food is delicious. Bars are becoming increasingly common, especially in places where there are discos. There are some good bars along the harbour promenade in Ierápetra.

DISCOS

Not long ago it was more difficult to find a disco on Crete than a needle in a haystack. Things have changed. Now there are so many places to dance, especially in the tourist centres, that it is not necessary to mention them all: in Iráklion around the Venizélos Square/Morosini Fountain area; in Haniá you can hear the music by the Venetian Harbour and along the nearby side streets; in Réthimnon on the Beach Promenade, in Arkadíou St., and Neárchou St., in Agios Nikólaos mainly at the port and in Martíou St., in Mália in the amusement street down to the sea. In Sitía there is one in Sórbas St., and another at the eastern end of the shore promenade. In Paleóhora every beach has its own disco: the "Studio" on the west side, and further to the east, the Camping Site Discos. The discos at camping sites are interesting and are usually more pleasant than the decibel-blasting inside discos.

NIGHTCLUBS

"Real" night clubs – the lower the lights, the higher the prices – are rare. Iráklion is to Crete what Athens is to Greece but this analogy doesn't make Iráklion a metropolis. You'll have to visit the clubs to make up your own mind about them. Most of them are around Venizélos Square. In other cities too, where there are clubs, they are usually in the centre. In Agios Nikólaos most of the nightlife takes place around Aktí Koundoúrou.

TAVLI

There are no casinos with roulette, blackjack and rows of one-armed bandits on Crete. There is no need for them, as all kinds of games are played in the kafenía, or kafeníon, where the atmosphere is electric. Apart from card games of varying complexity, the most popular of all games is *Tavli*, which is similar to backgammon. Of the various forms of the game played in the Mediterranean region, these three are the most usual in Crete: *Portes/Portas*, *Plakoto* and *Fewga*.

Cretans are enthusiastic and inquisitive. So if you want to join in a game of *Tavli* in a kafeníon, you won't have to wait long to find an opponent. You'll never beat an old hand at the game, but you'll have fun trying. As the three variations of the game are usually played one after the other, it is a good idea to learn the rules of each one.

Tavli is played by two players, each of whom has 15 white or black pieces and two dice. The one with the higher throw of the dice starts. After this, the dice are always thrown together. If both dice show the same number, the number is not just doubled but multiplied by four. But the throw cannot be played in one move, only in four single moves. Thus 2 and 2 on the dice does not merely mean 4, but 2 + 2 + 2 + 2. If the space for the first 2 is blocked, the whole throw is lost. If the space for the third 2 is blocked, you lose the fourth move. These rules apply to all three variations of the game played on Crete in the kafenía. However, there is a difference between the various games, even in the way the pieces are set out at the beginning.

The board is divided into four sections, A, B, C, D, each of which has 6 points: numbered 1-6 and 7-12, twice.

PORTES

Player I moves his pieces forward from sections A, B and C into D, where he collects them. Player II plays in the opposite direction, thus from sections D, C and B into A.

The most important rule: single pieces can be lost, and to avoid this it is better not to leave pieces single, but play the pieces double at least.

Player I could also move in this manner but it would be risky. If player II then throws 6 + 5, then with his 6 he could take the single black piece on the lower point 7, and with the 5, set his own piece on the safe point 12.

Player I must now get his piece back into play in section A, before he can continue to play his other pieces. If he throws 6 + 6, he would lose the turn as point 6 is in section A which is occupied by the opposing pieces.

It is important for each player to get his pieces into the last section as quickly as possible: player I into section D, player II into section A. Only from there can the players get their pieces off the board.

Bearing off can be done in three ways:

1. The pieces can be taken off according to the numbers thrown on the dice. But you don't have to do this. If you like you can move pieces in the last section, but it is in fact a waste of time. For example 1 to number 6: player I has thrown 1 + 4. He can then take off a piece from both points 1 and 4.

2. If the two numbers thrown do not fit, that is, there is no piece on the number thrown, those on higher points are moved forward. Example 2 to number 6: player II throws 2 + 2. As his point 2 is not occupied, he can either take pieces from point 4, 2 times 4, or move one piece forward two points from points 3 to 6, or take a piece from point 6, 3 times 2, and for the remaining 2 set a piece forward from point 3 etc. etc.

3. If the numbers do not fit, and there are no pieces to be moved forward, pieces may be taken off from the highest occupied point. Example 3 to number 6: player I throws 6 + 6. Two pieces can be taken from point 6, and two more from point 4. With a throw of 6 + 5, a piece can be taken from point 6 and another moved to point 1. If 5 + 5 is thrown, he must move the two pieces from point 6 to point 5. Then he can take two pieces from point 4 etc.

The winner is the player who first bears off

all 15 pieces. If the player accomplishes this before his opponent has removed any pieces, he gets a double win.

PLAKOTO

The players again play in opposite directions; only white begins in section A and black in section D. All pieces are stacked up on the first point.

This version is different from Portes in that opposing pieces are not taken, only stopped. That is: a single piece can be occupied by a single opposing piece. The occupied piece is converted to one of one's own pieces as the couple act as a block: the opponent cannot occupy this block. The occupier can put as many pieces as he likes on top of the first piece. The occupied piece can only move when his opponent has moved away. Only single pieces can be occupied. It is good to occupy as many points next to each other as possible, so that your opponent cannot pass.

Bearing off is the same as in Portes.

FEWGA

In this variation you can neither take nor stop a piece. A single piece can occupy a point and block the way for his opponent. The following rules apply:

1. No more than 4 points can be occupied in the last section or inner table, section B for black and section D for white.

2. Only when a piece has reached the first point of the opponent, can other pieces be brought into play.

In this variation a whole section can be occupied, if allowed, that is six pieces next to each other, but of course rule 2 must be obeyed. Almost as important are all points which should be so set that all numbers can be played.

SHOPPING

WHAT/WHERE TO BUY

There are plenty of souvenir and trinket shops in the tourist centres. Most are in Iráklion, of course, on Venizélos Square, Kalérgos Square and in Dédalos Street. Many of these shops sell very good quality woolen pullovers. If you don't feel like making the trip to Tílissos, you can buy the woolen garments right here instead.

Musical instruments of average quality are on sale at every street corner. Better quality instruments are harder to come by, but in Tsoúliki Street in Iráklion you should be lucky.

Neither Iráklion nor Agios Nikólaos is famed for anything in particular. You can get anything in Iráklion, and of good quality too, as it is the capital of the island.

Haniá is to be recommended for leather goods, especially in Skrídlof Street and in the old city in Réthimnon, where there is also a great selection of blankets. Anógia and Psichró are the places to go for carpets, while Kritsá offers fine woven articles and lace.

There also some good international bookshops in the centres:

Agios Nikólaos – R. Koundoúrou Street;
Haniá – at the Venetian Harbour;
Iráklion – Dédalus Street;
Réthimnon – Petiháki Street.

SPORTS

Sports on Crete is unique. Cretans love sports – but as spectators only. When there is a major football match on, the kafénia in the big cities will be full of enthusiastic supporters, and in Dédalos Street in Iráklion, obliging waiters will even arrange the chairs so that patrons can watch the game on the screen in the window of the TV shop opposite. But it is not easy to find active sportsmen among the Cretans. The main hindrance is probably the climate. There are sporting events, where great enthusiasm is shown, but there is no sports calendar. So if you are interested in sport, "do it yourself" on Crete.

There is plenty to do. There are the water sports, windsurfing, snorkelling, diving and water skiing, particularly on the north coast, from Iráklion to Agios Nikólaos/Eloúnda. Many of the big hotels have water skis and surfboards for hire. Some places, e.g. west of Haniá, hire out pedal boats. It is no use asking for diving gear, oxygen bottles etc. as diving is strictly forbidden. The penalties are becoming ever more severe, as archaeological interest increases. Even photographing archaeological objects underwater is now an offence.

Beach hotels in the upper price range usually have tennis courts. Less energetic are table tennis and mini golf, which can be played in smaller hotels too. There is a small stable on the beach at Amníssos-Kartéros where riding lessons are offered and horses can be ridden out into the countryside.

You can walk and climb all over Crete, but the higher reaches should only be attempted under the auspices of the Greek Mountaineering Club, the EOS. (See "GETTING AROUND, On Foot", page 249.)

Even skiing conditions are ideal on Crete: few tourists, empty runs and only two ski lifts on the whole island as opposed to the usual circus.

SPECIAL INFORMATION

SCHOOL CHILDREN/STUDENTS

In order to be eligible for reduced entrance fees to museums, exhibitions and tours etc., an international student's pass must be shown. Concessions apply to the places where local children would also be eligible for the reduced rates. The international pass is printed in five languages.

PHOTOGRAPHY

As Crete is exceptionally photogenic, bring along many rolls of film, and be careful of the X-ray machine at the airport. Film is expensive on Crete, so it is wise to buy before you go. There is also some risk in having film developed on the island, despite assurances from the photo shop. If you are staying for a long time, it may be better to send the film to Athens for developing. If your stay is short, bring the film home.

Photography is free in the archaeological sites, as long as no tripod or flash is used. Use of a tripod at an archaeological site costs 150 Drs; in museums, 700 Drs. per object. If cases are opened and objects moved, electricity used, then each article will cost 1,500 Drs. Such photography must be authorised by the museum administration in Athens. Permission cannot be sought on the island.

Short filming on archaeological sites costs 7,000 Drs. per site and in museums and archaeological collections 12,000 Drs. For longer filming, at least 150,000 Drs will be charged. Video-taping costs about half, depending on the length.

In monasteries and convents, anything may be photographed, apart from the interiors of the churches. Of course monks and nuns should not be included in pictures unless they have given permission. It is a general rule that people should be asked if they mind having their picture taken. In some areas, e.g. Kritsá and Mirtía there is in fact hostility to cameras now. In Sfakía it has been known for a man to rip a film from a camera. The old trader and flute player on the parking place at Agía Triáda near Festós who has featured on several book covers as a noble Cretan, has now decided only to allow his picture to be taken if you buy something at his stall. This may be an excellent individual solution, but it would be sad if eventually all Cretans decided to hide, or charge for photos. So one should proceed with caution when taking pictures of locals.

Military installations may neither be photographed nor looked at through a lens. Prosecution can be the consequence.

Addresses for special permits: National Archaeological Museum, 1 Tositsa Street, Athens, tel. 01/82 17 717; Byzantine Museum, 22 Vas. Sofias, Athens, tel: 01/71 11 027

USEFUL ADDRESSES

EMBASSIES & ADDRESSES

Honorary Consulates of the Federal Republic of Germany:

71110 Iráklion: 7 Grafou St., P.O. Box 1083. Tel 08/226288. Telex 262207

73100 Haniá: 64 Dakalogianni St. Tel : 0821/57944. Telex: 291168

Vice Consulate of Great Britain:

Iráklion: 16 Papalexandrou St. Tel 081/ 224012

Consulate of The Netherlands:

71202 Iráklion: 23, 25th August St., P.O. Box 1031. Tel 081/283820, 284820. Telex: 262107

Consulate of Norway:

71110 Iráklion: 24 Ag. Dimitrou Square, P.O. Box 71. Tel: 081/220536

The diplomatic missions of other countries are located in Athens.

ART/PHOTO CREDITS

INDEX